Theologies of Failure

edited by
Roberto Sirvent
and Duncan B. Reyburn

James Clarke & Co

James Clarke & Co
P.O. Box 60
Cambridge
CB1 2NT
United Kingdom

www.jamesclarke.co
publishing@jamesclarke.co

Paperback ISBN: 978 0 227 17713 6
PDF ISBN: 978 0 227 90714 6

British Library Cataloguing in Publication Data
A record is available from the British Library

First published by James Clarke & Co, 2020

Copyright © Wipf and Stock, 2019

Published by arrangement
with Cascade Books

All rights reserved. No part of this edition may be reproduced, stored electronically or in any retrieval system, or transmitted in any form or by any means, electronic, mechanical, photocopying, recording, or otherwise, without prior written permission from the Publisher (permissions@jamesclarke.co).

We dedicate this book to every one of our students who never made it to the top of the class, who came in late, managed their time and work badly, dropped out, chose the wrong career path, and lost faith. Your journeys through failure will always prove to be better teachers than we could ever hope to be.

"So we do not lose heart. Even though our outer nature is wasting away, our inner nature is being renewed day by day. For this slight momentary affliction is preparing us for an eternal weight of glory beyond all measure, because we look not at what can be seen but at what cannot be seen; for what can be seen is temporary, but what cannot be seen is eternal."

—2 CORINTHIANS 4:16-18, NRSV.

Contents

Acknowledgements ix

Contributors xi

1. Theologies of Failure: An Inadequate Introduction 1
   Duncan B. Reyburn and Roberto Sirvent

PART 1: FAILING WELL

2. Yes, And: Let Us Learn from Improvisers the Power to Fail 17
   Heather C. Ohaneson

3. A Popular Blogger's Theology of Failure:
   Glennon Doyle on the Redemptive Act of "Showing Up" 35
   Mariana Alessandri

4. Someone Must Lose: A Theology of Winning in Sport 45
   Lincoln Harvey

5. Failure and Natural Selection 54
   Kara N. Slade

PART 2: FAILING BETTER

6. Mimetic Failure and the Possibility of Forgiveness 71
   Duncan B. Reyburn

7. A Moral Theology of Technological Failure 84
   Michael S. Burdett

8. Christ the Failure: Bonhoeffer
   and the Paradoxical Power of Weakness 95
   Matthew D. Kirkpatrick

9. Orgasmic Failure: A Praxis Ethic for Adolescent Sexuality 107
   Kate Ott

10. Please Don't Go Out and Change the World:
    An Interview with William T. Cavanaugh *119*
    Roberto Sirvent

PART 3: FAILURE AS RESISTANCE

11. "A Strange Kind of Slavery": David Foster Wallace's Enslaved Self 133
    Dennis F. Kinlaw III

12. Blessed Are the Failures: Leaning into the Beatitudes 141
    Rebekah Eklund

13. The Uselessness of God: Failure as Political Resistance 151
    Silas Morgan

14. Pink Blankets, Sexual Violence, Moral Paralysis,
    and Christian Vocation 171
    Elisabeth T. Vasko

15. Failure and the Modern Academy 184
    Elizabeth Newman

PART 4: FAILURE AND LIBERATION

16. Rival Powers: US Catholics Confront the Climate Crisis 197
    Rosemary P. Carbine

17. The Body of Christ Given Up for the Ashamed:
    Rethinking Shame after the Sinking of the Ferry Sewol 216
    Min-Ah Cho

18. "Love Never Fails": Rereading 1 Corinthians 13
    with a Womanist Hermeneutic of Love's Struggle 230
    Mitzi J. Smith

Acknowledgements

The idea for this volume was sparked back in 2015. After a few minor disasters—including rejected proposals, missed deadlines and late submissions, submissions from authors that never arrived, and the like—it is finally done, and we are immensely grateful to everyone who made it possible. We wish to thank, first of all, every scholar who participated in the project and took time to consider failure in terms of the concerns of their own academic projects. We are grateful to them for their willingness to undertake the task at hand, their consideration of our suggestions, and their dedication to excellence. We have been enriched by working with each one. Then, we wish to thank everyone at Wipf and Stock who saw in our proposal the promise of good things, and took the risk of taking the bad along with the good. Special thanks to Lindsay Reyburn, for helping us to get the manuscript ready, and to our editor, Rodney Clapp, for seeing the process through to its conclusion. In particular, Roberto would like to thank his brilliant wife, Krista, who puts more creative work into decolonizing education than he ever could in a thousand lifetimes. Duncan would like to thank his wife Linda and his daughter Isla for their constant and illuminating presence, persistent love, and unfailing support.

Contributors

Mariana Alessandri is Assistant Professor of Philosophy at the University of Texas, Rio Grande Valley in the Borderlands between South Texas and Mexico. Her failures include burning caramel corn, killing ivy plants, and stubbornly believing that every task will only take thirty minutes. She plays the piano and wants to learn sign language.

Michael S. Burdett is Research Fellow in Religion, Science and Technology at Wycliffe Hall, University of Oxford. He was once an engineer in the aerospace industry, but gave up an exciting and well-paid job designing robots and satellites to be an academic vagabond in the declining field of academic theology. He has probably only read half the books on his shelf, but they do look impressive as decorations.

Rosemary P. Carbine is Associate Professor of Religious Studies at Whittier College. She specializes in constructive Christian theologies, focusing on comparative feminist, womanist, and Latinx/mujerista theologies, theological anthropology, public/political theologies, and teaching and learning in theology and religion. She has coedited three books and published numerous articles and essays, most recently appearing in *Planetary Solidarity: Global Women's Voices on Christian Doctrine and Climate Justice* (2017). Within the American Academy of Religion, she is a presidentially appointed member of the Teaching and Learning Committee and member of the steering committee for Women and Religion. Carbine's vertigo-inducing fear of heights perhaps accounts for her feminist and public theological studies of grassroots social movements.

Min-Ah Cho is currently a novice of the Society of the Sacred Heart (RSCJ), a congregation of religious women in the Roman Catholic

Church. After four years of teaching at St. Catherine University, St. Paul, Minnesota, she joined the Society, since she found herself deeply desiring the life in a community in which she could pray, eat, and envision a future together. As of the 2018 fall semester, she is going to teach at Manhattan College, NYC. She hopes that the public transportation in NYC gives her a relief and confidence in her mobility because she has never been a good driver.

Rebekah Eklund is Associate Professor of Theology at Loyola University Maryland in Baltimore. She likes to cook but doesn't understand how yeast works. Despite her best efforts, she never learned how to graph a parabola.

Lincoln Harvey is Assistant Dean at St Mellitus College, as well as being Lecturer in Systematic Theology. He has contributed to a number of books and journals, and has also written *A Brief Theology of Sport* (2014). Alongside his work in theological education, Revd Dr Harvey is currently a Licensed Preacher Under Seal in the Diocese of London.

Dennis F. Kinlaw III is Assistant Professor of English and member of the Honors College at Houston Baptist University in Houston, Texas. He carried out his graduate studies at the University of St. Andrews, Scotland—a town celebrated as the "home of golf." To the chagrin of private instructors, fellow golfers, and his father-in-law, his golf game actually worsened during this time. To this day, he tends to golf alone.

Matthew D. Kirkpatrick is Lecturer in ethics and Christian doctrine at Wycliffe Hall, University of Oxford. He is author of *Soren Kierkegaard* (2013), *Bonhoeffer's Ethics: Between Pacifism and Assassination* (2011), and *Attacks on Christendom in a World Come of Age: Kierkegaard, Bonhoeffer, and the Question of Religionless Christianity* (2011).

Silas Morgan is a political theologian who lives in Minneapolis, Minnesota, and works for Fortress Press. He worked hard at academic life, but no university would hire him. He hated the idea of being an independent scholar, so now he works in publishing. He reads at night and writes on the weekends, and still can't figgure out how to avoid typos.

Heather C. Ohaneson is an Assistant Professor of philosophy and religious studies at George Fox University, where she also serves as a William Penn Honors Program faculty fellow. She is a cautious driver, a middling cook, and an altogether dreadful camper.

Kate Ott is Associate Professor of Christian Social Ethics at Drew University Theological School in Madison, New Jersey. She was a part-time athletic department employee who spent more time watching games than ushering or controlling the crowd, which taught her about participatory pedagogy. In sexuality education workshops, she routinely defaults to the term *lover* as keeping up with relationships statuses like *seeing*, *talking*, *going out*, and *together* confuse her.

Duncan B. Reyburn is Senior Lecturer in Information Design and a researcher in philosophical theology and mimetic theory at the University of Pretoria, South Africa. He is the author of *Seeing Things as They Are: G. K. Chesterton and the Drama of Meaning* (2016). He used to be a professional designer and illustrator, but ended up in academia because of a bad life choice. If it weren't for GPS, he would get lost all the time, because he doesn't have a very good sense of direction.

Roberto Sirvent is Professor of Political and Social Ethics at Hope International University in Fullerton, California. He used to work for a US senator, but his obsession with the cafeteria's caesar salad and pecan pie made him a very unproductive employee. Even though he likes to teach and write about movies, he often relies on his wife to explain their endings.

Kara N. Slade is Theologian in Residence and Associate Chaplain at the Episcopal chaplaincy to Princeton University and Seminary, and Associate Rector of Trinity Church. She is a recovering and repentant bureaucrat, having also served as a research engineer and test manager for the National Aeronautics and Space Administration. With a doctorate in mechanical engineering as well as theology, she can correctly assemble IKEA furniture approximately 50 percent of the time.

Mitzi J. Smith is a tenured Professor of New Testament and Early Christian Studies at Ashland Theological Seminary. Her most recent book is *Womanist Sass and Talk Back: Social (In)Justice, Intersectionality and*

Biblical Interpretation (2018). In another life, she could have been a comedian. She sees the comical in situations that others do not, and this occasionally gets her in trouble when her laughter interrupts what others have thought to be a serious moment.

Elisabeth T. Vasko is an Associate Professor of Theology at Duquesne University in Pittsburgh, Pennsylvania. Prior to entering academia, she served as a youth and youth adult minister in the Chicago area. While her enthusiasm for working with young people remains, she simply did not have the stomach for all the pizza, donuts, and potato chips required for ministry life.

1.

Theologies of Failure
An Inadequate Introduction

DUNCAN B. REYBURN AND ROBERTO SIRVENT

"I never failed once. It just happened to be a 2000-step process."
—THOMAS EDISON.

FAILURE, BY ITS USUAL definition, refers to what falls short of a standard or does not conform to an ideal. Its mere presence announces a dichotomous relationship with its obvious opposite, *success*, and other synonyms of success: attainment, triumph, victory, and so on. In everyday usage, failure tends to resonate with pejoratives like *collapse, loss, negligence, omission, dysfunction, dissolution,* and *defeat*. Whatever we might conceive of as a failure depends a great deal, therefore, on the standard or ideal that we have in our sights.

It would be fair, for example, to distinguish between bad apples and good apples, since we have in mind an ideal—the form of the good apple—and thus a logical desire to balance the symbolic equation. However, misunderstanding the ideal or choosing the wrong ideal may lead us to make any number of false comparisons, and thus also to draw erroneous conclusions. G. K. Chesterton explains, via a metaphor, that we perceive falsely if we "think first of a Briareus with a hundred heads, and then call every man a cripple for having only one."[1] The point he makes is simple enough: if the ideal we measure something against is poorly selected, or if the analogical relationship between something in one category and something in another is misaligned, we will end up denigrating something unjustly; we will, at a fundamental level, misunderstand its very being.

The possibility that we might be setting up deceitful comparisons—comparing, as it were, apples with oranges—points out that the category of failure is not nearly as univocal as it may first appear. Failure can be said in many ways. Its meaning may turn out to be equivocal, for instance, in which case a precise value judgement about its quality or outcome would be difficult to make. And beyond the equivocal is the dialectical sense; and beyond that is the paradoxical or, to follow William Desmond, the metaxological. It may, in other words, include various meanings while also suggesting an inevitable surplus of meaning. Failure, in this paradoxical sense, points beyond itself, to more than itself, to what transcends failure completely—to the very context within which a dialectic between failure and success is established.

Failure may even have, in its paradoxical form, sacramental value. The broken body or text reveals a divine reality beneath and/or beyond the obviousness of our human assignments of meaning. This is demonstrated, for instance, in the paradoxical idea that what is regarded as a failure according to one standard or articulation may end up being a roaring success according to another. Failure is, if not entirely then at least to a significant degree, in the eye of the beholder.

The paradoxical voice of failure is wonderfully, if incompletely, captured in *James Acaster's Classic Scrapes*, a book with the tag line, "To err is human. To err enough to fill a book isn't." In that book, Acaster, a comedian by profession, recalls numerous life events that he refers to as "scrapes." Scrapes can be thought of as misfortunes that are nevertheless—and perhaps to the reader's relief—funny. After 300 pages of recounting a variety of personally experienced disasters, many of which had been owed to his own inability to properly consider his options and their possible consequences,[2] Acaster concludes:

> I once saw a poster in an office that read, "Your best teacher is your last mistake" and it filled me with pride. I may not have

---

1. Chesterton, *Collected Works, Vol. 1*, 68.
2. Acaster, *James Acaster's Classic Scrapes*, 2.

gone to university but my god, have I been educated. My professors were a skydiving instructor, a French porcelain salesman, a nobhead named Alistair and a nine-year old boy with unlimited access to cabbages. They are the ones who set *my* exams. And yes I failed those exams but in failing them I actually passed them because that's the way you pass an exam about mistakes—you fail. And all the people who "pass" the exam are the ones who actually fail the exam in the end. But in doing so maybe they also end up passing them because they failed. I don't work on an exam board; maybe everyone passes because everyone fails. And isn't that what life is all about? We are all failures and as such we are roaring successes. Each and everyone of us.[3]

There is something in failure, as Acaster alludes, that points beyond itself; that transcends itself, and thus reframes and rearticulates failure as something beneficial rather than detrimental. Not all failures work like this, of course, but some failures do. As many of Acaster's so-called scrapes reveal, failure is paradoxical also in the sense that it is something we avoid even though the seeds of failure can be found in many of the things that we actively seek out.[4] This is to say that, while trying to avoid failure, we are always moving towards it. Sometimes, in fact, the avoidance of failure, the very tentativeness of our steps towards any given goal, may exacerbate failure. Every movement towards success is always potentially a movement towards failure. This is evident, too, in Viktor Frankl's notion of "paradoxical intention," which suggests the possibility that it is precisely in striving for a goal that we ensure that the goal will not be reached. The more we might try to be happy, for example, the less likely it will be that we acquire happiness. And the more we try to control the world, the more it will spin out of control. Sometimes, it is precisely because we reach out for success that we fail. And yet not trying at all may render failure in even more catastrophic terms.

One example of a confusion of failure and success is found in reference to the so-called "*Citizen Kane* of bad movies,"[5] Tommy Wiseau's *The Room* (2003). According to generally accepted standards of good film-making—coherence in narrative, crisp dialogue, originality of content, consistent character motivation, realism in portrayal, etc.—it is quite simply a filmic disaster. But this apparently terrible creative production

---

3. Ibid., 302.
4. Juul, *The Art of Failure*, 2.
5. Morrin, "The *Citizen Kane* of Bad Movies."

is more talked about and widely enjoyed today than the film that won the Academy Award for Best Picture in the year that *The Room* was made and released.

The Room is acclaimed for various reasons, including its sheer entertainment value, its usefulness as a tool for educating new filmmakers, and its ability to unmask Hollywood vacuity. To this day, some speculate that everything in the film was put there deliberately by Wiseau to challenge the success standards of the American film industry. Since this is merely speculation, it cannot be taken entirely seriously, but it raises the oxymoronic possibility of a *successful* failure—a failure that succeeds precisely by virtue of being a failure. Others argue, of course, that even if everything in the film were to have been intentionally put there, there are more or less objective standards of excellence that must have escaped the notice of its creators. So even if it succeeds on one level, and succeeds by virtue of being a failure, it still fails completely in other respects. This reveals that failure and success can exist simultaneously, unified in a paradoxical coincidence of opposites.

In *The Disaster Artist* (2013), authors Greg Sestero (who acted in *The Room*) and Tom Bissel have a lot to say about failure, either directly or by implication. In their book we find these words: "*The Room* is a drama that is also a comedy that is also an existential cry for help that is finally a testament to human endurance. It has made me [Sestero] reconsider what defines artistic success or failure. If art is expression, can it fail? Is success simply a matter of what one does with failure?"[6]

This is simplistically put and philosophically naive. Art cannot be defined as mere expression. Cussing after stubbing one's toe accidentally is expression, but it certainly isn't art. Still, the example of *The Room* remains instructive and complements the idea at the heart of the present collection of essays, which is that often failure is the very thing that throws into question the dialectic of success and failure. In this sense, failure functions as rhetorical defamiliarization.[7] By throwing our familiar perspectives into question, it allows us to see things anew, as if for the first time. This is precisely the defamiliarization at work in much of the present book.

Of course, many have already written about failure, and considered it from various perspectives, often in keeping with failure's many voices.

---

6. Sestero and Bissel, *The Disaster Artist*, xxx.
7. See Reyburn, *Seeing Things as They Are*, 172–83.

Scott Sandage, for instance, has written extensively on failure in terms of its historicity in *Born Losers*. Sandage notes, for instance, that the now commonplace reference to failure as something that can be applied to human subjects is a very recent historical intrusion.[8] Failure had been, prior to the mid-eighteen hundreds, a term applied to business, rather than a metaphor applied to the denigration of people. Thus, economics became the measure of the self and Sandage points out that success has consequently become something of a trope in America's ideological landscape—often linked to issues of wealth and status.[9] Failure, as a designation of human worth, has thus often been a tool for existential formation. Whether one agrees with Sandage's assessment of capitalism or not, he nonetheless indicates something along the lines of St. Augustine's theologically informed insight concerning use and enjoyment in relation to people. Great evils are committed when people are regarded (as successes or failures) in terms of their use-value, rather than seeing people in terms of their intrinsic value.

Other writers have considered the category of failure in terms of its ability to challenge and disrupt accepted modes of interpreting the world. Jack Halberstam, in particular, opens up the possibility of regarding failure as a counter-hegemonic strategy.[10] And while his work is not in any formal sense theological, it opens up a number of theological possibilities. By embracing failure, for instance, we may discover more surprising ways of being in the world and of doing theology; or perhaps of recovering a childlike wonder that is unafraid of mistakes and therefore also disrespectful of strictly "grown up" seriousness when it comes to encounters with the Divine. Perhaps, as Halberstam considers, failure might offer a useful dose of chaos to that which is overly ordered.

But when it comes to genuinely exploring the theological implications of failure, we find something of a lacuna. *Theologies of Failure* aims to inadequately address this lacuna in theological discourse, namely the idea that *failure*, as a theological category with a variety of possible meanings and interpretations, is largely untapped. This is not to claim, of course, that theologians have not grappled with various forms of failure, but rather that failure has, for the most part, tended to be something of a peripheral concern. By highlighting failure itself—by isolating the

---

8. Sandage, *Born Losers*, 2.
9. Ibid., 12.
10. Halberstam, *The Queer Art of Failure*.

notion and by letting it be itself, albeit within the context of specific value structures, and without trying to completely undermine existing theological imperatives—the contributors in this book invite us to reflect on the meaning of failure in their own theological journeys. Some of the reflections allow for the whimsy evident in the examples provided above. Others are far more serious, dealing with failures that are truly weighty, and often difficult both in their existential resonances and in their theological formulations. To borrow the words of Raúl Coronado, we find in the essays that follow a provisional attempt to rethink theology's own potentially "overpowering categories of analysis" so that we might learn from a "history of false starts, of dreams that failed to cohere."[11] It should go without saying, however, that the perspectives in this book cannot fully account for the plurivocal possibilities of failure as a theological category. Nevertheless, they do manage, if only sometimes implicitly, to ask the reader to turn inward, perhaps even contemplatively and prayerfully, to consider the meaning of failure for her or his own life and thinking.

Our example for grappling with failure is found, most importantly, in the fact that many of the biblical authors seem to think failure worth dwelling upon. Second Corinthians 4, for instance, offers a theological musing on the existential perplexities of embodied entropy. There, we find a careful consideration of human afflictions, bafflement, persecution, and the like, not as causes of despair, but as signs that we are "[a]lways bearing the body of the dying Jesus, so that Jesus's life might be made manifest in our mortal flesh" (2 Cor 4:10, DBH).[12] Here we have, as suggested above, an example of a paradoxical failure that transcends the usual bounds of the dialectic of failure and success. That which fails is, in a sense, what overcomes the very distinction between what succeeds and what does not.

Similarly, in the same letter, Paul contemplates a mysterious "thorn in the flesh," which he regards not as something to be dismissed or gotten rid of but rather as having an androgogic function; it prevented him from being "excessively exalted" (2 Cor 12:7, DBH).[13] In a moment of revelation, Paul recognizes how true power is that which works beyond categories of both power and weakness, such that "power is perfected in weakness" (2 Cor 12:9, DBH).

11. Coronado, *A World Not to Come*.
12. See Hart, *The New Testament*.
13. Ibid., 367.

Such an acceptance of failure is mirrored in the message of Jesus, which can be understood, as Robert Farrar Capon intimates, as being in praise of the last, lost, least, little, and dead. In a particularly provocative passage, Capon writes that "[t]he work of Jesus in his incarnation, life, passion, death, resurrection, and ascension makes no worldly sense at all."[14] It is, in its own way, something that fails to communicate in terms that support the logic of the given dialectical world order. Thus, both theology *and* failure become strategies by which the ways of the world are refused. Capon continues: "The portrait the Gospels paint is that of a lifeguard who leaps into the surf, swims to the drowning girl and then, instead of doing a cross-chest carry, drowns with her, revives three days later, and walks off the beach with the assurances that everything, including the apparently still dead girl, is hunky-dory."[15]

Capon has a gift for pointing out something of the unpalatable darkness at the core of the illumination of the Gospels, which is failure. No Eden is possible without a serpent in it. As Capon's popular theological articulations highlight, Jesus doesn't simply overcome sin the way that a superhero might overcome the villain—by force or, in a gesture of supreme authority, by remaining completely immune to and above the villain's schemes. Rather, he "becomes sin" (2 Cor 5:21, DBH). He enters into and succumbs to death itself; he dies like a common criminal, thereby adopting something of the identity of a criminal (Phil 2:8). By all appearances, he lets corrupt ideologies succeed; he lets evil win. And yet this is not the real story. This is only the story as it *appears*. To continue Capon's image, Jesus doesn't save the drowning girl *from* death but saves her *in* and *through* death, both his and hers. Failure is not avoided but embraced as a component of the transcendence that outranks the very distinction between life and death. This embrace doesn't merely rush past the difficulties of existence as mere trifles but instead attentively acknowledges the trauma they produce and carefully considers what such traumas might mean, given their concreteness within existential reality.

However, of course, the point of the present book is that all of this is up for theological debate, and our brief exploration above of how failure is approached in Scripture, certain writers, and in the work of this one theologian cannot be assumed to be the universally adopted perspective in and on the message of the Gospels. And yet, we have highlighted all

14. Capon, *Kingdom, Judgement, Grace*, 39.
15. Ibid.

of this because through it we find an insight into the profound realism in the Gospels, which, as in much of the biblical canon, make no attempt bypass the deficiencies and losses affecting the human experiment. However we might read the Gospels and interpret their meanings, along with the other Scriptures, we cannot avoid the centrality of failures of all kinds to their theological and narrative arc. Failure, as the above suggests, does not have only one meaning or one application, and for that reason it is vital that we make an attempt to consider failure from multiple perspectives, through various hermeneutic postures and procedures. Some of these, of course, tend towards the univocal, where failure remains failure in its common, everyday sense, while others will consider the equivocal, dialectical, and paradoxical voices of failure—separately or together—to reveal entirely new interpretive possibilities and even, perhaps, moral and existential directives.

The different paradigms of the contributors to this book allow fresh perspectives on familiar ideas. All in all, the authors of these essays have in their own way contributed to a larger idea. *Theologies of Failure* asks how failure can challenge a world obsessed with power, prestige, privilege, and various other articulations of success, whether vaguely or clearly understood. It asks us if we have perhaps on occasion misunderstood certain failures, or overlooked their theological importance. It explores the ways in which theologies can help navigate, overcome, transcend, endure, and even embrace failure, depending, of course, on the kind of failure in question. In keeping with their various theological and philosophical commitments, the contributors encourage us to adjust our customary modes of perceiving the world and our being in the world. In doing this, they demonstrate that failure is something that must always be reconsidered or perhaps, to use the theological language of Irenaeus, *recapitulated*. To recapitulate is to relive, to remember, and to re-member. It is to put together what has been experienced and perceived as disintegrated.

This book deals with a range of pertinent topics, grouped under a few theme headings. And it is important to keep in mind that, through the review and editorial process, our aim has been to ensure that the voice of each writer be maintained, rather than setting up the policing of different positions to conform to a single one. For this reason, the reader will find essays that she or he both agrees with and disagrees with. This diversity of views, we believe, is vital for the sake of generating healthy, critical, informative, and insightful discussion. Such a diversity of views implies that the conversation needs to continue. With failure in our sights, we become more aware of the limits of our own positions and perspectives, and thus become open to considering and weighing up the viewpoints of others.

Part 1: Failing Well begins with Heather C. Ohaneson's reflection on failure through the lens of improvisation theory and the key idea of "overaccepting." Ohaneson argues that improvisation is far from simple. It includes moments of challenge, resistance, combativeness, and care, among other things, and always calls for skill and discernment. In theological terms, it requires grace and to be graced, to keep the play going. Following this is Mariana Alessandri's essay on Glennon Doyle's popular theology of failure. Alessandri pays attention to the voices of Augustine, Aquinas, and Kierkegaard, and aims to articulate a way of loving as "showing up" that is uniquely and beautifully reconciled to failure. In this, Alessandri reconfigures success and failure around the issue of showing up, rather than around measurements like wealth or status, and thus proposes a "Marian theology of failure" that invites us to receive forgiveness and extend love.

Lincoln Harvey takes on the subject of competitive sport from a theological perspective and ventures the proposal that sport, as an unnecessary but meaningful activity, helps us to celebrate our nature as unnecessary but meaningful creatures who have been summoned into life by God out of nothing. Given this proposal, Harvey maps winning and losing onto the dynamic ontological profile of the human creature, with losing becoming a vital component of the celebratory event of our subjective reality. In the last essay in this section, Kara N. Slade takes a look at something that may at first appear neutral—Big History—but which is in fact laden with an insidious ideology that can easily infect any form of theological thinking, especially around contrived divisions between what fails and what succeeds. The temptation to co-opt the supposed neutrality of Big History for theological purposes is unmasked as a participant in a form of epistemological arrogance. Slade offers a very Kierkegaardian reflection on what it means to fail to achieve a moment of self-transcendent reflection through reason.

Part 2: Failing Better starts off with Duncan B. Reyburn's critical reflection, through the lens of mimetic theory and interdividual psychology, on the inner logic of forgiveness. In particular, he uncovers what makes a shift from negative reciprocity (*ressentiment*, vengeance, and the like) towards positive reciprocity (forgiveness, love, and so on) possible, given the relational economy of desire. He posits that forgiveness itself becomes possible only after we have failed and accepted that failure. The acceptance of failure is also at the heart of Michael S. Burdett's essay, which explores failure as a constructive issue with regard to the question of technology. Jacques Ellul's work features, along with that of Tillich, Heidegger, and others, as a way of exploring how efficiency itself fails, as well as how inefficiency can be thought of as a kind of success. Among other things, Burdett demonstrates that it takes a kind of failure to be able to participate in virtue, and to genuinely care for our fellow human beings. Following this is Matthew D. Kirkpatrick's examination of the paradoxical power of failure in the life and work of Dietrich Bonhoeffer. Bonhoeffer can be considered, in some ways, more of a failure than a success, and Kirkpatrick aims to unpack some of the virtues of these failures, especially in terms of an identification with Christ himself.

Kate Ott explores the question of adolescent sexual ethics, which, in its most commonly articulated form, still tends to prioritize particular modes of self-mastery as the measure of success. In questioning the narrative of self-mastery, Ott places failure at the center of sexual ethics, and thus argues for the importance of a particular erotic attunement that promotes a healthier relationship with the self and with the body. Concluding this second section of the book is Roberto Sirvent's interview with political theologian William T. Cavanaugh, which begins by looking at advice that might be genuinely instructive at any commencement address, namely the advice to not give too much credence to exhortations to "change the world." As Cavanaugh explains, it is easy enough to presume a false empathy that dislocates the ethical impetus behind moral action. What is needed is a critical, although not cynical, posture that asks how political theology can become intimate with the more personal and circumstantial concerns of people. When Cavanaugh advises, "please *don't* go out and change the world," he exposes the hubris of so many well-meaning Westerners who presume a God's-eye view of the world—that they themselves have been given a unique, privileged, and even divine revelation about how people of other countries and cultures should conduct their affairs.

Part 3: Failure as Resistance begins with Dennis F. Kinlaw III's exploration of the work of David Foster Wallace, in which we find extended reveries on various kinds of failure, and through which we also discover that failure may present us with the possibility of genuine renewal. One of the editors of this book[16] tried and failed to read through Wallace's *Infinite Jest*, and Kinlaw argues that even such a failure may not have been entirely without merit. Rebekah Eklund's essay complicates the way that we might read the beatitudes, taking seriously the subversive, challenging, and often ambiguous meanings of the various kinds of failure that the beatitudes point to. Eklund's focus is a feminist reading of the beatitudes that allows us to see them in the context of community, rather than as confirmations of individualist ethics.

This is followed by Silas Morgan's apology for the uselessness of theology as a protest against a neoliberal ideology, which renders the world intelligible only in terms of competitive economic practices, use-value, and instrumental reason. In particular, Morgan brings critical theory and queer theory into dialogue with political theology, and in so doing argues for an artful, critical, queer theology of failure. In her essay, Elizabeth T. Vasko unpacks how accounts of self-love have not properly taken into account the practical effects and intergenerational impact of moral paralysis and self-hatred (the internalization of oppression). In particular, and in the context of sexual violence, and to highlight love's potential to dismantle cycles of violence, she outlines important considerations for ecclesial identity and Christian vocation. As Vasko argues, a genuinely compassionate love is one that embraces failure. The final essay of this third part of the book is Elizabeth Newman's, which provides a serious examination of the gnosticism—a failed theology—that underpins and undermines the modern academy. She offers, as a response to this failed and failing theology, the idea that genuine openness to the *logos* within our various academic cares and concerns requires the recognition of an ontology of communion that considers faithfulness as having priority over an "objectivity" that is ultimately neutral only in appearance.

With reference to feminist, ecological, and public theologies, Rosemary P. Carbine's essay commences *Part 4: Failure and Liberation*. Carbine considers reactionary religious and political responses to climate change from the US political right to Pope Francis's encyclical on the climate crisis, *Laudato Si'*. In this, Carbine argues that Pope Francis's attempt to address a widespread moral failure has some failings of its own, especially in terms of persuading conservative politicians. In the penultimate essay in the book, Min-Ah Cho examines shame, as that which suggests not only having failed but feeling like a failure. She asks if

---

16. It was Duncan.

shame cannot, in some way, be transformed into something constructive and even life-giving. In particular, Cho looks at Edward Schillebeeckx's thinking around the Eucharist, which takes seriously the embodied tension between remembrance and anticipation without collapsing the paradox or ignoring failure. The ambiguity within this tension takes seriously the human experience, and the hope that our self-awareness and capacity for compassion might be increased.

Finally, concluding the fourth section and the book itself, is Mitzi J. Smith's reconsideration of Paul's famous discourse on love in 1 Corinthians 13 and its literary context through the lens of a womanist hermeneutics of suspicion. She considers the possibility that Paul's theology of love is a theology of failure in a very particular sense. It is, in Smith's estimation, a theology that fails, since, among other things, it does not sufficiently take into account the struggle against problematic hierarchies and oppressive ideologies. Smith offers some instructive solutions to Paul's ideological framework in keeping with a womanist ontology of wholeness.

Taken together, the chapters in this book consider failure as that which has been, perhaps unfairly, submerged under a variety of dominant narratives. And yet, as the contributors have pointed out in many and varied ways, failure is in fact not hidden at all. It is, instead, something profoundly ordinary—something that we all know intimately, albeit from our own unique perspectives. It is part of the factical texture of our everyday engagements and, therefore, something that ought to be carefully considered as we work out our various theologies in fear and trembling. To say the least, the implications of taking failure seriously are ontological, epistemological, and teleological. Failure has implications for ethics, psychology, and politics, and any number of other human endeavors. In other words, failure speaks not only to what happens, but to what life itself is. Also, in terms of the frame provided in this introductory chapter, failure asks us to rethink how we have perceived things, as well as how we might still perceive things. It is thus not merely a pronouncement of the end of anything, but a condition of possibility. Perhaps it is even one of the conditions for the possibility of theology itself.

Bibliography

Acaster, James. *Jame Acaster's Classic Scrapes*. London: Headline, 2017.

Capon, Robert Farrar. *Kingdom, Judgement, Grace: Paradox, Outrage, and Vindication in the Parables of Jesus*. Grand Rapids: Eerdmans, 1989.
Chesterton, G. K. *Collected Works, Volume 1: Orthodoxy, Heretics, The Blatchford Controversies*. San Francisco: Ignatius, 1986.
Coronado, Raúl. *A World Not to Come: A History of Latino Writing and Print Culture*. Cambridge, MA: Harvard University Press, 2013.
Halberstam, Jack. *The Queer Art of Failure*. Durham, NC: Duke University Press, 2011.
Hart, David Bentley. *The New Testament: A Translation*. New Haven, CT: Yale University Press, 2017.
Juul, Jesper. *The Art of Failure: An Essay on the Pain of Playing Video Games*. Cambridge, MA: MIT Press, 2013.
Morrin, Ross. "The *Citizen Kane* of Bad Movies." https://www.rossmorinfilm.com/the-citizen-kane-of-bad-movies.html.
Reyburn, Duncan B. *Seeing Things as They Are: G. K. Chesterton and the Drama of Meaning*. Eugene, OR: Cascade, 2016.
Sandage, Scott A. *Born Losers*. Cambridge, MA: Harvard University Press, 2005.
Sestero, Greg, and Tom Bissel. *The Disaster Artist*. London: Little Brown, 2013.

Part 1

Failing Well

2.

Yes, And

Let Us Learn from Improvisers the Power to Fail

Heather C. Ohaneson

"Failing, doing something that is morally reprehensible, that is a great sin—well, many people will never come back from that. But the Christian way would be to get up and try again. Maybe not consciously, but you get yourself into a situation where you can make another choice." —Martin Scorsese.

"'You're not very good at this game,' I say. 'It'll take you twice as long to learn it!' This treats their failure as survivable, whereas if I said, 'But you must master this!' I would be adding to their despair."
—Keith Johnstone, *Impro for Storytellers.*

Christians are free to fail. The grace that marks Christian living means that Christians can, and occasionally do, find hope and joy amidst present circumstances—apart from success. Jesus' own failure, I speculate, is the linchpin of that freedom. Mindful of Jesus' victory, which came through the failure called death, and of their own freedom, Christians should live openly, modeling a wonderfully un-serious acceptance of and identification with others: those deemed failures *and*, what may be harder, those who have won at all costs. In doing so, Christians should continuously look to and rely on the example of Christ's self-sacrificial, compassionate identification with humankind. That will enable Christians to risk failure comfortably, graciously, and rigorously, without giving up.

I imagine that you may be uncomfortable even broaching the thought that Jesus failed. (Freedom to speculate ends at sacrilege!) In what follows, drawing on the Jesuit theologian John Navone, I will attempt to make that christological possibility less troubling. The first section of this chapter, then, will address the paradoxicality of Jesus and his death in light of various senses of failure. The claim that, in its creativity and vitality—i.e., in its commitment to life—Christian freedom bears a strong resemblance to the power of improvisers will be forwarded in the second section through a treatment of practices central to improvisation. Improvisers continue playing in the face of failure, often through practicing variations of the "Yes, and" principle known as overacceptance.

If, for Christians, life eternal and abundant is the chief value, then for improvisers, "play's the thing." Through their expertise and will to play, improvisers keep the play going by receiving, responding to, and redeeming the contributions of their fellow players. Rather than let their performance come to an end at the first sign of difficulty, they make choices that will allow for further choices. They persevere. Failures or mistakes are even appreciated as opportunities for virtuosity and as potential sources of extraordinary beauty; they can be the occasions of remarkable, creative feats, which bring forth transcendent "flow" experiences that surpass alternate (safer, more direct, less interesting) routes to excellence. In the conclusion, I return explicitly to theology. After underscoring similarities between Christians and improvisers, I attempt a further step into speculative theology. It is not only that Christians stand to learn how to fail from Jesus and from improvisers but that all people straining to live well amidst limitations are in a place to emulate God, who is the ultimate improviser insofar as God "will devise plans so as not to keep an outcast banished forever from his presence" (2 Sam 14:14b). God accomplishes a glorious feat and demonstrates an incredible commitment to the continuance and enhancement of life as God receives, responds to, and redeems the actions and accidents of humanity. God makes good on the enormous loss that came through human sin by saying, "Yes, and I have a Son."

Jesus' Paradoxical Failure

Failure, and its purported antonym, success, may be understood in a variety of ways. Failure may be conceived as and perhaps differentiated from error, mistake, fault, and shortcoming. It likely bears a negative connotation as something (deeply) undesirable, while holding an association with negativity (as in deficiency and lack). It may be dreaded. We may seek to avoid failure at all costs, unless we work in Silicon Valley, in which case we are permitted to fail fast. A bad act may spill over into a general state of being: from having failed in particular instances, I may *be* a failure. In discussions of failure, Samuel Beckett may be quoted; clichés may be trotted out and even believed. Alternatively, clichés may be ardently denied as writers hold up harder-edged truths to view. Thus, David Zahl unveils "silver-lining-itis," and Stephen Marche encourages us to fail better because failure is all there is.[1]

Furthermore, failure may be spliced into categories, arranged into types. Of these, I appreciate Mike Ford's threefold classification of (1) terminal failure, which causes an activity to cease; (2) temporary failure, from which one may recover; and (3) felicitous failure, which increases rather than impairs the degree of the activity's success.[2] In what follows, in addition to relying on Ford's typology, I will move between distinctions between paradoxical failure and "real" failure, and between graceful failure and failure marked by a lack of grace.

The sense of literal or final termination is reflected in one of the definitions of the verb "to fail," viz., "[t]o become extinct; to die out, lose vitality, pass away."[3] Perhaps this is why discrete experiences of failure within an individual's lifespan appear so threatening psychologically: in presaging the physiological inability of the human body to persist, failures expose our existential vulnerability.[4] Or, as Jack Halberstam summarily states, "To live is to fail, to bungle, to disappoint, and ultimately to die."[5] The sequence of mistakes, weaknesses, and foibles within a life

---

1. Zahl, "Failed Confessions of a Success-o-holic." As Marche puts it, "To fail better, to fail gracefully and with composure, is so essential because there's no such thing as success. It's failure all the way down." Marche, "Failure is Our Muse."

2. Ford, "'To Act or to Keep on Acting, or to Stop Acting,'" 4–6.

3. *OED*, 2nd ed., s.v. "fail, v.," I.2b.

4. Contrariwise, God is celebrated in the New Testament book of Hebrews for God's years never failing (1:2).

5. Halberstam, *The Queer Art of Failure*, 186–87. Cf. Navone, *Theology of Failure*, 13. John Williams, moreover, writes of death as "the slow, quiet attrition of time against

culminate in death; death appears as the terminus of such a spectrum of failure, the last stop. It is "loss without the possibility of being found."[6]

In theological terms, however, human imperfections are thought to exact death; death is the cost of sin (Rom 6:23). But how should failure be understood in relation to biblical concepts of sin? Do "falling short," "missing the mark," and "failing to hit the target"—phrases used to explain the meaning of the ancient Greek term *hamartia* as it occurs throughout the New Testament—count as proper failures? When Jesus takes on human sin without sinning as 2 Corinthians 5:21 suggests, does Jesus also accept human failing without failing? And could a sinless life produce the "end" of death?[7]

Dying was one of the ways in which Jesus failed—and, paradoxically, how he succeeded—according to Navone.[8] Jesus reached the end, the end that all human beings reach when our bodies expire. He thus relates to the full extent of the human experience because he himself met the limitation of the mortal body in death. The remarkability of Jesus' thorough identification with humanity bears further reflection. In his deity, Jesus neither made himself immune to the vulnerability and weakness people experience when we confront death, nor did he exempt himself from the ignominy of public crucifixion. He did not call a legion of angels to deliver him from the humiliation of execution or its excruciating pain; rather, he humbled himself to the ultimate possible extent (Matt 26:53; Phil 2:8). It is precisely in offering his body as a sacrifice that Jesus did *not* fail to fulfill the will of God.[9] He was obedient to the end. Conversely, if Jesus had ascended into heaven before the resurrection, i.e., without undergoing death, he would have *appeared* victorious by ordinary human standards and yet he would have failed to know the human condition perfectly.

But there is a greater paradox than Jesus' successful endurance of the ultimate human failure of the loss of life. It is precisely through dying that Jesus transcended death as such (1 Cor 15). To reiterate: if he had not died or if he had died in a sinful state, he would have "really" failed by not

---

imperfect flesh." Stoner, 41.

6. Schulz, "When Things Go Missing."

7. Note two possible senses of "end" and how they affect the meaning of the question. Would a sinless life not result in death because it lacked the cause of mortality? Would sinlessness or faultlessness be required for overcoming death once and for all?

8. Navone, *Theology of Failure*, 13, 100.

9. Ibid., 12.

completing his salvific mission (John 12:27).[10] The stakes were cosmically high, even as they were predicated on a puzzle. Jesus secured victory by losing his life; in his death, Jesus proved to be a perfect failure. In that way, he moved the boundary, replacing the marker of mortality with "life without end." By laying down his life, he made the end a no-end.

When Christians relate the resurrection to Passover, they do more than acknowledge the historical context of Jesus' death, which occurred during that festival. They proclaim another exodus. As Moses led the people of Israel out of the slavery of Egypt, Jesus carved a path of freedom for all peoples from the enslavement to death. He initiated "a new exodus act which creates and reveals the way of liberation from the condition of failure and its apparent finality."[11] To use the language of Ford's schema, we may say that Jesus canceled terminal failure.

That is why Christians are people of hope; through Jesus, they have faced the worst of all failures and seen beyond them to triumph. Knowing death as it has been transformed into the gateway to life, they have a future-oriented, life-oriented vision that allows them to imagine the reworking of any mistake—even the gravest of errors. As Navone writes: "This is the lesson of the cross, where the very symbol of failure and death has been transformed into a symbol of love and life. Love overcomes failure by reversing its meaning, by giving it a new meaning, a positive, redeeming meaning that becomes the message and good news of the disciples of Jesus."[12] An enormous theoretical and structural question remains, however. Why are the paradoxes of victory through loss and life through death effective? Did God have to put death to death through death? Was there another way for God to undo sin and transcend its effects, through sheer, unadulterated victory, say? Was there a crossless path to redemption? Perhaps the dual identity of Jesus as the God-man accounts for or, more strongly, demands the framework of apparent contradictions. It may be, further, that Jesus' drive to compassion was so strong that he chose a form of victory to which fallible human beings could relate.

Navone is bold enough to consider a second mode of failure on Jesus' part, which Navone describes as Jesus' historical failure. The fact that Jesus did not see the success of the movement of his followers within his own lifetime is relatively obvious. Such a lack of success frequently

---

10. Note, "really" failing may be contrasted with paradoxically failing.
11. Navone, *Theology of Failure*, 15.
12. Ibid., 3.

goes overlooked and unstated, however. Navone makes his point without mincing words: Jesus "died a failure."[13] In dying, Jesus not only experienced the failure of the mortal body to perdure, he suffered social condemnation as an unsuccessful leader.[14] As Navone explains it, Jesus accepted his failure to convert Israel within his lifetime, trusting that the Father loved him apart from his deeds. He committed the result of his work to God. In that, he modeled a radical freedom. Using the language of ultimacy (which may be related to finality), Navone expounds:

> Jesus submits to the disgrace and opprobrium of historical failure in a way that, through the gift of his Spirit, reveals to [hu]mankind that its historical failure is not absolute, ultimate, or meaningless. Jesus' acceptance of failure and death is a sharing in the universal human condition which, through the gift of his Spirit of love at Pentecost, is revealed as a hopeful condition because love rather than failure is the ultimate possibility for all [hu]mankind.[15]

At least three facets of Navone's theology of failure are pertinent here with respect to improvisation. The first is Jesus' radical *openness*. Jesus opened himself to failure and death in accepting—instead of resisting—them. A second, related idea is that of Jesus' *perseverance*. Instead of being paralyzed by fear, he moved forward, made new decisions, took further actions. He looked beyond history, rejecting the imminent end as the last word. Thirdly, in pressing through undesirable realities, Jesus exercised a dependence on the Father that was beautiful and freeing. Navone convincingly claims that genuine human freedom is incompatible with the crippling fear that surrounds the possibility of failure.[16] When we succumb to anxiety, we experience a paralysis that prevents the free making of further choices. Conversely, when we fail epically, we experience a release, which often proves extremely liberating.[17] On Navone's account, Jesus achieved true freedom by relying on the love God had for him (1 John 4:16).[18] As long as we cling to the goal of uniform success,

---

13. Ibid., 11.
14. Ibid., 12.
15. Ibid., 15.
16. Ibid., 13. Cf. Moltmann, *Theology of Play*, 14.
17. Mark C. Taylor makes a similar point with respect to vulnerability and invulnerability. *Field Notes from Elsewhere*, 270–71.
18. The theologian of play David L. Miller observes that people do not always win by winning or lose by losing. His argument is, in part, etymological. The English word

then, we are not truly free. While we are caught up in the pursuit of short-term acclaim, we are blinded to the ultimate power and importance of love, which becomes the final goal of life. As Navone charges, the person "who cannot accept the possibility of complete, radical, personal failure in the carrying out of his Christian mission is not sharing that absolute poverty of spirit which characterized the *freedom* of Jesus to accept the divinely appointed means for his mission."[19]

Thus, Jesus' failure and his attitude toward failure provide a deep source of freedom for his followers. Yes, Christians are liberated from having to worry about succeeding, thanks to the belief that God *succeeded* for humankind, in our place. (This "positive" substitution is usually expressed in the idea the Jesus lived a perfect, sinless life, the victorious and virtuous status of which he is willing to give away.) And, what happens if the standard theological position is thought in reverse? May people also be relieved that God *failed* in the place of humankind? If God took on the ultimate accomplishment *and* the ultimate failure, then individuals no longer have to worry about failing that badly.[20] Alongside or within the freedom to fail, there is the amazing comfort that Jesus identifies with failures and losers, all those of us who have disappointed ourselves and others. God, through Jesus, put an end (as it were) to the once-terminal failure of death, replacing death with love. Such a gospel message has always had currency among the poor in spirit; in fact, that very appeal is part of the good news' goodness. I am simply reframing it in the language of failure and loss.[21]

Note, there is an apparent consistency across the paradoxes of Christianity. Christ is the God-man who identifies with sinners and thus grants a righteousness that must be appropriated in what Søren Kierkegaard calls earnest jest.[22] Grace balances grace. Having an attitude of grace towards God's grace thus leads to a rigorous way of being in which

---

win derives from the German verb *gewinnen*: to gain by effort. The English word *lose* traces its origin to the ancient Greek verb *luein*: to release, set free, detach. "Playing the Game to Lose," 105–6.

19. Navone, *Theology of Failure*, 11, emphasis added. Cf. Wells, *Improvisation*, 67–69.

20. Paul in Romans 6 emphatically denies that grace is grounds to sin. Similarly, this freedom is not a license to fail in the "real," ultimate, or non-graceful senses of failure.

21. Cf. Miller, "Playing the Game to Lose."

22. Roberts, "Smiling with God," 173.

one's actions are regarded as tremendously important but nevertheless non-salvific. They are meaningful actions but they are free because they do not proceed from the necessity of attaining salvation. Failure is possible—even nonthreatening—because success in the most important things is assured, having already been secured externally by God.[23] In the light of Jesus' life, Christians are free to "live forward," facing the future with hope, unbeset by shortcomings, unchained from past mistakes, unafraid of death, and confident in the endless triumph of love.

Additional support for the view of perseverance as a peculiarly Christian ethic comes from the perhaps surprising source of Hollywood director Martin Scorsese. In Scorsese's long-awaited movie adaptation of Shusaku Endo's novel *Silence*, one encounters the character of Sebastian Rodrigues, a Jesuit priest in seventeenth-century Japan. Through Rodrigues's story, *Silence* addresses fundamental questions concerning the nature of faith, including the question of whether even apostasy can be survived and put to redemptive use. In other words, what counts as ultimate failure? Is there any failure from which a Christian cannot rebound? As Scorsese shares with Paul Elie for his *New York Times Magazine* article on the director:

> "It goes back to what Father Principe was telling me the last time I saw him, a couple of years ago," [Scorsese] said. "Failing, doing something that is morally reprehensible, that is a great sin—well, many people will never come back from that. But the Christian way would be to get up and try again. Maybe not consciously, but you get yourself into a situation where you can make another choice. And that's the situation Rodrigues is in—he can choose to save the lives of others by renouncing his faith, the act he considers most reprehensible of all."[24]

---

23. At the same time that he celebrates the transcendence of death, Paul urges followers of Christ to pursue excellence—a stance with which Kierkegaard's view on the gracious reception of grace accords. "The sting of death is sin, and the power of sin is the law. But thanks be to God, who gives us the victory through our Lord Jesus Christ. Therefore, my beloved [brothers], be steadfast, immovable, always excelling in the work of the Lord, because you know that in the Lord your labor is not in vain" (1 Cor 15:56–58). Once again, we are attempting to walk along the razor's edge of excellent failure. In this model, the freedom to fail does not entail laziness; it does not produce willful sin. It leads one to implant one's work in the Lord, so to speak, performing it for the Lord's sake, and entrusting its meaning and results to the Lord (cf. 1 Cor 3:5–9).

24. Elie, "Redemption," 47.

There may be a number of reasons why Scorsese identifies getting up and trying again as "the Christian way." Perhaps divine attributes such as patience and grace, as well as the assurance of forgiveness, allow Christians to overcome past failures and "move on." But maybe perseverance is quintessentially Christian because of how Jesus kept going. Did he stop at death? No! He rose again! By accepting the failure of death, Jesus set himself up to make the next choice, to exercise the power to conquer death and rise again to life. In passing through the cross, Jesus reached the resurrection and secured the unsurpassable victory: the victory over death as such (1 Cor 15:26).

These approaches toward choice, failure, and risk are directly relevant to the art of improvisation, where the joint value and practice of perseverance is particularly evident.

Improvisation: The Play's the Thing

A number of characterizations of improvisation reappear across the literature, not only in technical "how-to" guides and training manuals but also in theoretical investigations. Among these are freedom and spontaneity, which are frequently said to exist alongside formal structure and constraints; the notion of practice in the twofold sense of discipline and ongoing exercise—an unfinished process that is therefore able to resist commodification; making and accepting offerings; novelty and repetition; risk and responsibility; attentiveness; the careful listening and negotiation of power that accompany antiphony (patterns of call and response); losses of layers of self and time; and the ability to be surprised by accomplishing things unknown or previously thought impossible.

The spirit of improvisation is movingly conveyed in a monologue by Herbie Hancock, in which he describes an experience of playing with Miles Davis in Stuttgart, Germany around 1963. He narrates and reflects:

> I remember that we were playing "So What," one of Miles' compositions from the late 50s I guess. Um, uh, and Tony Williams, Tony Williams was playing drums, Ron Carter bass, Wayne Shorter saxophone. And it was a really hot night. The music was, was tight. It was powerful, it was innovative, and fun. We were having a lot of fun. And it was, the music was *on*. Tony Williams was burning on his drums. And, um, so right in the middle of Miles' solo, when he was playing one of his *amazing* solos, and I'm trying, you know, I'm in there, and I'm playing.

Right in the middle of his solo, I play the wrong chord—a chord that was . . . it just sounded completely wrong. It sounded like a big mistake. And I did this and I went "ehhh," like this, I put my hands around my ears. And Miles paused for a second, and then he played some notes that made my chord right, he made it correct, which astounded me. I was, I couldn't believe what I heard. He—Miles was able to make something that was wrong into something that was right with, with the power of his, of the choice of notes that he made and that feeling that he had. And so I couldn't play for, for about a minute. I couldn't even touch the piano. You know. But, uh, what I realize now is that Miles didn't hear it as a mistake. He heard it as something that happened, just an event. And so that was part of the reality of what was happening at that moment. And he dealt with it. He found something that, um, since he didn't hear it as a mistake, he felt it was his responsibility to find something that fit. And he was able to do that. That, that taught me a *very* big lesson about not only music but about life. You know, we can look for the world to be as we would like it to be as individuals, you know, make it easy for me. That idea. We can look for that. But I think the important thing is that we grow. And the only way that we can grow is to have a mind that's open enough to be able to accept situations, to be able to experience situations as they are and turn them into medicine, turn poison into medicine. Take whatever situation you have and make, make something constructive with it. That's what I learned from that situation with Miles.[25]

The theologico-improvisatory acts of receiving, responding, and redeeming appear within this powerful recounting of an experience of generous virtuosity. According to Hancock, in that set in Stuttgart, Miles Davis displayed a number of admirable qualities that have ethical resonance. Davis accepted or received a mistake in a gracious way that did not make the offender (namely, Hancock) feel ashamed. In responding to the purported failure of Hancock's "offering," *Davis* took responsibility. Davis applied his expertise—his power and choice of notes—to redeem what had come before without judging or trashing it; in his acceptance of Hancock's chord, he transformed the poison into medicine. While Hancock was stuck in what might be conceived as retrospective paralysis over his mistake—or perhaps was struck by awe at what Davis was doing to overcome it—Davis was keeping the play in motion.

25. This is my transcription of Herbie Hancock's remarks, which may be heard at https://www.youtube.com/watch?v=FL4LxrN-iyw. I thank David Williams for bringing this video to my attention.

Key to redemption, then, is reappropriation. Davis did not move on by leaving Hancock's playing behind and creating something entirely new. Rather, he exercised innovation in how he salvaged what came before.[26] Such technique may be conceived as commitment. Commitment to accident (rather than the accident itself) is what is partially determinative of the excellence of improvisatory acts. It is not so much the quality manifested by the initial offering itself that matters—which is precisely why Davis did not judge Hancock's mistake as a mistake—but what is done with it—whether the players commit to the offering by reappropriating it.

"Commitment" to the contributions of one's fellow players may be described in the language of improv 101 as the practice of overaccepting (the "Yes, and" technique of this chapter's title), which includes integrating the offerings of others—including their real or merely perceived mistakes—into an unfolding work. Overaccepting is distinguished from ordinary accepting in its active character. Rather than passively taking something entirely on someone else's terms, a player who practices overaccepting exerts power by shaping the other's offering as she receives it. Forward movement is stalled if a choice (whether good, bad, or neutral) is rejected in an outright fashion or ignored—as an inappropriate (i.e., unrelated and nonsensical) response or a non-cooperative "No" would represent.[27] Timing and patience are important here in developing patterns and reimagining contexts. "Blocking" offerings would bring play to a halt, leading to a series of stunted, short segments. Not giving each other enough time to explore and develop improvisatory lines would prevent great moments from emerging. Perhaps counterintuitively, accepting some merely okay thing by following through on it may prove value-enhancing.[28]

To give an example of how radical acceptance provides a way forward in play: In a blues song with the typical AAB line structure, the first line "A" that someone spontaneously throws out into the improvisatory arena may be quite weak on its own. Alternately, it may be considered

26. Cf. "Scrap Yard Challenge—Junkyard Wars" in Peters, *Philosophy of Improvisation*, especially pages 17–19.

27. Furthermore, by moving forward and focusing on the next move, one resists the forming of judgements, which lingering on the past affords. Bailey, *Improvisation*, 35.

28. Many sources attest to this forward-pressing practice. See, for example, Taylor, *Notes and Tones*, 52, quoted in Bertinetto, "'Do Not Fear Mistakes—There Are None,'" 90–91.

as something of a merely neutral quality until it is engaged—insofar as it is what follows that determines its merit or significance. The line can *become* impressive and gain artistic meaning simply by players' committing to and building upon it. Repetition is a sign of this acceptance *and* a means of improving. In playing the less than stellar line a second time, the players announce a willingness to build their play around that accidental choice and to strengthen it by investing further creativity in it. All of a sudden, it gains in aesthetic value. The confirmation of the line "A" lays the path for further surprises, enabling additional turns, which are potentially deeply gratifying, to emerge. This is how repetition links to novelty, how it even opens up the path to difference. When an alternate line (line "B") is grafted onto the "A-A" string, the song begins to take shape. Other layers are woven around the initial offering as the play continues. More choices are made, taken up, and repeated. The AAB structure of blues collaboration is a version of the "Yes, and" procedure.

Repetition does not allow for sentimentalism, however. When players (such as actors, musicians, dancers, or comedians) reach a collective place of excellence, when they have a moment of achievement, they must resist the temptation to remain in it too long or recreate it. Boredom lurks and safety dulls. Thus, improvisers are relentless in moving forward to produce new things, allowing acts or sounds or interactions to emerge that build on the direction of the current energy of the performance and, thus, that are "true" or appropriate to the new moment. Improvisational offerings, even excellent ones, are not safe from the spirit of creative destruction. Thus, in improvisation, there are contradictory impulses towards and away from repetition (and the past). On the one hand, repetition is resisted insofar as it is in tension with novelty, energy-bestowing risk, and the value that improvisers place on authentic responsiveness. On the other hand, repetition solidifies and even "makes good on" first offerings.

Despite idealized portraits, playing is not all acceptance, all the time. As the philosopher Gary Peters makes clear, there is a spectrum of combativeness and interpersonal care along which performances of improvisation occur. Challenges, posturing, and assertion are important aspects of improvisation.[29] At the end, after chaos and coherence have

---

29. Peters, *Philosophy of Improvisation*, 51, 53. In challenging sentimentalism, Peters states, "There is an idealism in improvisation that is heart-warming but misguided. The terminology that inhabits and informs the hegemonic dialogical language of care, enabling, sharing, and participation is only aesthetically productive to the extent that

mixed, there may be peace—a freedom-infused moment of stillness before the new round is taken up—but along the way there is struggle.[30] In addition to being a practice of freedom, improvisation is a practice of contestation.

This combativeness relates in crucial but not immediately apparent ways to what may be thought of as "good failure" and the grace that allows play to continue. The push and pull between power and freedom introduces a significant dynamism into improvisation, a competitive destabilization that takes the focus off of the individual players and, according to Peters, redirects their interests to the origin of their work of art. In addition to being a site of destruction out of which novelty may be coaxed, then, failure is a crucial element of improvisation because it provides improvisers the opportunity to value play above themselves. To return to Ford's framework, failure is felicitous when it increases the success of an event.[31] And, in my estimation, failure draws on the actual powers of improvisation—i.e., the skillful, genuine, and spontaneous responding to events so as to elevate the continuation of play above sheer or shallow success.

Peters develops these claims concerning the edginess that keeps improvisation vital by engaging the techniques of Keith Johnstone, the founder of Theatresports and author of *Impro for Storytellers* and *Impro: Improvisation and the Theatre*. In his work training improvisers and putting on shows of improvisational competition, Johnstone *depersonalizes* the players' experiences of fear, power, loss, and success. "It is the shifting of the balance of power that is crucial, not who has it. It is the possibility of failure or success that gives improvisation its edge rather than who succeeds or fails," to quote Peters's analysis.[32] By valuing "the happening of the artwork" more than any one person or personality, the improvisation expert and troupe leader spurs on a form of play that is both gracious and anticipatory. Referring to and building on Johnstone's writing, which contains the language of grace, Peters states:

> To fail "gracefully" is to fail successfully. It is to recognize that such failure is necessary for the work to continue. Such failure

---

it confronts the far from ideal reality of the work, where the necessity of singularity plays havoc with any dreams of universal consensus." Ibid., 50.

30. Ibid., 36.
31. Ford, "'To Act or to Keep on Acting, or to Stop Acting,'" 6.
32. Peters, *Philosophy of Improvisation*, 59.

is liberatory in two ways but also tragic on account of this very dualism. The sacrifice of performers is a necessary part of the work's happening (for Johnstone, the avoidance of boredom), but this failure liberates the artist from the task of trying to gather and hold together both the origin and the event or performance of the work within the temporality of aesthetic production: the duality of creation and preservation. And the artist *needs* to be liberated from this task in order to fully recognize its impossibility and, thus, its significance. In this sense such liberation might be best understood as an emancipation from the illusions of success that, in their foregrounding of the artist, obscure and trivialize the origin of the work of art. The liberation of the artist releases, in turn, the artwork from the gathering grasp of the singular artist, allowing it to return to its origin, which continues to happen as the singularity of production ebbs and flows. It is the liberation of the artwork from the cramped intentionality of the singular artist that ensures the continuing presence of the origin in the unfolding of the work, and it is the graceful failure of the artist that is required to keep this origin in play. To fail without grace is to lose sight of the origin, obscured or displaced by the success of the work.[33]

If for Johnstone the highest commitment is to keeping the play going, the preeminent consideration for Peters as these lines evince is the continuing presence of the origin as the work of improvisation unfolds. Everything seems to flow for Peters from the distinction between the *concealment* and the *presencing* of the origin (the Heideggerean references being explicit for him).[34] Under the undesirable, concealing side of the dichotomy would fall the individual artist along with intentionality and what I will refer to as "plain success" (versus Peters's version of the success of failure). Their venerable contrasts, which are indicative of the ongoing presencing of the origin, include the following: not artwork *tout simple* but artwork-and-artist-in-co-emergence; the impossibility of the dual performance of creativity and preservation; and successful failure—i.e., graceful failure.

---

33. Ibid., 60–61, original emphasis. An unusually novel aspect of this treatment of improvisation is Peters's willingness to rethink originality itself. Peters contributes to discussions of improvisation by drawing readers' attention to the prehistory of an aesthetic work (1).

34. "[I]t is not simply that the origin is lost in the destructive preservation of tradition and then mourned as a perpetual absence but, rather, that the 'founding leap' (*ursprung* [sic]) of origination is always present as the call of the work's future." Ibid., 62.

Failure and success might get tangled in an interpretation of this passage, so it is important to be clear. Failure, not plain success, is the friend of play. (Success might be the friend of the player.) This is because success hinders the proper continuing of play by drawing attention to the player ("the singular artist") over and above the origin. Other theorists of play have pointed out that success is the enemy of play in that winning puts games to an end. The sense of loss after one has won—for the play is lost then—leads to alternate forms of playing, such as speed-running in video games.[35]

Failure rises above plain success in Peters's estimation because failure denies the illusion that the artist could ever hold the origin and the ongoing event of art together. But the two, fundamentally different kinds of failure hinge on grace. Not surprisingly, the relation to origin is determinative of this status. Peters privileges graceful failure because it "keeps [the] origin in play." It does this by releasing the *artwork*—not the artist—from being "cramped." It is the artist, after all, who is failing. This is the manner in which Peters, by way of Johnstone, introduces grace to improvisation, though parallels with Jesus' graceful failure are apparent.[36]

Conclusion

As the principle of the givenness of redemption, grace finds expression in improvisation in players' prizing of play over product, i.e., in their affirmation that "the play's the thing," or perhaps even more strongly, *failure's the thing*.[37] It is not that all improvisation has a graceful sheen; very often, the discomfort (and thrill) that one senses in watching an improvised performance is the keen awareness that the players might not "pull it off." What they do is hard. Routinely that difficulty is not disguised. But perseverance scales up: Even the (purported) failures that are not success-

---

35. More than some analogue games, video games are structured so that if a player wants to stretch the possibility of play for the sheer joy of it, or keep the play experience going even after a victory, she can. See Franklin, "'We Need Radical Gameplay, Not Just Radical Graphics,'" 170–76. Cf. Taylor, *Field Notes from Elsewhere*, 269.

36. The themes of failure, play, and grace reverberate with Hugo Rahner's discussion of the mystic's willing surrender in *Man at Play*, 55–58.

37. Marche once more: "If there are to be any claims to greatness, they are to be found only in the scope of the failure and persistence in the face of it. That persistence may be the one truly writerly virtue, a salvation indistinguishable from stupidity. To keep going, despite everything. To keep bellying up to the cosmic irrelevance. To keep failing." "Failure is Our Muse."

fully overaccepted within a performance do not bring improvisation as a practice to an end. Where failures persist, improvisation may be found.

I would wager to say that where grace appears in improvisation in general is in the attitude towards risk. Because improvisers and Christians have the freedom to fail, and because failure itself is freeing, they can countenance risk. (Imagine Christian improvisers!) The assurance of redemption, salvability, is the ground of this freedom. An overall sense of security paradoxically spurs dangerous choices and chanciness. These issues not only relate to freedom but also extend to *work* in the following, colloquial manner.

During improvisation, attempts at creativity might not "work out." We have noted that, in addition to being thoroughly permissible and expected, failure may be necessary for novelty. Knowing ahead of time that any improvisatory line or offering can be saved (in the sense of being salvaged, not preserved) does not lead to laziness. Instead, it allows the players to keep the play going long enough to benefit from their risks and failures. Paradoxically, it is this order of value—play over product—that enables the creation of groundbreaking art. Such commitment to continuance sounds similar to the character Rodrigues's desire not to stop at his renunciation of faith but to give space to his failure so as to eke blessing from it. Abiding is key (John 15:1–11).

The persistence of improvisation both in the face of failure as well as in the face of the freedom to fail parallels what I understand the apostle Paul, Søren Kierkegaard, and other Christian theological thinkers to have maintained about Christianity as a strenuous but unstriving faith. Christ's once-and-for-all success—which came, not incidentally, through loss—determines the way of life of believers. Knowing that all of their past and future failures are comprehended and covered, they can (and do) undertake difficult callings such as denying themselves and loving their enemies (Luke 9:24; Matt 5:44). They live salubriously in the simultaneity of heeding Jesus' commands and falling short of them.

What undergirds this framework for human existence, including Jesus' human existence, which incorporates failure, improvisation, and redemption, may be the ongoing play of God. God may be said to make the rules up as God goes along (à la Wittgenstein and 2 Samuel 14:14), concocting, say, the incarnation in order to save lives.[38] What virtuosity in adaptability! Or, as the biblical scholar Terence Fretheim proposes,

---

38. Wittgenstein, *Philosophical Investigations*, §83, quoted in Bertinetto, "'Do Not Fear Mistakes—There Are None,'" 95.

in entering into human history and responding to human needs, God "works with what is available at any moment, with human beings as they are, with all their foibles and flaws, and within existing societal structures and possibilities, however inadequate."[39] The divine acceptance of the limits of human beings entails openness to criticism and failure.[40] Rather than diminish divine sovereignty, the countenance of cosmic risk heightens the visible power of God. God is turning poison into medicine.

The "Yes, and" ethic that characterizes improvisation—and which seems to account to an extent for God's actions in the world—has implications for the walk of faith. Christians' overriding commitment, rather than the accomplishment of any one thing, is to remaining in Christ and continuing the journey towards conformity to him—persisting in the freely productive play of faith, victory after victory, failure after failure, life without end (John 15:4–10; Rom 8:29).[41] They are not alone, however. Johannes Climacus goes so far as to say that God "in his resolution" is "now obliged to continue" in his venture, as if a player no less than God is committed to keeping the play going.[42]

Bibliography

Bailey, Derek. *Improvisation: Its Nature and Practice in Music*. Boston: Da Capo, 1993.
Bertinetto, Alessandro. "'Do Not Fear the Mistakes—There are None': The Mistake as Surprising Experience of Creativity in Jazz." In *Education as Jazz: Interdisciplinary Sketches on a New Metaphor*, edited by Marina Santi and Eleonora Zorzi, 85–100. Newcastle upon Tyne: Cambridge Scholars, 2016.
Elie, Paul. "Redemption." *New York Times Magazine*, November 27, 2016, 44–67.
"Fail, v." *Oxford English Dictionary*. http://o-www.oed.com.patris.apu.edu/view/Entry/67654?result=3&rskey=8401lg&.
Firestein, Stuart. *Failure: Why Science Is So Successful*. Oxford: Oxford University Press, 2016.
Ford, Mike. "'To Act or to Keep on Acting, or to Stop Acting': Human-Computer Improvisation and Three Types of Failure." New York: n.p., 2017.
Franklin, Seb. "'We Need Radical Gameplay, Not Just Radical Graphics': Towards a Contemporary Minor Practice in Computer Gaming." *Symplokē* 17.1–2 (2009) 163–80.
Fretheim, Terence E. "Divine Foreknowledge, Divine Constancy, and the Rejection of Saul's Kingship." *Catholic Biblical Quarterly* 47 (1985) 595–602.

---

39. Fretheim, "Divine Foreknowledge," 601.
40. Ibid., 601–2.
41. Kierkegaard, *Concluding Unscientific Postscript*, 80–86.
42. Kierkegaard, *Philosophical Fragments*, 55.

Halberstam, Judith. *The Queer Art of Failure*. Durham, NC: Duke University Press, 2011.

Hancock, Herbie. "Miles Davis According to Herbie Hancock." https://www.youtube.com/watch?v=FL4LxrN-iyw.

Johnstone, Keith. *Impro for Storytellers: Theatresports and the Art of Making Things Happen*. New York: Faber and Faber, 1999.

Juul, Jesper. *The Art of Failure: An Essay on the Pain of Playing Video Games*. Cambridge, MA: MIT Press, 2013.

Kierkegaard, Søren. *Concluding Unscientific Postscript to Philosophical Fragments*. Vol. 1. Translated by Howard V. Hong and Edna H. Hong. Princeton, NJ: Princeton University Press, 1992.

———. *Philosophical Fragments*. Translated by Howard V. Hong and Edna H. Hong. Princeton, NJ: Princeton University Press, 1985.

Marche, Stephen. "Failure is Our Muse." *New York Times*, July 25, 2014. https://www.nytimes.com/2014/07/27/opinion/sunday/failure-is-our-muse.html.

Miller, David L. "Playing the Game to Lose." In *Theology of Play*, attributed to Jürgen Moltmann, 99–110. New York: Harper and Row, 1972.

Moltmann, Jürgen. *Theology of Play*. Translated by Reinhard Ulrich. New York: Harper and Row, 1972.

Navone, John. *A Theology of Failure*. Mahwah, NJ: Paulist, 1974.

New Oxford Annotated Bible: New Revised Standard Version. Edited by Michael D. Coogan. Oxford: Oxford University Press, 2001.

Peters, Gary. *The Philosophy of Improvisation*. Chicago: University of Chicago Press, 2009.

Rahner, Hugo. *Man at Play*. Translated by Brian Battershaw and Edward Quinn. New York: Herder and Herder, 1972.

Roberts, Robert C. "Smiling with God: Reflections on Christianity and the Psychology of Humor." *Faith and Philosophy* 4.2 (April 1987) 168–75.

Schulz, Kathryn. "When Things Go Missing: Reflections on Two Seasons of Loss." *The New Yorker*, February 13 and 20, 2017. http://www.newyorker.com/magazine/2017/02/13/when-things-go-missing.

Taylor, Arthur. *Notes and Tones: Musician-to-Musician Interviews*. Boston: Da Capo, 1993.

Taylor, Mark C. *Field Notes from Elsewhere: Reflections on Dying and Living*. New York: Columbia University Press, 2009.

Wells, Samuel. *Improvisation: The Drama of Christian Ethics*. Grand Rapids: Brazos, 2004.

Williams, John. *Stoner*. New York: New York Review Books, 1965.

Wittgenstein, Ludwig. *Philosophical Investigations*. Translated by G. E. M. Anscombe. Malden, MA: Blackwell, 2001.

Zahl, David. "Failed Confessions of a Success-o-holic." *Mockingbird*, July 30, 2014. http://www.mbird.com/2014/07/confessions-of-a-success-o-holic/.

3.

A Popular Blogger's Theology of Failure

Glennon Doyle on the Redemptive Act of "Showing Up"

MARIANA ALESSANDRI

WHEN GLENNON DOYLE MELTON was asked by Oprah Winfrey about her impending divorce from her husband of twelve years, she refused to call it a failure. Instead, she declared:

> My marriage was/is a raging success . . . A marriage isn't a success just if it lasts until you die; as a matter of fact a marriage is *only* a success if it lasts until you die *if* you are both happy and having a good time and wanting to be there, but my marriage is a success because it was two people who sat together inside of love and pain and allowed it to make us wholer and braver and kinder and better people, and so we leave each other whole.[1]

Doyle runs a blog called *Momastery*, through which she is able to share her ideas about God, love, failure, addiction, etc. with millions. Followers have read her posts for the past eight years, during which time she also published two *New York Times* best-selling memoirs: *Carry on Warrior* (2013) and *Love Warrior* (2016). Just before the release of her second book, which deals with her husband's adultery and her previous decision to remain in the marriage, Doyle announced her divorce.

---

1. Melton, "I'm Live with Oprah Winfrey."

People routinely describe divorces as failed marriages, but Doyle is intent on quixotically transforming hers into a (raging) success, and in so doing develops and disseminates a fascinating theology of failure. In her response to Oprah's question above we can see that Doyle and her husband are pioneering a new kind of public separation: a loving divorce. She refuses to call it a failed marriage because she believes that "love never fails." For Doyle, no matter how much a divorce may resemble failure, as long as love is present, the marriage is and was a success; a married couple's separation doesn't automatically render their unity a failed project. Moreover, her attempt to redefine success and failure applies to areas outside of marriage and divorce. Based on her "field research of one," Doyle reveals a sophisticated, if non-scholarly, theology of failure, rooted in the idea that "God is forever tries," or, put differently, that turning back towards God is always possible.

In this short essay on Doyle's theology of failure, I argue that, while Doyle's definition of failure as the refusal to "show up" is largely rooted in traditional Catholic and Protestant theologies of sin and despair, she ultimately surpasses them, in part, by penetrating the culture of social media and reaching a secular audience. Doyle's fresh theology of failure is as compelling as it is accessible to non-theologians, who make up most of her followers. Academic theologians would do well to consider the work of Glennon Doyle, despite her non-traditional, non-academic status, since her popular theology has given the secular public what religious communities typically have: a way to redemption based on the deceptively simple task of showing up.

Doyle's Theological Lineage

Traditionally, sin and despair both refer to turning away from God. Doyle does not use the term *sin*, and only occasionally uses *despair*, but if she did, it would be easier to recognize her theological ancestry.[2] Although she no longer identifies with any specific Christian denomination, she was raised Catholic, and her writing reveals this. If Doyle used the word *sin* to describe the times we fall short, she would be explicitly tapping into a long and familiar Catholic theological lineage, one that locates sin

---

2. Doyle uses the terms *failure* and *not showing up* doubtless, in part, because her secular audience is more comfortable using these than the more explicitly theological terms, *sin* and *despair*.

in turning away from God, in the form of the Holy Spirit. Blasphemy is the ultimate, unforgivable sin, according to St. Augustine, consists in "sinning against the Holy Spirit," which, for Catholics, means spurning Truth.[3] In *Dominum et Vivificantem*, Pope John Paul II uses Augustine and Thomas Aquinas to explain why it's impossible for God to save someone who has turned away:

> Blasphemy against the Holy Spirit consists precisely in the radical refusal to accept this forgiveness, of which he is the intimate giver and which presupposes the genuine conversion which he brings about in the conscience. If Jesus says that blasphemy against the Holy Spirit cannot be forgiven either in this life or in the next, it is because this "non-forgiveness" is linked, as to its cause, to "non-repentance," in other words to the radical refusal to be converted.[4]

For Catholics, failing to turn to God who offers salvation constitutes sin. I suggest that Doyle holds the same position but replaces the term *sin* with the terms *failure* and *not showing up*, since she is blogging her theology for a secular world. The result is less problematic and perhaps more compelling, as I argue below.

If, on the other hand, Doyle used the term *despair* instead of *failure* or *not showing up* she would be aligning herself with someone like Søren Kierkegaard's Protestant pseudonym Anti-Climacus, who describes despair as the failure to accept the idea that one is not one's own, but was created by another. For Anti-Climacus, despair entails turning away, and when one is not "at every moment destroy[ing] the possibility of being in despair," then one is sinking deeper into it. He writes: "Every actual moment of despair is traceable to possibility; every moment he is in despair he is bringing it upon himself. It is always the present tense; in relation to the actuality there is no pastness of the past: in every actual moment of despair the person in despair bears all the past as a present in possibility."[5] For Anti-Climacus, when we are not turned toward God, we are necessarily turned away from God. For her modern, often nonreligious readers, Doyle calls this act of turning away "failure," and it includes turning away from God but also *Love*, *Truth*, and *Life*, terms she uses interchangeably.

3. Augustine, "Sermon 71, On Selected Lessons of the New Testament."
4. John Paul II, *Dominum et vivificantem*, 46. Thomas Aquinas called this sin *blasphemy*, and declared it unpardonable "in so far as it removes those things which are a means towards the pardon of sins." Aquinas, *Summa Theologica*, II, q.1, a. 3.
5. Kierkegaard, *The Sickness Unto Death*, 15, 17.

In short, for traditional Catholics and Protestants, sin and despair involve turning away from God; for Doyle, failure means refusing to "show up" to God and/or one another.

Doyle's Redefinition of Success as "Showing Up"

If we take Doyle's interpretation of her marriage and divorce as demonstrating the logic of her theology of failure, then the only way to fail, according to Doyle, is to not "show up." In other words, if she believed that divorce were itself a failure, then she could not hold the position that her marriage "was/is a raging success." For Doyle, there are ways to succeed while divorcing and, likewise, to fail while remaining married. Her marriage, separation, and divorce are successful because she and Craig are "showing up" to and for one another and for their children. For example, Doyle tells Oprah that her kids "will never see us speak poorly of each other," which is common enough, except for her reasoning.[6] Her refusal to trash-talk her cheating husband is not primarily a stifling of the angry self for the sake of her three kids, as it is for many divorcees. On the contrary, Doyle still loves her husband, but not in a scripted way, wherein the forsaken Christian wife tries to rescue her husband from his wayward, sinful path. Doyle explains that she and Craig will not speak poorly of each other because "we don't think poorly of each other. I actually think that Craig is kind of a hero to me—he's my kind of hero. He made a mess of things and then he stayed in it and fought for it, and he's better for it now, and so I respect the heck out of him."[7] Here Doyle uses "staying in it" and "fighting for it" to measure success. Most often, though, she calls it "showing up." One example Doyle uses from her separation is that Craig, having moved out of the house and having no reason to expect reconciliation, began to buy the groceries for the family and leave them on the front stoop. Instead of turning away from Doyle and his marriage, which would constitute sinning, despairing, failing, or just plain "not showing up," Craig's act of buying groceries was a way for him to "show up" to Love, his marriage, and Doyle.

---

6. Melton, "I'm Live with Oprah Winfrey."
7. Ibid.

Doyle's Life as a Failure

Long before her marriage ended, Doyle experienced what most people would call a series of failures. She became a bulimic at the age of ten. Her list of addictions quickly grew to include alcohol, drugs, and sex. She's received at least one DUI, been arrested five times, and had an abortion.[8] On Mother's Day in 2007, upon finding out that she was pregnant again, Doyle decided to have the baby, which for her meant deciding to immediately stop drinking, drugging, and purging. While both Doyle and society might agree to call her new self a "success" and her old self a series of "failures," it would be for significantly different reasons. From Doyle's point of view, what makes her current life a success is not her bestselling books, her awards, or even her children; it is *only* the fact that she "shows up" to it. Likewise, her *only* failure in life consisted in not showing up, in having hidden from life in her addictions. There is only one way to fail, for Doyle, and it is the same every time: to refuse to show up. Likewise, there's only one way to succeed: to show up. As difficult as it is to do, Doyle writes that she can only show up because she believes that "God is forever tries."

God is Forever Tries

The cycle that Doyle describes in *Love Warrior*—which began with her lying about her various addictions, and, when discovered, turned into begging her family's forgiveness along with earnestly promising to stop, only to end in deeper addictions—was a cycle that actually prevented her from changing. She wondered how many times she could reasonably ask to be forgiven, and how meaningful her promise could have been if she had made a similar one a month before. In a word, Doyle considered herself "unforgivable," which Anti-Climacus describes as yet another "movement away from God."[9] Doyle remembers thinking: "I've run out of tries. I can't ask for forgiveness again. I'm out of forgiveness. I've used up so much more than my fair share. I should do everyone I love a favor and just disappear."[10] Even Doyle's very forgiving parents reached the end

---

8. Melton, *Carry On Warrior*, 5; Melton, *Love Warrior*, 42–43, 47.

9. Kierkegaard, *Sickness*, 111–12.

10. Melton: "Hey loves. Look! This is what a survivor looks like." Anti-Climacus calls the act in which a person in despair declares himself unforgivable just a "substitute for humbly beginning by humbly thanking God that he helped him to resist

of their patience. In what seemed to be a final attempt to help her by using "tough love," Doyle's parents made her an appointment with a priest. But before she even talked with him, Doyle realized that "God is forever tries" (though that precise formulation came later).

This theological insight came inside a Catholic church. While staring at a painting of Mary, Glennon felt that Mary understood Doyle's rock-bottom predicament, and that she loved her anyway. Mary, who on that night Doyle describes as God-as-mother, represented endless, unconditional mercy. In contrast, the priest, whom Doyle describes as an "administrator" of God, explained to her the standard equation whereby her repentance was necessary for God to forgive her sins. Glennon noticed, however, that Mary hadn't demanded repentance; she had only invited Doyle to rest. Mary's free forgiveness elicited a childhood memory in which Doyle witnessed a boy mischievously crawl into an ice cream truck and begin to hand out free popsicles from the back, unbeknownst to the ice cream seller who continued to charge for the popsicles through the window. Mary was the mischievous boy: that night she offered Doyle forgiveness for free while the priest charged for it in the confessional.[11] That night, with no help from God's administrator, Doyle showed up to God.[12] In front of Mary she ceased to be ashamed; she believed that Mary "saw the good me trapped inside."[13] Until then, Doyle had believed that love only belongs to those who are clean and therefore loveable. That night, Mary taught her that she was lovable exactly as she was: unshowered and shoeless; Mary taught her that God is forever tries. This meant that she could turn back to life, to truth, to God, to love, but less as a penitent and more as a participant. By showing up, Doyle learned that she was already redeemed.

"Showing Up" as Redemptive

To get out of sin, Catholics say one must repent, or turn back toward God. To get out of despair, Anti-Climacus advises one to "rest transparently

---

temptation for so long a time, acknowledging before God and himself that it is already much more than he deserved, and then humbling himself under the recollection of what he has been." Kierkegaard, *Sickness*, 112.

11. Melton, *Love Warrior*, 56.
12. Ibid., 54–55.
13. Ibid., 59.

in the power that established" one.¹⁴ To stop failing, Doyle advises us to show up, even if it means failing again and repeating the process: *"As [a child of God] you are free to dream and risk and love and fail and lose and rest and try again, forever. A child of God's birthright is: Forever Tries."*¹⁵ Doyle insists that showing up simply means accepting the difficult burden of life. But the trick is that, as her predecessors stressed, turning back, or trying again, is never a one-time effort. As Anti-Climacus puts it, we must "at every moment destroy" despair.¹⁶ Doyle's encounter with Mary taught her that she is worthy of love as is, which gave her the strength to show up time after time, which, time after time, destroys the possibility of despair.

In a blog post on suicide prevention day, Doyle writes: "Apparently the way you avoid suicide is not to become a different person (!) or fix yourself (!) or HEAL (?) or become amazing (!!!) yadda yadda. Survival is actually not that complicated or shiny or exciting. *The way you avoid suicide is you don't commit suicide.*"¹⁷ Showing up is not glamorous for Doyle; you can show up in your pajamas. She writes: "here is the truth: THERE IS NO RUNNING OUT OF TRIES. LIFE IS FOREVER TRIES. Every heartbeat is proof that you've got another try."¹⁸ Every heartbeat is a chance to turn back, but all you really need to do is show up. Love, God, and life are all forever tries. Simply put, for Doyle there is no way to fail if you show up. Perhaps this is why Doyle's favorite label, "recovering," suits her theology of failure best. As a recovering addict Doyle is, at every moment, fighting herself to get herself to show up; i.e., she is always recovering herself.

The Difficulties of Dancing Sober

When she realized that she no longer had to feel ashamed of her jail record but could use it to make a connection with others, a world opened up for Doyle. Becoming a "reckless truth teller" meant that Doyle would eschew small talk in favor of exposing hers and others' sadness, difficulties, and

---

14. Kierkegaard, *Sickness*, 14.
15. Melton, "The Gift of the Green Blob."
16. Kierkegaard, *Sickness*, 15.
17. Melton, "Hey loves."
18. Ibid.

dark sides, or what she calls "monsters."[19] She began to collect virtual friends by telling the truth about herself, and this process shows no signs of stopping, eight years later. By humbling herself, she inspires others to humble themselves; by showing up she inspires them to show up.

Doyle calls life "brutiful"—beautiful and brutal—and insists that life's being hard is not an indication that you are doing it wrong.[20] Life is just hard. Just as failure shouldn't be measured by our status in life, *success for Doyle does not mean doing great things or "becoming" someone great; it just means showing up to life.* About her own experience, she writes: "Am I able to do it (make a thousand women laugh and cry and Remember Hope) because I beat the monster? Because it leaves me alone now? NO! Still speaks to me. It's just not the BOSS of me. I just say: Oh, shut up. You lie. Pain comes and goes like clouds. LOVE IS THE SUN."[21]

Even before becoming a "reckless truth teller," she always already *was* telling the truth, albeit into the toilet.[22] She believes all addicts tell the truth about life: that it's hard to bear, and that, as hard as it is to live as an addict, it's easier than showing up. Doyle believes that addicts are not wrong in their estimation of life as hard to bear, and she shares their confusion at the fact that non-addicts seem to handle it better. (She even goes a step further to venture that these seemingly perfect, Pinterest-worthy people are in fact not handling it all perfectly.) She often reiterates the claim that life's being difficult doesn't mean we are doing it wrong. If we could embrace our messy lives, then more people could "dance sober," which Doyle defines as "honest, passionate living."[23] As an addict, Doyle could only dance when she was intoxicated; now she feels free to be her "messy, clumsy, crutchless" self.[24] Knowing that she doesn't have to get it right, she can just show up.

---

19. Ibid.
20. Melton, "I Need to Tell You Something."
21. Melton, "Hey loves." In *Carry On, Warrior*, Melton likens God to the sun, always there and always inviting, but never pressuring us to show up (18).
22. Melton, *Love Warrior*, 27.
23. Melton, *Carry On*, 25.
24. Ibid.

Conclusion

If Doyle's divorce didn't render her marriage a failure, this suggests that there is a crucial distinction to be made between things typically taken to be failures—endings, dissolutions, discontinuations—and true failure—i.e., the failure to show up. Doyle masterfully brings a religious message to a largely secular public: failure always takes the form of not showing up, and success should be understood as genuinely showing up. Craig is a successful husband because he showed up for Doyle despite his adultery; they are a successful couple because they show up to love despite their divorce. Doyle's simple metric for success illustrates just one of the theological insights that makes her so popular with women in the US. If the public—religious and otherwise—could be convinced that the only way to fail is to not show up, then perhaps people would cease to measure their success by wealth or status, but rather by whether or not they show up daily to Love, God, and each other. And perhaps this formulation would invite them to show up rather than shame them into turning away.

Not everyone can answer the shame-laden traditional call to repentance, but Doyle's disarming invitation for us to show up without shame has enough power to make the impossible seem possible. That night in the church, Mary and the priest both seemingly wanted Doyle to be forgiven, but only Mary invited her; only Mary offered her shameless redemption. Doyle's Marian theology of failure is compelling insofar as it is simultaneously personal and universal. Her decision to replace the terms *sin* and *repentance* with the economically charged terms *failure* and *success*—and with the even less churchy terms: *not showing up* and *showing up*—is typical of her theology for a secular audience. More scholarship devoted to Doyle's popular theology would doubtless reveal her as a formidable, if non-academic, theologian.

Bibliography

Aquinas, Thomas. "Summa Theologica." http://www.sacred-texts.com/chr/aquinas/summa/sum269.htm.

Augustine. "On Selected Lessons of the New Testament." Edited by Philip Schaff and translated by Rev. R. G. MacMullen. http://www.ewtn.com/library/PATRISTC/PNI6-7.TXT.

John Paul II. *Dominum et vivificantem*. Encyclical Letter. Vatican City: Libreria Editrice Vaticana, 1986. http://w2.vatican.va/content/john-paul-ii/en/encyclicals/documents/hf_jp-ii_enc_18051986_dominum-et-vivificantem.html.

Kierkegaard, Søren. *The Sickness Unto Death*. Translated by Edna and Howard Hong. Princeton, NJ: Princeton University Press, 1983.

Melton, Glennon Doyle. *Carry On Warrior*. New York: Scribner, 2013.

———. "The Gift of the Green Blob." *Momastery* (blog). http://momastery.com/blog/2015/08/04/the-gift-of-the-green-blob/.

———. "Hey loves. Look! This is what a survivor looks like." *Momastery* (blog). https://momastery.com/blog/2016/07/05/survivor/.

———. "I'm Live with Oprah Winfrey." Video conversation on Facebook. https://www.facebook.com/glennondoylemelton/videos/10154496620664710/.

———. "I Need to Tell You Something." *Momastery* (blog). http://momastery.com/blog/2016/08/01/i-need-to-tell-you-something/.

———. *Love Warrior*. New York: Flatiron, 2016.

———. *Momastery* (blog). http://momastery.com/blog/.

4.

Someone Must Lose

A Theology of Winning in Sport

Lincoln Harvey

Victory and Defeat in Sport

In every sport, the unwritten rule is that you must try to win. Put otherwise, victory is the aim of the game. There is therefore no place in sport for the player who deliberately attempts to lose a match, perhaps being motivated by a financial inducement offered by a secret betting syndicate. Sport is darkened with the names of many shamed heroes whose misdemeanors cut short their dazzling careers: South African cricket's Hansie Cronje, for instance, or virtually the entire Chicago White Sox baseball team in 1919. Match-fixing is anathema. You *must* play to win.[1]

This unspoken meta-rule means that sport is played with the utmost seriousness. You must put everything into winning, entering fully into the physical struggle, and genuinely competing with the opposition. No one should play at playing, as one philosopher put it.[2] Of course, the desire to win can be taken too far, quickly mutating into a *win at all costs*

---

1. I am indebted to the philosophical work of Steven Conner here, whose analytic clarity on the unwritten rule in sport is well worth a read. See Conner, *Philosophy of Sport*, 171–82.

2. Ibid., 172.

mentality. This mind-set has its own hall of shame: Lance Armstrong, Ben Johnson, and all other hyperbolic cheats who are prepared to break the rules in their disordered desire to win. But victory must never come at the expense of the game. Sport is serious, but it's not *that* serious.

The meta-rule of playing to win does have a downside: not everyone *can* win. There will always be at least one loser for every winner, and that loser must face the pain of defeat; and that's no fun. We need only remember the last time the television cameras zoomed in on the tear-strewn face of a defeated player, inconsolable in grief as opponents lift the trophy. Defeat certainly hurts, so no one in their right mind would want to celebrate it.

But losing comes with this territory. There will always be losers in sport because competition is integral to it. In fact, competition is one way to distinguish sport from other leisure activities. You can't lose at art or music, for instance, and you can't win at ballet, even if these activities can have competition imposed on them. We need only imagine a television show such as *Strictly Come Dancing* or *American Idol* to confirm the point, or imagine the competitive nature of the job market. But in these instances, competition is somewhat artificial, although that isn't to say that you can't dance or play music badly, missing the beat or singing out of key. Still, the act of dance or music does not require someone else to lose in order to be done well.[3] With sport things are different: competition is intrinsic to the game.[4]

As we might suspect, the competitive nature of sport also differentiates it from other forms of play. The work of Allen Guttmann is helpful here.[5] Guttmann makes good use of a classificatory system, succinctly dividing play into four types. Our play can be *spontaneous*—an impulsive action that is unplanned and unregulated. We catch sight of this when the serious business of life is unexpectedly interrupted, perhaps during a formal presentation when the speaker makes an unscripted remark in which, according to Guttmann, "an ecstatic sense of pure possibility"

---

3. I am grateful to Duncan Reyburn for helping to clarify this distinction.

4. See Harvey, *A Brief Theology of Sport*. I remain grateful to Peter Nicholas at *Christians in Sport* for originally suggesting a succinct way to talk about the imposed nature of competition in the arts, and to Duncan Reyburn for helping to clarify the distinction.

5. See Guttmann, *Sports*.

opens up before the audience.[6] In this sort of incident, our play suddenly breaks into events.

If our play isn't spontaneous then it will be *regulated*. As the adjective suggests, regulated play is determined by a set of rules. The rules define the purpose of the activity and the means by which that purpose is achieved, as well as the way the players' success at achieving it is to be measured. Rules can vary enormously across games, ranging from the formulized regulations of a governing body, to the unspoken "*imagine as if . . .*" that enables children to play at make-believe. But whatever form the rules take, regulations mean that we are playing a *game*. Games are regulated play.

Guttmann shows that the rule-defined category of games can also be split, the divide now centering on whether or not the game is competitive. Some games do not produce winners, a point Guttmann backs up with a reference to leapfrog. In leapfrog, a player must run up towards their co-player, place their hands on their back and spring over them, before landing and assuming their own crouched position, to be leapt over in turn. The rules here define the activity, but they are not designed to produce winners and losers. Leapfrog is a non-competitive game.

Other games, however, are designed to produce winners, and these sorts of games are called *contests*. This subdivision can again be divided, with the final separation centering on whether the contest is designed to measure mental or physical ability. Guttmann argues that some contests, such as chess matches, measure the players' intellects, though obviously a physical element remains (in that pieces must be moved around the board). Even so, the game is decided by the quality of the mind, unlike in sport, where the players' physical prowess is the primary determinant for what ought to settle things.

In sport, the physical prowess of the players is measured by the creation of artificial impediments or obstacles that the players have to overcome in pursuit of the objective. Of course, there remains an intellectual element in sport, with particular players often celebrated for their ability to overcome brute force with clever skills and quick thinking. Nonetheless, sport is primarily a physical contest, and that's what makes it different from a game like chess; you can't simply think the ball into the net.

Having established that competition is intrinsic to sport, we can see that there will always be losers in sport. A sport is designed to measure

6. Ibid., 1.

which players are performing best on a particular occasion, thereby automatically generating a distinct class: the defeated. Therefore, in the remainder of this essay, I will explore how Christians should understand the nature of winning and losing in sport, drawing on Christian theology to construct a vision of competition in which losing can be embraced positively (whilst remaining something we want to avoid). To that end, we must first reimagine what competition is, thereby overthrowing a common stereotype that dominates popular understandings of sport.

Competition Is Dance, Not War

Competition can be understood in a number of ways, but it is often linked conceptually to war. A simplistic narrative of the survival of the fittest is often behind such accounts, with reality being pictured as a warlike struggle to adapt to the environment, usually at the expense of each other. This metanarrative is then allowed to influence our understanding of sport, with George Orwell's soundbite capturing the core thesis: *sport is war minus the shooting.*[7]

On Orwell's reading, sport functions as a domesticated form of war, enabling us to let off some evolutionary steam without having to kill each other in the process. Supporting evidence for the thesis is easy to gather, with the recurring violence both on and off the field explained in its light. But that doesn't mean Orwell is right. Christians believe that reality is most basically peaceful, rather than war-like, having been established by a loving God. This narrative opens up a new way of imagining competition, one that is more faithful to the gospel because of its nonviolent character.[8]

The work of George Lakoff and Mark Johnson is helpful in getting us started.[9] Lakoff and Johnson analyze how metaphorical language works in poetry and prose, showing that it functions as a literary device that enables the meaning of one thing to *carry over*—literally *meta-pherein* in

---

7. Orwell, "The Sporting Spirit."

8. Of course, the fall destroys this peace, setting us at war against God and each other, but the point remains (or at least can be remade eschatologically). John Milbank and David Bentley Hart, amongst others, have argued persuasively for the ontological primacy of peace in dialogue with the pervading nihilism at the heart of much contemporary philosophy. Milbank, *Theology and Social Theory*; Hart, *The Beauty of the Infinite*.

9. Lakoff and Johnson, *Metaphors We Live By*, 4–6.

the Greek—to inform the meaning of another. But Lakoff and Johnson argue that the dynamic of exchange extends way beyond language, with our behavior shaped by a number of conceptual pairings. In making their case, Lakoff and Johnson offer numerous examples, including the way modern culture functions as if *time is money*. By systematically linking these two concepts, time becomes a limited resource with an intrinsic value that can be wasted, spent, borrowed, invested, used profitably, or put aside. But of primary interest for this argument is the way Lakoff and Johnson focus their attention on another conceptual metaphor, the belief that *argument is war*.[10]

Lakoff and Johnson claim that the reality of war informs the way that we argue, thereby giving rise to commonplace phrases that populate our speech. Points can be indefensible or right on target, ground can be gained, at other times lost, and our positions attacked and sometimes shot down, with people acting aggressively or defensively as they struggle to win. But Lakoff and Johnson invite us to picture a different way of arguing. They ask us to imagine a culture where argument is conceptualized as *dance*. The language of attack and defense immediately disappears, the protagonists now imagined as disciplined performers who aim to create an aesthetically pleasing outcome through a series of precise steps, regulated gestures, and adopted positions, which combine to create an elegantly free movement of thought. Now there is motion, pace, ebb and flow as the partners engage in a cooperative act of instantiating the beautiful reality that the argument communicates step by step. In effect, the revised conceptual metaphor transforms the nature of debate. Argument is no longer belligerent.

But what difference would Lakoff and Johnson's conceptual move make—with the necessary changes—to our understanding of sport? To answer this question, we first need to take a step back, thereby analyzing the nature of sport, before giving it a theological twist. In so doing, we will see that sport is also a dance, one in which we pivot between life and nothingness, in tune with our identity as creatures.

---

10. Of course, there are obvious differences between arguing and war. War involves tanks and planes, rather than the nouns and verbs that populate our arguments. Nor do Lakoff and Johnson maintain that this one conceptual metaphor exhausts the way we understand the nature of arguing, though it is surely dominant in the public square. See ibid., 90–91.

Life, Loss, and Nothingness in Sport

Sport is an unnecessary but meaningful act.[11] It punctuates the serious business we're all caught up in, interrupting the great chain of necessity that fills our waking hours. We catch a train to go to work to sit in meetings, to get our salary, to buy our food, supply our drinks, heat our homes, and pay our rent; a repetitive—though variable—cycle that is reset each night by the inescapable requirement of sleep. Simply put, our lives serve our needs.

But sport doesn't serve our needs in this way. No commodity rolls off a conveyor belt, no crop ripens on the pitch, and no artifact hangs on the wall; sporting events simply happen, with nothing produced. As a result—from a utilitarian perspective—there really isn't any point to them.

Of course, this conclusion is wrong. Sport *does* have a point. In fact, every sport has a goal or target, points to be won or a line to be crossed; sports are always ordered towards a specifiable end. But the end of a sport is always *internal* to the sport itself. No ulterior motive dictates the action in question, as if a player kicks the ball past the goalkeeper in order to gain extrinsic reward. Though some now make a fortune out of it, the average player knows that we only kick the ball at the goal because a goal is the point of the game; it constitutes the meaning of this unnecessary act. That's precisely why we don't like sports being set to serve outside interests, say when commercial and political agendas come into play. We sense that such encroachment undermines the sport, polluting the essentially autotelic nature of the event. Sport—on this account—is radically non-instrumental.

The theological link to be made here is relatively straightforward.[12] Because it is an unnecessary-yet-meaningful act, our sport expresses something of our unnecessary-but-meaningful nature. That's because, just like a sport, we too are unnecessary, in that God did not need to create us. He certainly wasn't obliged to act, as if there was another god forcing his hand, insisting that he make a world to satisfy their needs. Nor for that matter was there an intrinsic compulsion at work in God, as if he had some itch to scratch or yearning to fill. We are not that serious, so to speak, being set to serve neither extrinsic nor intrinsic need. We are

---

11. To this, the simplest reference is again to some of my earlier work: see Harvey, *A Brief Theology of Sport*, 61–75.

12. Again, the points made here find explicit and extensive support in the relevant chapters of my previous work: see Harvey, *A Brief Theology of Sport*, 76–100.

instead summoned into existence *freely*—graced!—rather than resulting from irresistible necessity.¹³

But make no mistake. We are not capricious. The act of creation was not haphazard or whimsical, somehow void of a plan. God instead determined the creature towards a specifiable end, enabling it to participate in the loving fellowship that is his eternal life in Jesus Christ. Love is the intrinsic meaning of the unnecessary creature.

Clearly, two doctrines have been set to work to establish the point here: the doctrine of the Trinity, and the doctrine of creation *ex nihilo*. The belief that the creator God is Father, Son, and Spirit—and just therein perfectly fulfilled—means that God keeps his own eternal company, so to speak, meaning that the act of creation addresses no deficiency in him: the Father, Son, and Spirit were certainly not lonely, they were instead endlessly bestowing and receiving identity in relationship, an eternal act of communion in which the one God is infinitely satisfied and simply complete. As a result, when the triune God creates, he does so freely.

In addition, the act of creation is no self-deception. The triune God does not break off a piece of his God-stuff, rebranding it as a creature and fooling himself that something different now exists. Nor for that matter did he make us out of any pre-existing materials, as if there was something lying around in eternity that he just had to use. Instead, the one triune God freely summons the creature into existence *out of nothing*, thereby establishing us in distinct relation to himself.

Now, with those two doctrines in view, a constructive proposal can be ventured. Given the nature of God's creative act in summoning us out of nothing, we can say that we have a particular ontological profile: the creature is not God, neither are we nothing; we are instead substantially plotted between the two. And it is this ontological profile—in its dynamic trajectory—that needs to be kept in mind in what follows.

Sport needs to be understood as an unnecessary-but-meaningful event in which the unnecessary-but-meaningful creature celebrates its identity. Sport enables the creature to resonate with its primary constitution, celebrating that we are unnecessary-yet-purposeful, summoned from nothing into a life of love by the God who is love. As a result, this celebratory event requires two dynamic movements that are directed towards our ontological horizons. Thus, at the end of the game, the winners embrace *life*, the joyful reality into which we are invited. The losers—at

---

13. For the idea of non-serious creatures, see Williams, *A Silent Action*, 71–82.

precisely the same moment—face the nothingness from which we've been summoned. But only together, as winners and losers, can the players capture our trajectory, not at the expense of each other but in the joint enterprise of celebrating the nature of our being. In other words, the winners and losers require each other if the event is to resonate with our identity, because the game involves them existentially pivoting towards the dual perimeter of our being. *That* is the dance of sport.

On this reading, sport can be seen as true *entertainment*, as Joseph L. Price has argued. That is to say, the players pivot gracefully between the two poles of their existence.[14] The game is the tensed reality of our existential identity, held between God and nothingness. This insight helps us to understand why we prefer close sporting contests to one-sided affairs. The best games are rarely a walkover, where victory is all but decided from the start. We instead prefer a tense struggle, a match that is decided by the final throw, the last kick, extra time, even penalties, because the closest contests enable the players to live the question of existence for the maximal time, thereby embodying together our reality as those summoned into existence out of nothing.[15]

And—again, on this reading—losing is a vital component of the dance. Of course, we still prefer to win. God has judged existence—life!—to be good, and deemed nothingness to be the negation of this goodness. Winning is therefore directed towards our true end as creatures, whereas losing faces the derelict nothingness that marked our contingency. And *that* is why we must still play to win—because the competitive struggle is no pretense, it is real. But just therein losing plays its part: it is an essential element of the event in which we celebrate our identity as creatures, even if we rightly want to avoid it.[16]

And so, on the basis of their faith, the Christian can fully embrace defeat. Yes, winning is to be preferred, and that is why we strive for victory. But sport would not be what it is without the defeated, because—as

---

14. Price draws on the work of Victor Turner to excavate the etymology of the word *entertainment*, noting how the French words *entre* and *tenir* signify a holding between two realities at the edge of existence: Price, "Playing and Praying," 77.

15. Harvey, "Sport, Competition and Creatureliness."

16. A disclaimer here may be necessary: This account of winning is not intended to validate the sports-world's rather merciless focus on winning. It relativizes winning by underlining its positive function only in companionship with losing in which both are equal in that together they capture our profile.

a dance of our identity—sport is more important than winning. That's why there's no shame in losing. And that's why there is no need to cheat.[17]

Bibliography

Conner, Steven. *A Philosophy of Sport*. London: Reaktion, 2011.

Guttmann, Allen. *Sports: The First Five Millennia*. Amherst, MA: University of Massachusetts Press, 2004.

Hart, David Bentley. *The Beauty of the Infinite: The Aesthetics of Christian Truth*. Grand Rapids: Eerdmans, 2003.

Harvey, Lincoln. *A Brief Theology of Sport*. London: SCM, 2014. "

———. "Sport, Competition and Creatureliness." *The AllRounder*, October 6, 2014. http://theallrounder.co/2014/10/06/sport-competition-and-creatureliness/.

———. "A Theology of Sport: On the Rebound." *First Things*, November 17, 2014. http://www.firstthings.com/blogs/firstthoughts/2014/11/a-theology-of-sport-on-the-rebound.

Lakoff, George, and Mark Johnson. *Metaphors We Live By*. Chicago: University of Chicago Press, 2003.

Milbank, John. *Theology and Social Theory: Beyond Secular Reason*. Oxford: Blackwell, 1990.

Orwell, George. "The Sporting Spirit" (1945). http://orwell.ru/library/articles/spirit/english/e_spirit.

Price, Joseph L. "Playing and Praying, Sport and Spirit: The Forms and Functions of Prayer in Sport." *International Journal of Religion and Sport*, vol. 1 (2009) 55–80.

Williams, Rowan. "Not Being Serious: Thomas Merton and Karl Barth." In *A Silent Action: Engagements with Thomas Merton*, 69–82. London: SPCK, 2013.

———. *A Silent Action: Engagements with Thomas Merton*. London: SPCK, 2013.

---

17. In personal correspondence, Roberto Sirvent asked me whether failure is sometime to be preferred, "in the sense that 'losing' or 'failure' can be an act of refusal, resistance, or counterhegemonic strategy? After all, if the dominant culture determines what is 'success' and a 'win', then aren't we as Christians encouraged to resist dominant ideologies of success? In the sports-world, that might mean favoring other goods over winning (e.g. cooperation, aesthetic pleasures, etc.)." This is a good question, although deliberately losing would turn the player into a spoilsport, undermining the meta-rule of playing to win. Though I am in principle opposed to sport being instrumentalized in this way, sometimes protest will be rightly judged necessary, although that doesn't mean the protester isn't a spoilsport, but instead a justified spoilsport. For more on this, again, see Harvey, *A Brief Theology of Sport*.

5.

Failure and Natural Selection

Kara N. Slade

Physical science is proving more and more the immense importance of Race; the importance of hereditary powers, hereditary organs, hereditary habits, in all organized beings . . . She is proving more and more the omnipresent action of the differences between races, how the more favored race (she cannot avoid using the epithet) exterminates the less favored, or at least expels it . . . and, in a word, that competition between every race and every individual of that race, and reward according to deserts is (as far as we can see) a universal law of living things.

—Charles Kingsley, *The Natural Theology of the Future.*

To write a pamphlet is frivolity—but to promise the system, that is seriousness and has made many a man a supremely serious man both in his own eyes and in the eyes of others.

—Søren Kierkegaard, *Philosophical Fragments.*

In the beginning was a TED talk. At the TED 2011 Conference in Long Beach, California, historian David Christian in eighteen minutes told the story of what he called "Big History," an encyclopedic evolutionary account of all time from the Big Bang to the present day. Christian may have been a relatively unknown professor at the time, but the man who introduced his lecture was well known to the audience and to the world of technology to which the TED series appeals. That man was Bill Gates. In the five years since, what Christian dubbed the Big History Project has become a slickly packaged, Gates Foundation-funded effort to bring its sweeping metanarrative and its "framework for all knowledge" to elementary and secondary schools around the world—especially in the United States.[1] Big History, in the estimation of Christian and Gates alike, has the benefit of explaining human origins and human history from the objective standpoint of scientific truth. Here, there is no place for the politics or the superstition of religious stories of origins. There is only scientific fact.

This is neither a new nor a unique idea. The methodology of the Big History project itself, with its underlying philosophy of "Universal Darwinism," is only one of the most visible, and most easily unpacked, examples of a common impulse in both secular and modern Christian thought. It can be seen in contemporary theological projects that range from the evangelical BioLogos foundation, supported by former NIH director Francis Collins, to the liberal Protestant-Unitarian vision of Michael Dowd's *The Great Story* project.[2] In each case, the working assumption is that the story that tells us who we are, where we have come from, and where we are going as human beings is assumed to be the story of the beginning: the beginning of time, the beginning of the material universe, the beginning of the species. Only by grasping the story of the beginning, so the argument goes, can we understand the story we inhabit now.

However, this story is far from innocuous. In this chapter, I examine how the narrative that plumbs human origins and evolutionary history to explain human existence is a narrative written from the standpoint of evolution's winners: as individuals and as groups. Behind the category of failure lies the category of success. The latter stands as the measure of the former. And, as I explore in the pages that follow, in evolutionary narratives it can function theologically as a boundary that marks some as elect and others as biologically reprobate.

1. "Big History."
2. See, for example, http://biologos.org/about-us/ and http://thegreatstory.org/home.html.

A "Framework for All Knowledge"

As it is taught in schools, the grand narrative of Big History traces a story of progress through eight threshold or transition points that function as the keys to understanding the past, present, and future. The first five are the unremarkable subject matter of eighth-grade science classes: the Big Bang, the emergence of stars, the proliferation of chemical elements, the beginnings of earth and the solar system, and the first organic life on earth. Only in the last three do human beings enter the picture. The entirety of human life, past, present, and future, is encompassed and determined by three transition points: collective learning, agriculture, and the emergence of a globalized industrial modernity. The latter is described in one teaching resource in terms that leaves much unsaid:

> When humans began to take advantage of advances in transportation, exploring unknown parts of the world, they ushered in an exchange of people, ideas, plants, animals, and diseases among formerly separate regions. By the early 19th century three factors—the interconnected world zones, the expansion and the importance of commerce, and the discovery of fossil fuels—began to rapidly transform some societies. Several of these regions found their wealth and power grew at an enormous rate, setting the stage for the first truly modern societies.[3]

The pedagogical and political effect of such an account is clear, marking histories of oppression as well as the political and economic status quo as natural and inevitable in precisely the same way as the emergence of chemical elements.

The narrative of Big History functions ideologically, even as it explicitly describes itself in terms of a secular, scientific, and objective origin story and a source of meaning intended to complement, if not to replace, that of the Christian story. It is a doctrine of creation for those who have progressed beyond creatureliness, where Providence unfolds in the spread of globalized capitalism that marks the success of some and the failure of others. In the words of the project website, "Since the earliest humans, we've struggled to make sense of our world and understand where we come from. Big History, which presents a perspective based on modern science, is simply another attempt to answer the big questions about our beginnings."[4] At first glance, such an effort might seem

3. "Crisscrossing and Connected."
4. "What is Big History Project?"

harmless enough, or at the most it may appear to be the latest instantiation of a creeping secularization that can do without God. However, to understand what precisely is wrong with such a project, it is necessary to think outside the binaries left over from the fundamentalist-modernist controversy. The problem is not that Big History can do without God, but rather with how the theoretical pathologies of Big History (and similar projects) travel into theological thought.

The first difficulty with this account has already been alluded to. The metanarrative presented by Big History, especially in its popularized forms, downplays or ignores the role of racialized colonialism in favor of a unified narrative of the unfolding of globalization.[5] Yet this problem does not exist in isolation. The role that race plays in scientific metanarratives or origins is enmeshed with its other problematic aspects, namely, its appeal to scientific authority and its inhuman time scale, at the deepest level.

Homo Scientificus and the Transparent "I"

The role played by the determinative scientific authority—the figure of "scientific man" who stands at the apex of reason—is another problematic aspect of this account. Claims to scientific authority, and by scientific figures seen as authoritative, take on the significance of priestly proclamation. The effects of this appeal to authority can be seen in venues that range from the aforementioned works on human origins to articles in the popular press that breathlessly report the latest findings of neuroscience or the latest evolutionary explanation for modern Western social behavior.

Moreover, scientific man also occupies a particular place on a temporal trajectory, at the apex of progress in the position of contemporaneity. From this vantage point, he is able to catapult himself outside of time to envision time and history on the most massive, Hegelian scale. And, from there, the authority of science and of scientific man is deployed to arrange other human beings on a trajectory of primitivism and progress.

5. The connections between liberal narratives of globalization, the universal account of human rights, and colonization within modernity have been commented upon in detail by many. See, for example, Lisa Lowe's argument that "the forgetting reveals the politics of memory itself, and is a reminder that the constitution of knowledge often obscures the conditions of its own making." In Lowe, *The Intimacies of Four Continents*, 39.

Actual human beings, existing at the time scale of a human life, can too easily be disregarded and even disappear at the scale of Big History. The operative logic in such an account participates at the deepest level in what historian Jenny Reardon names as a defining feature of modernity: "the entanglement of rules that govern what can count as knowledge with rules that determine which human lives can be lived."[6]

Writing in *Toward a Global Idea of Race*, Denice Ferreira da Silva describes how scientific universality and the figure of scientific man does work that once was performed by theology, governing the modern production of Western man as a transparent "I." *Homo scientificus*, da Silva's term for the version of "man" that emerged in the nineteenth and early twentieth centuries, is a philosophical descendent of Hegel. But it differs from Hegel insofar as scientific universality makes transcendental *poesis* the "rewriting of reason as a transcendental force," a "matter of the body rather than of the spirit."[7] The difference between the Hegelian *homo historicus* and the later Darwinian *homo scientificus* is that the latter "assumes that in the body of man resides the causes for the emergence of the self-determined 'I.'"[8] Da Silva argues that this shift could only take place after "scientific projects" of the "truth" of "man" had sought to "rewrite the mind as an object of scientific reason"[9] As she explains, *homo scientificus* posits himself as "the transparent 'I,'" who "rewrites its bodily and social configurations as signifiers of transcendality."[10]

The distinction between white, Western *homo scientificus* and other human beings, then, is not merely a matter of cultural difference that can be overcome by liberal rhetorics of inclusion. It is the chasm between the transcendental and the immanent, the mark of the creature who has placed himself in the position of the Creator. And so it is also the ultimate distinction between evolutionary success and failure. The implications of this transcendental move become clear as da Silva turns directly to the work of Darwin. The transparent *I* within which Darwin includes himself, Newton, Shakespeare, and the English colonial project is set apart from the forces of nature as the victor. She writes,

6. Reardon, *Race to the Finish*, 5.
7. Ferreira da Silva, *Toward a Global Idea of Race*, xvi.
8. Ibid., 94.
9. Ibid.
10. Ibid.

> When he explicitly writes the transparent I ... outside—always already the winner—of the "struggle for Life," Darwin introduces an element absent in previous ... descriptions of the global as a site of human differentiation, namely affectability. In the same statement, his version of the science of life safely places post-Enlightenment Europe in the moment of transparency and writes the "savage races" in the same way Newton has described the bodies of physics, as doubly governed by exteriority, that is, the exterior regulating force (productive nomos) and coexisting more powerful human beings, that is, the "Caucasian races." In other words, they are always already losers in the "struggle for existence" against the European "races of men," the ones whose social configurations testify to their competitive advantage.[11]

While the "savage races" are subject to both the laws of nature and the domination of other, more powerful, humans, the transparent *I* of post-Enlightenment Europe is subject to neither.

Of Trowels and Backhoes

To the extent that Christians have engaged with this project, they have predictably done so in ways that remain captive to the assumption that epistemology is the only ground of contention that matters in the relationship between science and Christian faith. One recent engagement with Big History has come from Catholic theologian John Haught, for whom Big History represents "a sacramental opening" that renews "our sense of the infinity and personality of God." Blending the thought of David Christian with that of Pierre Teilhard de Chardin, Haught posits a Christian "metaphysics of the future" in which "the realities of evolutionary struggle, innocent suffering, and moral evil" are a regrettable but acceptable form of collateral damage in the great process of cosmic becoming.[12]

Meanwhile, for Ted Peters, the perspective of Big History is problematic only insofar as subjectivity fails to play a role within the story it tells. He writes,

> Any story of nature's history told strictly from within the scientific gaze requires an objectivist or third person perspective. . . . Now, please do not mistake me. I celebrate the scientific gaze.

11. Ibid.
12. Haught, "Big History, Scientific Naturalism, and Christian Hope," 80.

> This third person gaze has proved to be of inestimable value during the rise of the natural sciences in the modern West. Restricting itself to empirical research and rational reflection, the scientific method has demonstrated its fruitfulness beyond measure. Scientific research is progressive, leading daily to new discoveries and new knowledge. Modern civilization can only say "thank you" to our scientific method and to the energy of the devoted researchers among us. The price paid for this scientific advance, however, has been the sacrifice of meaning and the game of pretend that says subjectivity does not count in human knowing. We discover this when we shuffle our theological trowel below the soil surface. Here, we uncover an enormously influential assumption at work in modern science, namely, the exclusion of mind, consciousness, personhood, and, therefore, meaning.[13]

For Peters, a little "shuffling of the theological trowel" is needed to "dig around" and "expose" the "existential questions" that "are already buried within scientific accounts of our cosmos and the evolution of life."[14] But Peters's Tillichian solution is to dig under the surface to uncover a substrate of true and universal meaning that is already there. This project, on the other hand, assumes that a backhoe and not a trowel is needed to excavate what lies under, behind, and beneath the accounts of Big History and similar projects. The writing of European transcendality from a place at the apex of time, yet also outside it, marks the depth to which evolutionary accounts of human origins such as Big History cannot be made theologically harmless with a few cosmetic alterations. Rather, the problems go all the way down. Like the magi after encountering the newborn Jesus, we find that we must go home "by another road" entirely (Matt 2:12, NRSV).

"For then the whole thing would collapse"

The work of Søren Kierkegaard offers one such alternate route. One starting point along this path may be found in the often overlooked and fragmentary *Johannes Climacus*. This, the ostensible biography of the author of *Philosophical Fragments* and *Concluding Unscientific Postscript* is especially helpful in uncovering the connections between claims of

---

13. Peters, "Big History and Big Questions," 56–57.
14. Ibid., 48.

intellectual authority, the attempt to construct an encyclopedic Hegelian system of knowledge, and anxiety around securing a proper beginning for thought. On one level, it revolves around three theses: "(1) philosophy begins with doubt, (2) in order to philosophize, one must have doubted, and (3) modern philosophy begins with doubt."[15] But to read this text only as a meditation on doubt is, I believe, to miss the point entirely. On another level, it functions as a caustic commentary on Hegelianism and on the temporal relations contained in the Hegelian system.

The text begins with an easily missed parenthetical note that bears quoting in full. Under the heading, "Please Note," Kierkegaard writes,

> Someone who supposes that philosophy has never in all the world been so close as it is now to fulfilling its task of explaining all mysteries may certainly think it strange, affected, and scandalous that I choose the narrative form and do not in my small way hand up a stone to culminate the system. But someone who has become convinced that philosophy has never been so eccentric as now, never so confused despite all its definitions (much like the weather last winter when we heard simultaneously things never heard before at the same time—shouts of "mussels," "shrimp," and "watercress"—so that someone who was attentive to a particular shout at one moment would think it was winter, then spring, and then midsummer, while anyone who heard them all would think that nature had become confused and that the world would not last until Easter)—that person will surely find it in order that I, too, by means of the form seek to counteract the detestable untruth that characterizes recent philosophy, which differs from older philosophy by having discovered that it is ludicrous to do what a person himself said he would do or had done—he will find it in order and will merely lament, as I do, that the one who here begins this task has no more authority than I have.[16]

Here, Kierkegaard undermines his own authority at the same time as he contrasts his own writing in the form of a whimsical narrative with the building up of the Hegelian system from its secure beginning in idealized thought.

It is that reliance on Hegelian philosophy that is an underlying target of Kierkegaard's critique in *Johannes Climacus*. Climacus is described as a young man who is "ardently in love" with "thought, or more accurately,

15. Kierkegaard, *Johannes Climacus*, 132.
16. Ibid., 117.

with thinking."[17] His particular love, of course, is for systematic thinking that is constructed from a beginning point, and thus, he becomes obsessed with where to begin—so much so that he never finds the proper beginning he so desperately seeks. As Kierkegaard describes his predicament: "It was his delight to begin with a single thought and then, by way of coherent thinking, to climb step by step to a higher one, because to him coherent thinking was a *scala paradisi* [ladder of paradise], and his blessedness seemed to him even more glorious than the angels."[18]

And yet Climacus is constantly frustrated by the precariousness and instability of his own method:

> As long as he labored to climb up, as long as coherent thinking had as yet not managed to make its way, he was oppressed, because he feared losing all those coherent thoughts he had finished but which as yet were not perfectly clear and necessary. When we see someone carrying a number of fragile and brittle things stacked one upon the other, we are not surprised that he walks unsteadily and continually tries to maintain balance. If we do not see the stack, we smile, just as many smiled at Johannes Climacus, not suspecting that his soul was carrying a stack far taller than is usually enough to cause astonishment, that his soul was anxious lest one single coherent thought slip out, for then the whole thing would collapse. He did not notice that people smiled at him, no more than at other times he would notice an individual turn around in delight and look at him when he hurried down the street as lightly as in a dance. He did not pay any attention to people and did not imagine that they could pay any attention to him; he was and remained a stranger in the world.[19]

We smile, too, reading Kierkegaard's comic description of the difficulties entailed by piling one "coherent thought" upon another in the work of seamless system-building.

In the character of Johannes Climacus, we see a playful and poignant demonstration of a methodology of thought that depends on securing its own beginning and building the system from that point. It is a methodology that Kierkegaard identified in his many critiques of Hegel, of which *Johannes Climacus* stands as one. It is also a methodology that Denise Ferreira da Silva identifies with the Hegelian and Darwinian figure of

17. Ibid., 118.
18. Ibid.
19. Ibid., 119.

homo modernus, world-historic and scientific man. Under this framework, the question of beginnings, of origins, becomes temporal as well as philosophical. The beginning of thought that defines humanity, and human freedom, is conflated with the temporal beginning of humanity. Evolutionary history is mapped on to anthropology.

Meanwhile, Johannes Climacus confuses himself with the question of the beginning and who has the authority to make it. Is it a "religious" or "historical" question, "ethical" or "metaphysical"?[20] He reflects that "to the Greeks," philosophy "begins with wonder," but concludes that "a principle such as that can give rise to any historical consequence whatsoever."[21] Thinking further, he concludes that "modern philosophy" is "simultaneously the historical and the eternal" and "is aware of this itself." Indeed, he concludes that "it is a union similar to the two natures in Christ."[22] He continues along this quasi-christological vein, tying his thoughts on modern philosophy and the question of where to make a philosophical beginning explicitly to the relationship of time and eternity:

> That the single individual could become conscious of the eternal, he could perhaps grasp, and an earlier philosophy presumably had thought to have grasped it, too—that is, if there had been any such thing at all. But to become conscious of the eternal in the whole historical concretion, indeed, according to the standard that it did not involve only the past, this he believed was reserved for the deity. Neither could he grasp at what instant in time a person would become so transfigured to himself that he, although himself present to himself, became past to himself. He believed that this had to be reserved for eternity and that eternity was only abstractly present in time.[23]

For Climacus, eternity is "only abstractly present" in time, and so he takes recourse in an ecstatic meditation on the Hegelian unfolding of philosophy in a necessary chain:

> The individual philosopher must become conscious of himself and in this consciousness of himself also become conscious of his significance as a moment in modern philosophy; in turn modern philosophy must become conscious of itself as an element in a prior philosophy, which in turn must become

20. Ibid., 153.
21. Ibid., 145.
22. Ibid., 139–40.
23. Ibid., 141.

conscious of itself as an element in the historical unfolding of the eternal philosophy. Thus the philosopher's consciousness must encompass the most dizzying contrasts: his own personality, his little amendment—the philosophy of the whole world as the unfolding of the eternal philosophy.[24]

Kierkegaard's narration of the event continues with a wry depiction of the precariousness of a system that contains itself:

> It was a long time before Johannes managed to think this enormous thought correctly and definitely. Just as a man rolling a heavy load up a mountain is often overcome so that his foot slips and the load rolls down, so it went with him. Finally he was confident that he could make the movement with ease. He then decided to let the thought work with all its weight, for he made a distinction between the laboriousness of thinking and the weight of the thought. As a historical thought, he thought the thought with ease. He had collected new strength, felt himself whole and complete; he put his shoulder, as it were, to the thought—and look, it overwhelmed him and he fainted![25]

The section, "Modern Philosophy Begins with Doubt" ends with Climacus having made no progress towards understanding. It "cost him time and hard work," and he was "poorly rewarded for his troubles."[26] He concludes that his original thesis may have been "an impossibility," yet the sentence that follows is the most telling: "Yet he did not have the courage to believe this."[27]

In *Johannes Climacus*, we see the consequences of apprehending oneself as "a moment" in the necessary unfolding of the history of ideas. The recourse to systemic thought as the determinative "moment" in Climacus's own life evokes the "moment of transparency" in da Silva's work. In very different ways, both Kierkegaard's and da Silva's texts puncture the notion of the self-positing individual who achieves transcendence through reason. And both trouble the ways that an evolutionary or developmental temporal consciousness, fixated on the question of its own origins, can obscure rather than reveal how humanity might think of itself in time.

24. Ibid., 140.
25. Ibid., 140–41.
26. Ibid., 143.
27. Ibid., 143.

But what if we begin elsewhere, not with the aim of securing a foundation for a Hegelian ladder of paradise, but from the non-abstract, revealed "moment" at the intersection of time and eternity? We see this moment further discussed in *Philosophical Fragments*, a text which, along with *Concluding Unscientific Postscript*, was published under the pseudonym of Johannes Climacus. In this, one of Kierkegaard's most abstract works, Climacus contrasts what he calls "the Socratic," a system in which truth lies within each individual and is achieved by an ascent of knowledge, with a version of Christian theology made newly strange. "If, then, the unity could not be brought about by an ascent, then it must be attempted by a descent."[28]

Climacus repeatedly returns to the phrase, "If the moment is to have decisive significance," gesturing towards a "moment" that determines human existence in something other than a remote temporal origin.[29] Over against the moment of transparency described by da Silva, Kierkegaard focuses on the moment in which the human being receives herself by receiving the truth of her own sinfulness, and "discovers his untruth."[30] This is a knowledge that can neither be built up to by a Hegelian staircase or extracted from within the individual. Rather, it can only be received from the outside, and specifically from the Word made flesh, who took the form of a servant. And this, Climacus writes, is "the boundlessness of love, that in earnestness and truth and not in jest it wills to be the equal of the beloved, and it is the omnipotence of resolving love to be capable of that of which neither the king nor Socrates was capable."[31]

Unscientific Postscript

In the name of generating a seamless and systematic account that includes both the Christian tradition and natural selection, what has too often resulted has been a theology of success, written from the position of transparency by those who are always, already the winners in an evolutionary struggle. It has been the case since the early days of Darwinism, when the Rev. Canon Charles Kingsley delivered a lecture entitled "The Natural Theology of the Future" at Sion College in London. Kingsley, the

---

28. Kierkegaard, *Philosophical Fragments*, 31.
29. Ibid., 14.
30. Ibid.
31. Ibid., 32.

Canon of Westminster and chaplain to Queen Victoria whom science historian P. J. Hale calls "Darwin's Other Bulldog," based his remarks on the premise that "theologians [should] accommodate the latest findings of natural science with Scripture even if this ultimately meant revising traditional exegesis."[32] For Kingsley, the imperative of progress required that Anglican theology adapt itself to the latest developments of scientific thought, lest it become unattractive to an informed, modern populace. He draws a stark distinction between what he sees as the overly superstitious and *un*reasonable theology espoused by revivalists like Wesley and Whitefield with its suitably progressive alternative, noting that "there lingers about them a savor of the old monastic theory, that this earth is the devil's planet, fallen, accursed, goblin haunted, needing to be exorcised at every turn before it is useful or even safe for man."[33] For Kingsley, the planet was useful for only those with the ability and qualities to make use of it. In a passage with which this essay began, he writes:

> Physical science is proving more and more the immense importance of Race; the importance of hereditary powers, hereditary organs, hereditary habits, in all organized beings ... She is proving more and more the omnipresent action of the differences between races, how the more favored race (she cannot avoid using the epithet) exterminates the less favored, or at least expels it ... and, in a word, that competition between every race and every individual of that race, and reward according to deserts is (as far as we can see) a universal law of living things.[34]

Under this logic, the depredations of colonialism are naturalized by those who posit themselves as the transcendent success stories of evolutionary development. Evolution's failures, in this scenario, are getting exactly what they deserve.

Contemporary accounts of evolutionary development like Big History may be subtler in their language, but they still rely on the same distinctions between the successes and the failures of natural selection. As theologians negotiate—and renegotiate—the relationship between our discipline and the physical and biological sciences, we would be well advised to remember the history of our own failures to do so faithfully. And we would be well advised to ask ourselves this question before beginning

32. Hale, "Darwin's Other Bulldog," 1008.
33. Ibid.
34. Ibid.

such an effort again: What is the underlying logic of the human story? Is it a tale of agonism that separates success from failure by, in the words of Jürgen Moltmann, a "biological execution of the Last Judgment on the weak, the sick and the 'unfit'"?[35] Or is it a drama of love and redemption that proclaims a sacrifice to end all sacrifice and that upends all notions of success and failure? That is where we begin.

Biography

"Big History." The McLean School. http://www.mcleanschool.org/Page/SCHOOL-LIFE/Learning-Commons/Learning-Commons-Online/Transformative-Teaching-Strategies/Big-History.

"Crisscrossing and Connected: Trade, Fuel, and Globalization." Big History Project. https://www.bighistoryproject.com/chapters/5#crisscrossing-and-connected.

Ferreira da Silva, Denise. *Toward a Global Idea of Race*. Minneapolis: University of Minnesota Press, 2007.

Hale, P. J. "Darwin's Other Bulldog: Charles Kingsley and the Popularization of Evolution in Victorian England." *Science & Education*, vol. 21, no. 7, 977–1013.

Haught, John. "Big History, Scientific Naturalism, and Christian Hope." *Creation Stories in Dialogue: The Bible, Science, and Folk Traditions*, edited by Jan G. van der Watt and R. Alan Culpepper, 78–94. Leiden: Koninklijke Brill, 2016.

Kierkegaard, Søren. *Johannes Climacus*. Translated by Howard V. Hong and Edna H. Hong. Princeton, NJ: Princeton University Press, 1985.

———. *Philosophical Fragments*. Translated by Howard V. Hong and Edna H. Hong. Princeton, NJ: Princeton University Press, 1985.

Lowe, Lisa. *The Intimacies of Four Continents*. Durham, NC: Duke University Press, 2015.

Moltmann, Jürgen. *The Way of Jesus Christ*. Minneapolis: Fortress, 1980.

Peters, Ted. "Big History and Big Questions." In *Creation Stories in Dialogue: The Bible, Science, and Folk Traditions*, edited by Jan G. van der Watt and R. Alan Culpepper, 48–77. Leiden: Koninklijke Brill, 2016.

Reardon, Jenny. *Race to the Finish: Identity and Governance in an Age of Genomics*. Princeton, NJ: Princeton University Press, 2004.

van der Watt, Jan G., and R. Alan Culpepper, eds. *Creation Stories in Dialogue: The Bible, Science, and Folk Tradition*. Leiden: Koninklijke Brill, 2016.

"What is Big History Project? A Social Studies Course That Runs on Jet Fuel." Big History Project. https://school.bighistoryproject.com/bhplive.

---

35. Moltmann, *The Way of Jesus Christ*, 294.

Part 2

Failing Better

6.

Mimetic Failure and the Possibility of Forgiveness

Duncan B. Reyburn

Vivas to those who have fail'd!
And to those whose war-vessels sank in the sea!
And to those who sank themselves in the sea!
And to all generals who lost engagements, and all overcome heroes!
And the numberless unknown heroes equal to the greatest heroes known!

— Walt Whitman, *Song of Myself*.

In *The Human Condition*, Hannah Arendt offers that "the discoverer of forgiveness in the realm of human affairs was Jesus of Nazareth."[1] Although worth considering in its own right,[2] the historical verifiability of Arendt's claim is of less significance here than the implication that forgiveness enters the human drama as an apocalypse—as a startling new beginning, a revelation, and a discovery. Forgiveness is less the natural outflow of historical processes than an interruption of them.

As Arendt implies, forgiveness is a subversion and a reversion. It is an event that undoes and reframes our pain, our longing, and our very

---

1. Arendt, *The Human Condition*, 238.
2. See Wolterstorff, "Jesus and Forgiveness."

consciousness of our experience of and place in the world. It intimates something of an inherent impossibility: the undoing of what was done. It is therefore as much a political statement as it is an existential one, and as such it is central to interpretive understanding itself, especially with regard to understanding the message of Jesus to the hurt, broken, disenfranchised, lost, and forgotten, no matter their social status, ideological commitments, or political predilections. Jesus speaks to the losers, who are, precisely, *everyone*. "For all have sinned and fall short..." (Rom 3:23, DBH).[3] Forgiveness is also, as I aim to explore in this essay, central to understanding the logic of positive reciprocity, as well as how this logic participates in combating negative reciprocity.[4]

Perhaps the most startling expression of forgiveness in the New Testament comes from the mouth of Luke's Jesus while he is dying on a Roman execution stake: "Father, forgive them; for they do not know what they are doing" (Luke 23:34, DBH). Against critics of this legitimation, René Girard points out that it is the very furthest thing from a "trifling excuse."[5] Instead, it is loaded with profound theological and philosophical significance. To contend with this statement, as something announced out of unimaginable anguish, is to contend with what is at the heart of all theologies of the crucifixion. While the meaning of Christ's death is still debated today, with several interpretations contested and reconfigured, there is nevertheless a widespread agreement that it is to be understood as having to do with the forgiveness of sin.[6] Ultimately, the naked, bleeding, dying God-man, while hanging between two thieves, does not call for vengeance upon his persecutors. Rather, he prays for them to be let off the hook.

It is remarkable that Jesus' prayer for forgiveness is bound to that simple-sounding claim: "they do not know what they are doing." The perpetrators of violence against the innocent and condemned, Jesus

---

3. All quotations of Scripture are taken from David Bentley Hart's translation of the New Testament.

4. The logic of positive reciprocity is at the heart of the ethical teaching of Jesus, which seeks not to much to abolish the *lex talionis* as it does to improve upon it (see especially Matt 5:38–48). Obviously, this logic is not only limited to the issue of forgiveness, and much of what I say on the issue of forgiveness here would have implications for how we understand living out any other virtue, like, say, temperance, humility, and so on.

5. Girard, *The Scapegoat*, 110.

6. Heim, *Saved from Sacrifice*, 321. This idea is pivotal to how the writers of the New Testament interpreted it. See, for instance, 1 Peter 3:18 and 1 Corinthians 15:3–18.

suggests, are not acting according to some kind of epistemic clarity. Rather, they are acting in concert with something else—something akin to the psychoanalytic or cognitive unconscious, or perhaps some ideological or counter-ideological *Zeitgeist*, over which they have no power and about which they seem to have no perceptual awareness.[7] Notably, the gap between the personhood or being of the perpetrators and their understanding of their actions seems to be essential for making forgiveness possible. There is an interval between their being and their comprehension, and thus also, by implication, between their essential self and their performative self. Because of this interval, one can begin to ascertain a distance between the sin—that is, the act committed and the conscious, fallacious understanding of that act by its perpetrator—and the being of the perpetrators and sinners themselves.

This interval affirms a commonplace theological notion: Sin is the privation of being—an absence that detracts from, reduces, diminishes, and opposes being[8]—rather than an extension of being, which, as Aquinas suggests, is always the primary site of intelligible goodness. Sin, manifest in multiple ways, is therefore the opposite of love, since love is that which essentially affirms and thus seeks to redeem the goodness of created being.[9]

All of this and more, it seems, is recognized by Jesus in his plea from the cross. He regards people, not as utterly bound to their procedures and perceptions, but rather as somehow separate from them. This is captured even in the cliché that claims that we ought to love the sinner while hating the sin—an idea that, while familiar to us and thus easy to overlook, is in fact highly sophisticated and by no means obvious. However we may define it, forgiveness negates sin and thus also contends against the negation of being. It undoes that which seeks to violate wholeness. It reaffirms and reclaims being in the wake of any force of degradation or annihilation. Thus, here, at the center of the issue of forgiveness, is the idea that we need to recognize a parallel between what seems to be going on and what really is going on. There is a disjunction assumed by Luke's Jesus between what *appears* and what *is*.

In his forgiveness-prayer from the cross, Jesus connects forgiveness to the real or the actual, and the ignorance of his persecutors to what only

---

7. Girard, *The Scapegoat*, 110.
8. See Pieper, *The Concept of Sin*.
9. Pieper, *Faith, Hope, Love*, 169, 176.

seems or appears. When we forgive, we acknowledge the real over illusion. Thus, we participate in the real through a sacramental linguistic act and, in so doing, become real ourselves. One might even say, *we become ourselves*. Moreover, if we follow the work of Girard, it becomes clear that what only *seems*—that is, what resists giving into the real—follows a particular kind of logic; it is the logic of negative reciprocity. Knowing this, it becomes clear that it is this logic that forgiveness needs to break, or participate in breaking, so that a shift toward positive reciprocity becomes possible.

In this essay, I aim to explore how this shift from one form of reciprocal logic (negative reciprocity) to another (positive reciprocity) happens. My claim is a simple one, although it requires some elucidation, namely that this shift requires dealing with what may be termed *mimetic failure*. I argue that forgiveness is both hampered and helped by this mimetic failure, which is a compound of two failures, namely, first, the failure to break from imitating the vengeful other and, second, the failure to imitate the one who is the source of all forgiveness. With regard to the core issue of this essay, mimetic failure amounts to a failure to forgive. I argue that the *recognition* of this failure to forgive is vital for disarming mimetic failure; it is part of what causes mimetic failure itself to fail, and thus ensures the possibility of forgiveness. To clarify what I mean by this requires some detail on how, insofar as mimetic theory is concerned, the self is constituted through mimetic desire.

It is well known that Girard's mimetic theory—and the work of many of his disciples—dwells at length on the issue of negative reciprocity. As a result, mimetic theory has become, in the minds of many, a "theory of conflict."[10] In Girard's view, "[t]he principle source of violence between human beings is mimetic rivalry, the rivalry resulting from the imitation of a model who becomes a rival or of a rival who becomes a model."[11] Shared, copied, acquisitive mimetic desire—the central pivot of Girard's realism—gives rise to all manifestations of violence. But it is vital to notice that Girard distances himself from any view that would see violence as an "instinctual phenomenon" and thus inherently real.[12] To see violence itself as instinctual would be to ontologize it. What *is*

10. See Palaver, *René Girard's Mimetic Theory*, 33.

11. Girard, *I See Satan Fall like Lightning*, 11. In Girard, *Things Hidden*, 27, this idea is articulated in more detail as including the transformation acquisitive mimesis into conflictual mimesis.

12. Palaver, *René Girard's Mimetic Theory*, 33.

instinctual is thus not violence but rather our inability to generate desire spontaneously, as well as the correlating capacity for taking on the desires of others. This does not caricature human beings as mindless copycats but instead highlights that we are inherently and radically open to otherness in keeping with our distinct, unique capacities.

Mimetic desire—this instinct that we have to emulate not only the activities of others but even their very wishes and wills—is what gives rise to both negative and positive reciprocity. It is also, very importantly, what gives rise to the self. The self, as a locus and filter of shared desires, is constituted by the desire of the other. Apart from desire, there can be no self. Without desire there would only be an evanescent impermanence composed of disparate personalities, ideas, and modes of operating. Desire is, metaphorically speaking, the judge that calls the court (the self) to order. Put differently, desire is the central principle of human intentionality in its structural ontology. Given this inescapable dimension of our concrete, experiential being, part of the practical and ethical function of mimetic theorists, then, must be to discern ways to encourage the constitution of selves-of-desire that work in favor of positive reciprocity, since it is in positive reciprocity, such as what Jesus articulates in the Golden Rule, that the goodness of being is best affirmed.

Since both forms of reciprocity (negative and positive) hinge on mimesis, they are in many ways analogous in their structure. Starting from the seed of original mimesis, both can produce an escalation of shared desires. Both suggest a negation of or cost to the self—since the self that is gained through being constituted by mimetic desire results from the loss of a self that was constituted by other mimetic desires. Moreover, both assume that there is a price to be paid, although *when* and *how* this price is paid differs. Negative reciprocity pays the price later, by taking. Positive reciprocity pays the price first, by giving. Similarities in structure, however, do not mean equivalence in content or meaning. Even the smallest difference between these two modes of being is significant.

In particular, negative reciprocity prescribes immediacy. In the face of injustice, so-called justice "must" act swiftly, even if in its swiftness this so-called justice is very likely to be little more than the repetition or emulation of the prior injustice. Justice may quite easily be vengeance by another name; what is thought truly moral may be little more than a complex delusion of values produced by *ressentiment*.[13] Because of the sense

---

13. It is for this reason that mimetic theorists examine conflict, in personal and political spheres, in terms of dyads or doubles. To understand conflicts, it is never

of immediacy—this pressure to react *now*, to repeat injustice *promptly* in the name of so-called justice—the desiring subject is less likely to recognize her desire as an imitation of the desire of another. This is to say that, in negative reciprocity, the desiring subject is merged with her enemy or rival—her self-of-desire is precisely a self constituted in imitation of the enemy's or rival's desire, and is therefore a self that is entangled in, indeed *formed by*, what the enemy or rival wants. In negative reciprocity, the desiring subject assumes, mistakenly of course, that her desire is *hers* rather than someone else's.

In conflict, especially in an escalation toward extreme forms of negative reciprocity (rage, revenge, war, and so on), the mimetic field becomes entirely undifferentiated. Doubles appear everywhere and multiply, and the world-historical timeline becomes populated with unconscious attempts toward achieving perfect, total, homogenous symmetry, minus a few scapegoats. This is particularly well illustrated in Jean Giraudoux's retelling of the Trojan War. There, undifferentiation perpetuates negative reciprocity and negative reciprocity escalates undifferentiation. Hector kills Patroclus (the double of Achilles), and Achilles (the double of Patroclus) ends up killing Hector (Achilles's other double), and all people in the story function as synecdochic doubles of their nations, which are really doubles of each other. Giraudoux's Hector says, "In the past, those I was going to kill had seemed to me to be the opposite of myself. This time I found myself kneeling over a mirror. The death I was going to mete out was a little suicide."[14]

On this scene, which references the myth of Narcissus,[15] Mark Anspach notes that "[w]hen violence is at its height, opposition seems to

---

enough to focus on simplistic differences, which are often arbitrary. Rather, central to any conflict, and the main reason for its perpetuation through exaggerating differences, is the (acquisitive) desire shared by all parties. Irreconcilable differences may be cited as the core reason for the conflict, but the real source of the conflict is something more paradoxical: *irreconcilable similarity*. As is exposed by mimetic theory, for example, often counter-hegemonies and counter-ideologies are little more than mimetic copies of what they oppose, even while they wear a different mask. See, for example, Farneti, *Mimetic Politics*; Oughourlian, *The Genesis of Desire*; Tomelleri, *Ressentiment*.

14. Quoted in Anspach, *Vengeance in Reverse*, 30.

15. Narcissus may be taken as a symbol of the potential destruction that can arise from being bound up in the desire for and of a double. The myth itself suggests that Narcissus's desire was implanted, rather than spontaneous, and thus intimates that his trouble begins in the desire of the other. Narcissism, as such a reading would suggest, is not so much a form of solipsism as it is a form of excessive attachment to a particular kind of acquisitive mimesis.

be greatest, and yet the adversaries behave in the same way, each intent on killing the other because the other is intent on killing him. *The illusion of difference is accompanied by a structural symmetry that usually goes unperceived.*"[16] The paradox here is that a strong subjective sense of asymmetry (what *seems*), which is underpinned by ignorance, is likely to accompany an objective symmetry (what *is*), just as a stronger sense of symmetry (what *seems*) is likely to produce the differentiation of subjectivities (what *is*). The interval between the sinner and the sin is thus, in a sense, the interval between the subjective (a misperception of the real) and the objective (faithful attunement to the real). As conflict escalates, the symmetry between rivalrous others is rendered "ever more exact."[17]

In addition to exacerbating undifferentiation, negative reciprocity is always firmly rooted in repeating past misdeeds. Negative reciprocity is unforgiveness, since unforgiveness confirms all wrong done without undoing it. It dwells, not in possibility, but in a kind of historical paralysis, in the repetitive or obsessive mind-set of sheer victimhood. This is symbolized by the driving idea of Kurt Vonnegut's novel *Timequake*. Vonnegut's characters in the novel are transported back a decade while being forced to relive every moment of the previous decade—minus their free will.[18] In truth, negative reciprocity exaggerates this fictional conceit; it is a timequake, minus both free will and the awareness of what one is doing. Because of this, it is profoundly unimaginative and uncreative. It cannot do anything but denigrate being.

The self-of-desire constituted in negative reciprocity is closed to everything except the rivalrous desire of the other, and thus ensures the perpetual over-simplification of personhood—both of the self and the other. The enemy is rendered a two-dimensional copy of the subject's own destructive mimetic desire. In the process, the self becomes little more than the enemy's flatland dyad. Negative reciprocity seems to therefore insist, against the reasoning of Jesus' forgiveness statement in Luke 23, that no one can be forgiven, because they *are* precisely what they are doing. Whether they know what they are doing or not is not factored into the equation, since their sin has been deemed ontological. The ontological division of sin from sinner is impossible within a framework of negative reciprocity. Forgiveness, too, is rendered impossible.

16. Ibid., emphasis added.
17. Girard, *Oedipus Unbound*, 77.
18. Vonnegut, *Timequake*.

An insight from the mimetic psychology of Jean-Michel Oughourlian proves helpful for explaining why forgiveness becomes impossible within the undifferentiated mimetic field of negative reciprocity. Oughourlian points out that to understand all forms of reciprocity, a distinction between physical time and psychological time is essential.[19] The basic idea, which each of us is likely to understand on an intrinsic level but which we may easily forget in everyday life, is that our sense of time's meaning (*kairology*) is not time itself (*chronology*).

In physical time, Subject B perceives and receives the desire (D) of Subject A. The desire (D) is then replicated in Subject B as an echoed desire (d). Subject B's desire (d) is thus obviously neither spontaneous nor self-generated. However, this is not what Subject B perceives and experiences in psychological time. In psychological time, Subject B would perceive the secondary desire (d) as spontaneous, self-initiated, and preliminary. Thus, Subject B may easily regard Subject A's desire (D) as secondary and imitative—although it is also possible that Subject B will fail to recognize the presence of Subject A's desire (D) completely.

As this suggests, there is thus, in psychological time, something like "presentification" at work.[20] An aspect of the past is misremembered, and only the present conception of the past feels real. The past—Subject A's desire (D)—is replicated in the present but without having Subject B notice the process of duplication. Unfortunately, the concentrated emotional frame provided in the interplay of negative reciprocities only intensifies this presentification, such that any alternative view of time within psychological time becomes less acceptable from a subjective point of view. However else we might understand it, forgiveness must, at the very least, free us from the false narrative of psychological time with regard to the origin of our desires so that we might be connected once again to the real.

Again, the stronger the sense of asymmetry within the undifferentiated mimetic field of negative reciprocity, the less likely forgiveness—or any other expression of positive reciprocity—becomes. Arguably, nothing solidifies one's identification with the other—and one's reliance on the problematic aspects of the identity of the other—more than negative reciprocity. Since the self-of-desire within the mimetic field of negative reciprocities is gained by being lost in the negative desires of the other,

---

19. Oughourlian, *The Mimetic Brain*, 30.
20. Ibid.

it is, almost by definition, a self that cannot forgive. It is a self that renders the human subject entirely subservient to mimetic failure. And yet, in Jesus' metaphysical vision, forgiveness remains not only possible but necessary. If we are going to unpack how forgiveness is made possible, we need to better understand one of the fundamental goals of forgiveness, which is to embrace the logic of positive reciprocity.

I have already noted a structural analogy in negative and positive reciprocities, but, to clarify how a shift from negative reciprocity to positive reciprocity can take place, it is important to further articulate how these two forms of reciprocity differ. To begin with, negative reciprocity relies on lack as its primary motivator, and because of this it is bound to a psychology of scarcity that produces an all-consuming tunnel vision.[21] This tunnel vision or presentification as a psychological phenomenon essentially means the loss of perspective—an inability to see outside of a lack (brought about by negative reciprocity itself) that is perceived.[22] The focus in negative reciprocity is on what was taken—what is now lost, presumed irretrievable—and is consequently also a focus on taking or taking back, and on revenge. This explains, albeit partially, why it is so difficult to reverse or transcend the processes of negative reciprocity. No alternatives are provided by negative reciprocity. Presentification renders concrete and immovable what should in fact be in flux, including the self-of-desire. It solidifies mimetic failure.

By definition, positive reciprocity reverses the characteristics of negative reciprocity. Where negative reciprocity favors immediacy, undifferentiation, a focus on the past, a lack of imagination, scarcity, taking, and tunnel vision, positive reciprocity favors contemplative delay, differentiation, a future-focus, imagination, abundance, giving, paying-it-forward and an intentional, deliberate openness to otherness—even the absolute otherness of God. With regard to the last feature in particular—openness to otherness—positive reciprocity returns us to the realm of choice, in which we are able to recognize our desires as borrowed within physical time even when psychological time convinces us of something different.

21. See Mullainathan and Shafir, *Scarcity*. The psychology of scarcity is a fairly new field of and does not deal directly, to my knowledge, with what I am raising in this essay. My point here, in any case, is primarily philosophical one, although it would certainly have implications for phenomenology and psychology.

22. Something like this happens when oppositional groups report on the views of their "enemies." The actual perspective of the enemy is seldom reported fairly, since presentification has rendered the subject's capacity to reason at a distance (that is, apart from the mimetic dyad) defective.

We are then able to make conscious decisions concerning what we ought to emulate in others. Our ability to separate ourselves from the desires of others, to allow us to choose our mimetic models, is made possible.

However, the distance between negative reciprocity and positive reciprocity remains immense within the frame of negative reciprocity and/or vengeance. And so the question must be asked: *What makes a shift from negative reciprocity to positive reciprocity possible?* This question presumes a double gesture: stopping one social process (negative reciprocity) and starting another (positive reciprocity). Although many explanations may be provided for what would make this double gesture possible, I limit my own explanation to the core issue of this essay, namely, the requirement that the self-of-desire constituted by one form of mimesis (negative reciprocity) needs to be reconstituted (through positive reciprocity) as another self-of-desire. I argue that, to a significant extent, positive reciprocity is itself the solution to negative reciprocity; as such, it is also foundational for forgiveness. Since the problem of negative reciprocity and the option of positive reciprocity are both rooted in mimetic desire, it is perhaps helpful to know that we do not have to look too far for an answer.

To make this point clearer, it helps to refer to a story told by Corrie Ten Boom towards the end of her co-authored autobiographical book *The Hiding Place*.[23] Having gone through and survived a kind of hell at the hands of Nazis, Ten Boom became a leading voice against negative reciprocity and for healing. However, one day, after speaking to a group of people, she was confronted with a man who was an SS soldier at the concentration camp where she had seen her sister die. The man had thanked her for her talk, especially for her words about the forgiveness of Christ offered even to the worst of sinners. This startling confrontation with her enemy caused Ten Boom to recoil.

She knew that she must forgive, since this was so central to her faith, but she found that she could not. She prayed silently, admitting in that prayer that she could not forgive the man but needed "Jesus" to forgive him on her behalf. As Ten Boom describes it, it is precisely this recognition—"I cannot forgive"—that opens up the possibility of forgiving. Still, this can only be done through imitating the desire of another. After all, prior to such an imitation, the self-of-desire is trapped in a state of mimetic failure. Of course, it is highly likely that this is not the only

---

23. Sherrill, Sherrill, and Ten Boom, *The Hiding Place*.

way that forgiveness becomes possible but it is certainly, even from my own experience, a powerful catalyst for forgiveness.

The above account confirms mimetic theory's claim that the self, by being the result of the desire of another, is not autonomous. Girard's neologism for this self-of-desire is the "interdividual"—i.e., not the individual. Insofar as mimetic theory is concerned, the notion of an individual is a false theoretical construct—an illusory self that does not take into account the mimetic desires that constitute it. Thus, the recognition—"*I cannot forgive*"—is right. The "I" does not have this ability or capacity, precisely because it is an "I" constituted by the original rivalrous desires of the other within a mimetic field of negative reciprocity. Nevertheless, this admission of a failure to forgive is precisely what opens up the question: *Who, truly, is able to forgive?* For Ten Boom, the answer to that was Jesus. It was only in sharing, through faith, in Jesus' desire to forgive, and in letting that desire to forgive constitute a new self-of-desire, that she was able to offer forgiveness, and, moreover, break from the flow of negative reciprocity. It was only in adopting Jesus as a model of positive reciprocity that the way for positive reciprocity could be opened. But this could only follow from a simple moment of recognition.

In the Gospel of Mark, when Jesus heals the paralytic, he announces not only that the man is healed but that his sins have been forgiven (Mark 2:5). The healing is offered by Jesus as evidence "that the Son of Man has power to forgive sins on the earth" (Mark 2:10, DBH). Some scribes in the vicinity declare that Jesus is blaspheming, since their assumption is that only God can forgive (Mark 2:7). This story offers an interesting symbolic analogy for this discussion. Jesus forgives a man who has done no obvious wrong against him, which might be akin to, say, me forgiving a total stranger for stealing something that belongs to you. The absurdity of this is made more understandable, however, when one recognizes Jesus as a model of desire who opens the door to forgiveness. It is precisely his forgiveness of the other that may allow others to forgive in turn. The paralysis of negative reciprocity can be cured, not by some isolated Nietzschean will to power or mere self-made virtue, but by a participation in the goodness and grace modeled to us by Jesus.

It is possible to argue that, in his pronouncement of forgiveness from the cross, this same condition for forgiveness is evident. Jesus announces not "I forgive you" but a prayer that God the Father would be the source of forgiveness. In doing so, Jesus seems to locate the source of his forgiveness outside of himself—in an ideal origin of desire, in Absolute

Goodness. While we may be tempted to look only for the conditions of forgiveness in our perceptions of the other ("they do not know what they are doing"), my point has been, taking seriously Jesus' appeal to his Father, that we cannot find a way to forgive without a clearer experience of a self—the self, constituted through the desire of another—that hopes to forgive. Forgiveness, like any form of reciprocity, needs a mediator. And the mediator is Christ. In recognizing the mediator of positive reciprocity, the subject is no longer a self-of-desire caught up in what *seems*—that is, a self that is bound up in negative reciprocity and mimetic failure. Rather, the subject is transported into what *is* by becoming a self-of-desire constituted by the desire of the one who can and does love and forgive. In this, the subject, now participating in truth and in the affirmation of the goodness of created being, is made real.[24]

Bibliography

Anspach, Mark R. *Vengeance in Reverse: The Tangled Loops of Violence, Myth, and Madness.* East Lansing, MI: Michigan State University Press, 2016.

Arendt, Hannah. *The Human Condition.* Chicago: University of Chicago, 1959.

Farneti, Roberto. *Mimetic Politics.* East Lansing, MI: Michigan State University Press, 2015.

Girard, René. *I See Satan Fall Like Lightning.* Translated by James G. Williams. New York: Orbis, 2001.

———. *Oedipus Unbound: Selected Writings on Rivalry and Desire.* Edited by M. R. Anspach. Stanford, CA: Stanford University Press, 2004.

———. *The Scapegoat.* Translated by Yvonne Freccero. Baltimore: Johns Hopkins University Press, 1986.

———. *Things Hidden Since the Foundation of the World.* Translated by Stephen Bann and Michael Metteer. London: Bloomsbury, 2016.

Hart, David Bentley. *The New Testament: A Translation.* New Haven: Yale University Press, 2017.

Heim, Mark S. *Saved From Sacrifice: A Theology of the Cross.* Grand Rapids: Eerdmans, 2006.

Mullainathan, Sendhil and Eldar Shafir. *Scarcity: Why Having Too Little Means So Much.* London: Penguin, 2013.

Oughourlian, J-M. *The Genesis of Desire.* East Lansing, MI: Michigan State University Press, 2010.

———. *The Mimetic Brain.* East Lansing, MI: Michigan State University Press, 2016.

Palaver, Wolfgang. *René Girard's Mimetic Theory.* Translated by Gabriel Borrud. East Lansing, MI: Michigan State University Press, 2013.

---

24. I am grateful to Marno Kirstein and Leon Marincowitz for their constructive criticism on an earlier draft of this essay.

Pieper, Josef. *The Concept of Sin*. Translated by Edward T. Oakes. South Bend, IN: St. Augustine's, 2001.

———. *Faith, Hope, Love*. San Francisco: Ignatius, 2012.

Sherrill, Elizabeth, John Sherrill, and Corrie Ten Boom. *The Hiding Place*. London: Hodder & Stoughton, 1971.

Tomelleri, Stefano. *Ressentiment: Reflections on Mimetic Desire and Society*. Breakthroughs in Mimetic Theory. East Lansing, MI: Michigan State University Press, 2015.

Vonnegut, Kurt. *Timequake*. London: Vintage, 2011.

Wolterstorff, Nicholas. "Jesus and Forgiveness." In *Jesus and Philosophy*, edited by Paul K. Moser, 194–214. Cambridge: Cambridge University, 2009.

7.

A Moral Theology of Technological Failure

Michael S. Burdett

I MOVED TO THE United Kingdom about a decade ago. When I first moved, as can be imagined, I noticed many different things between my native USA and the UK. Despite speaking the same language, many words and phrases were different. Elevators are called *lifts*, pants are called *trousers*, and a car trunk is a *boot*. One of the most frustrating adjustments I needed to make concerned customer service, and the difference in expected household convenience and comfort. It took three months to get Internet hardware installed in our flat (our apartment), several more months to get a bank account, and I noticed that dishwashers and clothes dryers were a rarity. Things just took longer to get done and required more manual effort.

Whenever I would describe these differences to either my British friends or my American family back home I would recount how these differences in cultural practices expressed different cultural values. The British are very eco-conscious (I've been reproved on more than one occasion for putting too much water in the kettle because it takes more energy to boil the excess water I won't use) and have a great love of nature (besides crosswords, gardening and walks in the countryside are beloved pastimes and celebrated as markers of Britishness). They tend to be thrifty and value past generations and traditions. Institutions like the National Trust actively seek to protect the British heritage and identity through preserving old buildings and estates. People live in homes that can sometimes be centuries old (my last house was built in 1542) and, rather than tearing them down as might be the general custom in the USA, are often retrofitted generation after generation.

Traveling home to the USA many times during the past decade, I'm consistently reminded how comfortable life can be in contradistinction. Central heating can be found in the coldest of climates and one often doesn't need to face the chilly elements walking from one's car in the parking structure to the central shopping mall. Substitute central heating for air conditioning if you are in an oppressively hot climate. Houses tend to be brand new and the walls are free of out-of-use wires from previous occupants (they clutter most British homes). Such bespeaks the American valuation of comfort and efficiency. Indeed, it is this last value, efficiency, which has growing significance for our modern technological age and is the linchpin to a moral theology of technological failure. Simply put, and what I will be arguing for here, technological failure can be morally and personally constructive when a society, such as ours, places efficiency as the supreme good to be pursued. In fact, stated more seriously, we cannot lead Christ-honoring lives that exemplify his virtues unless we challenge and dethrone efficiency as the highest end of society and our individual pursuits.

Jacques Ellul and Efficiency as the Highest Value in Our Technological Society

Jacques Ellul is one who has thought deeply about the impact technology has made on present society, our valorizing of efficiency because of it, and what this means for the Christian faith. But Ellul's trenchant insights and criticisms regarding the technological society aren't primarily levelled at just the proliferation of mechanical objects that make our lives easier, they are just the material instantiations of a much larger force on society. Indeed, Ellul is most concerned with what is termed *technique* in French. *Technique* for Ellul is defined as the "totality of methods rationally arrived at and having absolute efficiency (for a given stage of development) in every field of human activity."[1] Essentially, Ellul comments on how the technological society is obsessed with the methods, means, and processes in society and how this focus is, in turn, transforming that society. So, *technique* can be applied to the ordering of governments to yield technocratic rule. It can be applied to the economy to streamline

1. Ellul, *The Technological Society*, xxv.

production systems and generate more capital or it can be applied to human psychological health and yield various therapeutic techniques (e.g., cognitive behavioral therapy or psychoanalytic therapy). None of these has technological apparatuses as its object because *technique* is about processes and the analysis of them.

It is easy to see, then, how efficiency relates to Ellul's characterization of the technological society. Let me explain. One of the characterizing features of *technique* in present society is its relation to rationality. When Ellul speaks of the rationalizing nature of *technique* he means that the processes themselves are transformed from illogical and spontaneous means to reflective and fine-tuned ones because of an explicit rational analysis of the processes. Ellul says this is most visible today in our "systemization, division of labor, creation of standards, production norms and the like."[2] Essentially, whereas a given domain might have had several different processes equally utilized in the past (e.g., perhaps different methods of fixing soles on to shoes was used), the rational character of modern *technique* does not allow for multiple means because one will be more logical than the others and will fare better than the others. Ellul says, "The choice is less and less a subjective one among several means which are potentially applicable. It is really a question of finding the best means in the absolute sense, on the basis of numerical calculation."[3] Therefore, when the processes are inspected, scrutinized, and refined using the measure of rational reflection, only the most efficient means remains. Human creativity and choice, therefore, have little to contribute to the overall development of technology and other systems. The hunt for the best means possible requires no creativity because unnecessary components of the process are abolished and deemed inappropriate.

Even more grave for present society is that this search for the most efficient means tends towards universalization in society. As new technologies are created and integrated into existing technological infrastructure, new areas of human activity are rationalized that have never been before. When Ellul speaks of the universalizing character of *technique*, he means that no area remains unchanged by its totalizing and rationalizing force. Why does the application of rationality necessarily lead to such propagation? First, inefficient means have no possibility of surviving against efficient ones in the marketplace of means. In a kind of

2. Ibid., 79.
3. Ibid., 21.

survival of the fittest scenario, only the most efficient will remain. Indeed as one commentator has claimed, "The entrance of technique into a non-technical milieu forces its transformation into a technical one, since efficiency renders all less efficient means obsolete."[4] Yet, Ellul also states that, second, humanity provides no resistance to the momentum technique has generated because we have been swept away by the technical revolution; we are bedazzled by it and have given up our freedom:

> On the other hand, all people in our time are so passionate about technology, so utterly shaped by it, so assured of its superiority, so engulfed in the technological environment, that they are all, without exception, oriented toward technological progress, all working toward it, no matter what their trade, each individual seeking the best way to use his instrument or perfect a method, a device etc.[5]

Ellul was writing this in the mid-twentieth century. Observing people line up in front of the Apple Store hours if not days before the new iPhone is released, Ellul might encourage us to ask now: How much more visible is our technological passion today than it was decades ago? And how much more difficult is it today to break from the exceeding technological pace in present society for fear of being left behind? We want things faster and done with less effort: the very definition of efficiency.[6] We live in a society where efficiency is the supreme virtue.

Diagnosis of a Society Concerned With Maximizing Efficient Means Rather than Pursuing Human-Affirming Ends

What is the problem with a society and people that elevate efficiency to the highest goal of society and individual lives? As so many have claimed: it is dehumanizing. Those in a technological society that solely focus on maximizing efficient means are in serious danger of losing sight of the true virtuous ends of a society and life. As David Lewin argues, "on the one hand technology presents pure ends to us by way of the interface,

---

4. Fasching, *The Thought of Jacques Ellul*, 17.
5. Ellul, *The Technological System*, 209.
6. For a more sustained treatment of Ellul's treatment of efficiency see Son, "Are We Still Pursuing Efficiency?" For an excellent treatment of how efficiency still figures prominently in contemporary society, owing to the force of technology, see chapter 7 of Alexander, *The Mantra of Efficiency*.

while on the other hand technology continually improves efficiency for efficiency's sake, thereby displacing the end for which efficiency strives."[7] When the final goals of a life or society are reoriented around the search for the best means, true ends are eclipsed and all kinds of moral issues arise because of disordered values.

An extreme example is visible in the testimony of Rudolf Höss, the Nazi commandant of Auschwitz, at the Nuremberg trials in 1946. What is horrifying in Höss's testimony and remarked on by trial psychologists is the cold, calm, and collected nature of his description of "processing" Jews in the concentration camp. What is so striking in reading his testimony is the excessive technical detail he gives to the court regarding the actual process of genocide at Auschwitz; how the "processing of so many bodies" was an incredibly technical task. Indeed, here is the leader of one of the most horrendous concentration camps at the center of one of the most egregious crimes against humanity the world has ever seen, and most of his testimony is made up of lists and technical production details. The expected remorseful disposition is instead replaced by a technocrat who worries about making the "process" more efficient. There is no feeling, there is just the work at hand that needs to be made more efficient.[8] Of course this liminal case is an extreme example of the consequences of focusing so intently on efficiency that is the product of our technological society. In spite of its severity, it does help throw into relief just how dangerous such radical obsession with efficiency can be when it loses sight of proper ends, when it becomes the paramount end for any domain of life.

In fact, it is precisely the elevation of the technological system in society, what others have called the mass society, over the human individual that has been criticized by so many critics and scholars the last two centuries. One of the most trenchant and long-lasting criticisms comes from existentialism. As Paul Tillich has argued, existentialism "rebels in the name of personality against the depersonalizing forces of technical society."[9] Tillich goes on to outline how critics as diverse as Kierkegaard, Marx, and Nietzsche, in their own way, fight for the dignity and common core experience of humanity in the face of debilitating technical forces. Kierkegaard addresses the single individual and claims "the crowd is untruth." Marx seeks to outline how the class system underlies the de-

---

7. Lewin, *Technology and the Philosophy of Religion*, 113.
8. Read more in Gilbert, *Nuremberg Diary*; Höss, *Death Dealer*.
9. Tillich, *The Spiritual Situation in Our Technical Society*, 123.

bilitating production system that all are slave to and how to emancipate the people in it for the sake of the individuals themselves. For Nietzsche, "man becomes . . . a cog in the all-embracing machine of production and consumption" and robs each individual of the "creative power of life."[10] Rather than seeking liberation through the "leap of faith" as Kierkegaard argued, or through social dialectics following Marx, Nietzsche turned to the "depth of personal life itself."[11] These critics, and many more like them, have sought to return to the human being its dignity that has been seriously eroded by the technological society. In spite of often diverging views, these critics invite us to ask: what are these technical means for (and indeed the study of the means) but to help human beings flourish? When human beings are functionalized and not treated as an end in themselves, this is the very definition of dehumanization. A society that elevates too highly efficiency is in danger of such dehumanization.

Of course, much more could be said that diagnoses the maladies that arise with a technological society that neglects humanistic values as its ultimate goal. One is worth highlighting, in particular, because it occurs so frequently amongst critics of technology in society and relates to faith and religion. Gabriel Marcel, Paul Tillich, Erich Fromm, and Martin Heidegger all note, in some way, that modern technology in present society has stunted robust spirituality in its individual members. Marcel refers to this as a "broken world"[12] where "the spirit of technology" has "become detrimental to the flowering of humanity" and works "adversely against the aspiration of the person toward its fulfillment in being."[13] What is most at stake for Marcel is that human beings lose their sense of orientation to transcendence and spirituality because of the "mass society." For Marcel, human fulfilment and deep inner spirituality are seriously in danger today. Fromm similarly diagnoses humanity and even suggests that only a shared common spirituality, with holistic humanistic aims and sensibilities, will be able to combat the destruction of psychological and spiritual health wrought by our technological society.[14] Tillich also warns that the "thingification" of persons and mass society reduce the human center of ultimate purpose and, hence, spirituality. In the process,

10. Ibid., 127.
11. Ibid., 128.
12. Marcel, *The Mystery of Being*, vol. 1, 18–56.
13. Gendreau, "Gabriel Marcel's Personalist Ontological Approach to Technology," 233. Also see chapter 3 of Marcel, *Man against Mass Society*.
14. Fromm, *The Revolution of Hope*, 48–64, 137ff.

the very kernel of humanity and its dignity is degraded.[15] Finally, Martin Heidegger contends that the present technological condition seriously limits our relation to the world and that we are in danger of losing sight of our relation to Being itself and, hence, are alienated from ourselves and everything around us.[16]

All of these figures recognize that technology has vast repercussions for humanity's inner spiritual life and indeed a deep connection with the rest of the world. We might say that the obsession with efficient means takes so much of our attention that it therefore distracts us from much more affirming, deep values and activities. The greatest vice in a technological society is boredom—the most inefficient use of attention. Yet, the avenue to a deep inner life begins with waiting, boredom's brother, and attending to things in a non-instrumental way. Indeed, technological life and keeping up with the exceeding pace it demands keeps us from lingering on those very important, but difficult, existential and spiritual issues and questions that are critical to a meaningful life. Questions like: Am I really making a difference? Am I doing the right thing? What is this all for? These kinds of issues resist quantification and because we don't live our lives under the weight of them we will never be fulfilled. We trade long-lasting fulfillment for immediate payoff. Being animated by modern technological efficiency keeps us from true shalom.

Breaking the Spell with Heidegger and Reordering Our Values with Augustine

If lauding efficiency to this degree has had such dramatic effects on ourselves and society, what is to be done and how might this all relate to the theme of this book on theological appropriations of failure? On the face of it, failure of any kind would seem to be detrimental to any form of human activity and to humanity's flourishing. Indeed, specifically technological failure can lead to great suffering and even death. More and more we entrust our lives to technology and the engineers that design them, whether riding in an elevator in a skyscraper or traveling over a bridge. Hence, we are more at risk today when they fail and this is to be lamented. Technological failure is a serious matter. However, the failure I am talking about is a failure of the very ethos of a technological society

---

15. Tillich, *The Spiritual Situation*, 118–21.
16. Heidegger, *The Question Concerning Technology and Other Essays*.

that has championed efficiency as the highest goal. Can the failure of certain kinds of technology be constructive, particularly when they fail at being efficient? I think they can because an inefficient, failed technology awakens us to the relation we have with that technology and to our task and environment. It causes us to assess our purposes and aims.

Heidegger is instructive here. In Heidegger's magnum opus, *Being and Time*, he describes a basic and central activity of any human being (*Dasein*): tool use. Specifically, he focuses on the relation the human being has to a particular tool, a hammer, during the process of use. Essentially, when one is engaged in hammering the hammer recedes into the background. It is not consciously being used as a thing that requires direct and abstract reflection. In a way, Heidegger points to how objective descriptions of the subject (human being) and object (hammer) are abstractions from the actual phenomenological tool use. Instead, the carpenter has no explicit awareness of the hammer as an object, nor the environment in which he works: the environment, tool, and person are caught up in one common action and relation. Now Heidegger goes on to explain why this matters for his existential analytic of *Dasein* but, for our purposes, what is most interesting is how the failure of the hammer awakens the carpenter to explicit awareness of the tool, environment, and purpose or intended aim for hammering. As Heidegger says: "But when an assignment has been disturbed—when something is unusable for some purpose—then the assignment becomes explicit . . . we catch sight of the 'towards-this' itself, and along with it everything connected with the work—the whole 'workshop' . . . ."[17] The failure of the tool awakens the individual from being caught up in their action and illuminates the network of relations they have, including their intended aim. The flow of the efficient action is interrupted by a tool not performing efficiently and this causes one to assess one's ends.

Heidegger's phenomenological account of technological failure can be expanded upon. For, the effect of technological failure, assessment of one's ends, has vast implications for the moral life. Heidegger surely means here that the tool user is made aware of their intended aims with just the present action and the particular piece of technology. However, once functionalist actions move to reflective teleological value-laden discourse, regardless of whether it begins with just the present technological action, we are then in the domain of moral deliberation: why pursue this

---

17. Heidegger, *Being and Time*, 105 [I.3.75].

goal instead of another? Why pursue a functional action rather than an artistic one, or rather than a spiritual one? Indeed, breaking free from the flow of efficient means we are then awakened to the fact that we aren't just *homo faber*, "man the maker," but are so much more: *homo aestheticus*, *homo religiosus*, and *homo spiritualis*.

If Heidegger helps us to break out of the technological circle to focus again on "ends" and "purposes," then Augustine helps us to recognize that anything but *caritas* as the supreme end of any human endeavor is doomed to dysfunction and dissatisfaction. Augustine famously speaks of human happiness and virtue by referring to what is the object of our love. Indeed, Augustine even speaks of sin in terms of love—preferring to speak of sin arising from loving the wrong things in the wrong ways. Indeed, the human desire to love is fulfilled and the human being is happy/flourishes when their loves are ordered properly and things are loved for their own sake rather than the utility that they afford to us.[18] In fact, Augustine puts it more strongly in a theological register when he says that one can never be happy unless God is loved as the supreme end and source, and God's creation is loved in light of God.[19] In this way, our happiness and well-being is not a final end alone but rather a product of loving God and because of loving God, loving all that he has created. To quote the oft-cited refrain of Augustine: "you made us for yourself and our hearts find no peace until they rest in you."[20] Therefore, any other value placed as the pinnacle of human achievement will ultimately end in dissatisfaction and dysfunction. Any society or individual that seeks to set its foundation on anything less is doomed.[21]

Conclusion

I've argued here that technological failure can be morally and personally constructive, particularly when that failure is embedded in a technological society that has placed efficiency as its supreme value. Ellul teaches that one of the animating characteristics of modern technology is the

---

18. Augustine, *City of God*, 637 [XV.23].
19. Kent, "Augustine's Ethics."
20. Augustine, *Confessions*, 21 [I.1].
21. For further reference to how Augustine and his followers understand how societies themselves are animated by what they love see Brock, *Christian Ethics in a Technological Age*, 193–210; O'Donovan, *Common Objects of Love*.

rationalizing and universalizing force it has on every area of human activity. Efficient means will triumph in any situation and particularly when this value is celebrated by members of such a technological society as ours. Technological failure—that is when it no longer contributes to efficient work and is not catastrophic to the well-being of people involved—can be morally uplifting because, as Heidegger intimates, it awakens the people embedded in the technological task to explicit reflection on the purposes and goals of those involved: it leads to moral and personal deliberation and can be the avenue to reorienting and reordering our lives and societies towards more loving and, hence, fulfilling ends.

In my move from the USA to the UK, I often catch myself grumbling about trains not being on time, my water heater running out of hot water prematurely while I'm in the shower, and the battery on my phone dying. But I have come to learn that these inefficiencies merely reveal a societal culture that has not become as bedazzled with efficiency as my native USA and that this can be an opportunity to recognize there can be more important values at work. I have learned to cultivate the virtue of waiting that gives me the space to do things like pray for my fellow delayed passengers. I might use the extra time not spent in the shower to read a story to my daughter. Or, instead of searching for a spot to recharge my phone, I could start a conversation with someone around me. The point is that the system and its continual efficiency as the supreme virtue does not matter as much as the people in it and their virtuous development that ultimately finds its source in a loving God. So, when you are frustrated because your computer is slow, angry when your car breaks down, or you choose to not to get the latest smartphone but instead keep your perfectly capable but less efficient one, remember that these moments can be acts of virtuous personal development and can help reorient you to the more important purposes and goals of life that will invariably help you flourish better.

Bibliography

Alexander, Jennifer Karns. *The Mantra of Efficiency: From Waterwheel to Social Control.* Baltimore: Johns Hopkins University Press, 2008.

Augustine. *Concerning the City of God against the Pagans.* Translated by Henry Scowcroft Bettenson. London: Penguin, 2003.

———. *Confessions.* Translated by R. S. Pine-Coffin. London: Penguin, 1961.

Brock, Brian. *Christian Ethics in a Technological Age.* Grand Rapids: Eerdmans, 2010.

Ellul, Jacques. *The Technological Society.* Translated by John Wilkinson. New York: Vintage, 1964.

———. *The Technological System.* Translated by Joachim Neugroschel. New York: Continuum, 1980.

Fasching, Darrell J. *The Thought of Jacques Ellul: A Systematic Exposition.* Lewiston, NY: Edwin Mellen, 1981.

Fromm, Erich. *The Revolution of Hope: Toward a Humanized Technology.* New York: HarperCollins 1981.

Gendreau, Bernard. "Gabriel Marcel's Personalist Ontological Approach to Technology." *The Personalist Forum* 15, no. 2 (1999) 229–46.

Gilbert, G. M. *Nuremberg Diary.* New York: Da Capo, 1995.

Heidegger, Martin. *Being and Time.* Translated by John Macquarrie and Edward Robinson. New York: Harper and Row, 1962.

———. *The Question Concerning Technology and Other Essays.* Translated by William Lovitt. London: Harper & Row, 1977.

Höss, Rudolf. *Death Dealer: The Memoirs of the SS Kommandant at Auschwitz.* Translated by Andrew Pollinger. Buffalo, NY: Prometheus, 1992.

Kent, Bonnie. "Augustine's Ethics." In *The Cambridge Companion to Augustine,* edited by Norman Kretzmann and Eleonore Stump, 205–33. Cambridge: Cambridge University Press, 2001.

Lewin, David. *Technology and the Philosophy of Religion.* Newcastle: Cambridge Scholars Press, 2011.

Marcel, Gabriel. *Man against Mass Society.* Translated by G. S. Fraser. South Bend, IN: St Augustine, 2008.

———. *The Mystery of Being.* Translated by G. S. Fraser. 2 vols. Chicago: Henry Regnery Company, 1950.

O'Donovan, Oliver. *Common Objects of Love: Moral Reflection and the Shaping of Community.* Grand Rapids: Eerdmans, 2002.

Son, Wha-Chul. "Are We Still Pursuing Efficiency? Interpreting Jacques Ellul's Efficiency Principle." In *Jacques Ellul and the Technological Society in the 21st Century,* edited by Helena Mateus Jerónimo, José Luís Garcia, and Carl Mitcham, 49–62. New York: Springer, 2013.

Tillich, Paul. *The Spiritual Situation in Our Technical Society.* Edited by J. Mark Thomas Macon, GA: Mercer, 1988.

8.

Christ the Failure

Bonhoeffer and the Paradoxical Power of Weakness

MATTHEW D. KIRKPATRICK

BONHOEFFER WAS SOMETHING OF a failure. Despite his significant legacy, Bonhoeffer's life could be better judged by what it didn't achieve than by what it did. His vocation as an academic or pastor was never ultimately fulfilled.[1] His significant efforts within the ecumenical movement yielded little fruit. His predictions about the rise of National Socialism and the plight of the Jews remained unheeded, and his own Confessing Church considered him more of a troublemaker than an astute political and social commentator.[2] The illegal seminary he founded was only active for a short period before it was shut down by the Gestapo.[3] Many of his students were imprisoned, conscripted, or killed, with as many as 85 percent of Confessing Church pastors taking the oath to Hitler.[4] By 1940 the Nazi state had robbed Bonhoeffer of his liberty to speak in public, and

---

1. Hans Richard Rueter refers to Bonhoeffer's *Habilitationsschrift*, *Act and Being*, published at the age of twenty-five, as his "last publication in the realm of professional academic theology" (Rueter, "Afterword," 177).

2. Many contemporaries developed a negative impression of Bonhoeffer due to the urgency of his call. Various biographers refer to him as having been considered a "heretic," "zealot," and "legalist" (cf. Bethge, *Bonhoeffer*, 521f, 569), or a "pessimist" and "inconvenient Cassandra" (Schlingensiepen, *Bonhoeffer*, 127, 167).

3. From April 1935 to September 1936.

4. As recorded in Pugh, *Religionless Christianity*, 40.

then, finally, to publish his work.⁵ His involvement in the attempted assassination obviously failed. But even his own personal task, to persuade the allies to support the German resistance, was just as futile, as Churchill had already decided that any such requests should be treated with the upmost suspicion.⁶ On the relational front, Bonhoeffer's engagement to Maria von Wedemeyer was also thwarted with his arrest and imprisonment just three months later.⁷ And, finally, Bonhoeffer was executed on April 9, 1945, just a few shorts weeks before the end of the war. So what *did* Bonhoeffer achieve during his lifetime?⁸

Such an introduction is clearly rhetorically framed. The fact that I am writing about Bonhoeffer over seventy years later, and able to draw on an extraordinary wealth of primary and secondary sources in such an endeavor, clearly reveals the profound success of Bonhoeffer's life and work in a certain regard. But this shouldn't distract us from the raw facts of his life, or his own experience and perception of them. As he reflected back upon his life from prison, what could he have held on to? Was it all for nothing? If we place ourselves in his shoes, would we have been able to fight back the despair of seeing our lives apparently left in meaningless ruins?

Bonhoeffer's letters from prison clearly reveal something of that existential concern. Bonhoeffer was no stoic. And yet what we find within his theology, forged in part as a result of his prison experience, is a profoundly countercultural message concerning our evaluation of success and failure, and how Christians have unwittingly embraced the perception of the world rather than that of Christ.

---

5. On August 22, 1940, Bonhoeffer was banned from public speaking, and on March 19, 1941, from publishing. In a letter to Walter Schmidt on March 31, 1941, Bonhoeffer wrote, "On the basis of the ban on public speaking, they have now also imposed on me a ban on writing, so there is very little left of my ministry" (Bonhoeffer, *Conspiracy and Imprisonment*, 184).

6. Cf. Dramm, *Bonhoeffer and the Resistance*, 79.

7. Bonhoeffer was engaged on January 17, 1943 and was arrested on April 5, 1943.

8. The situation is summarized by Eberhard Bethge, one of the people closest to Bonhoeffer during his life, in the preface to his peerless biography: "A man suffered shipwreck in, with, and because of his country. He saw his church and its claims collapse in ruins. The theological writings he left consisted of barely accessible fragments. In 1945 only a handful of friends and enemies knew who this young man had been; the names of other Christians in Germany were more in the limelight. When his name did emerge from the anonymity of his death, the response from the world of academic theology and the churches was tentative and restrained. Even today some Germans hesitate to accept him and what he stood for completely." Bethge, *Bonhoeffer*, xiii.

Christ the Failure

Bonhoeffer's prison theology has had a profound influence on a wide range of thinkers with its provocative and embryonic thought.[9] However, few themes have been as fruitful as his understanding of the weakness of Christ. According to Bonhoeffer, much of the development of Christian thought has been founded on an error. In the face of primitive humanity's ignorance about themselves, the world, and the meaning of life, the church has forged God into the ultimate and comprehensive answer to every question—a transcendent, all-powerful being, who rests outside of our experience, to dominate it all.[10] In doing so, the church has also guaranteed its own importance and control as God's minister. However, according to Bonhoeffer, such a God has never truly existed, and if we are to understand him rightly, we must begin where he reveals himself most clearly—with someone whose greatest achievement is to hang on a cross. As Bonhoeffer comments,

> God consents to be pushed out of the world and onto the cross; God is weak and powerless in the world and in precisely this way, and only so, is at our side and helps us. Matt. 8:17 makes it quite clear that Christ helps us not by virtue of his omnipotence but rather by virtue of his weakness and suffering! This is the crucial distinction between Christianity and religions. Human religiosity directs people in need to the power of God in the world ... The Bible directs people toward the powerlessness and the suffering of God; only the suffering God can help.[11]

In order to understand the importance of Christ's weakness, and its salvific potential, we must first understand the predicament that humankind is being saved from.

According to Bonhoeffer, the fall must be understood epistemologically. The problem for Bonhoeffer is not simply one of obedience—whether

---

9. Cf. Kirkpatrick, ed., *Engaging Bonhoeffer*.

10. The world, for Bonhoeffer, has now "come of age." As humankind has grown in maturity, so it has been able to understand more and more itself, with little need for cosmic answers. Such a God has therefore been pushed to the extremity of existence, and revealed to be nothing but a "stop gap" or "deus ex machina." As a last attempt to retain its central significance and control, the church has tried to preserve a place for God by emphasizing humankind's sins and need for forgiveness. But even this is failing, according to Bonhoeffer, as in its maturity the world has lost connection with its potentially guilt-inducing sense of a "religious a priori."

11. Bonhoeffer, *Letters and Papers*, 479.

Adam and Eve ate the apple or not—but rather one of perception. In his question to Eve—"Did God really say?"—the serpent leads Eve to stand in judgment on God's word. And in choosing to answer the question, humankind no longer simply accepts and enacts God's word, but rather evaluates it. In doing so, we no long stand under God as his creatures, but above God as those who act as the ground of his validity. For Bonhoeffer, this isn't a simple rejection of God, but a desire to get to God and be with him—but on our own terms.

God's response is equally nuanced. Quite apart from a simple rejection, God grants humankind their request and they receive the fruit of the tree of knowledge. However, as we have neither the capacity nor purity of the divine mind to receive and understand the full content of reality, such knowledge comes crashing down around us. Knowledge now lies shattered on the epistemological floor, robbed of its harmony and integration. Human reason is left to pick through the shards and build partial and partisan systems in its attempt to live out of itself rather than God. "Reality" is now recreated through the human ego in the place of God, and bears the marks of humankind's fear, insecurity, and sense of existential isolation. Consequently, power and violence become the foundations of our social interactions as we strive over one another to establish ourselves within the world, and success becomes the real measurement of our thoughts and actions.[12] Weakness and vulnerability are vilified and banished to the private realm as inconvenient reminders of our corruption. "Religion," for Bonhoeffer, is the essence of the fall, embodying the attempt by humankind to get to God on its own terms, and in its affirmation of power and success, it is precisely the transcendent, omnipotent, and impassable God that is created at its center.

Bonhoeffer describes this fabricated "reality" as the product of the *"cor curvum in se"* and the *"ratio in se ipsam incurve"*—the human heart and mind turned in upon themselves.[13] And it is as an answer to both of these that Christ comes. If we turn first to the mind, Bonhoeffer draws heavily on Kierkegaard's Christology to argue that Christ comes to over-

---

12. As he comments, "the majority fall into *idolizing success*" and "become blind to right and wrong, truth and lie, decency and malice. They see only the deed, the success. Ethical and intellectual capacity for judgment grow dull before the sheen of success and before the desire somehow to share in it. People even fail to perceive that guilt is scarred over in success, because guilt is no longer recognized as such." Bonhoeffer, *Ethics*, 89.

13. Cf. Bonhoeffer, *Sanctorum Communio*, 41 and 46.

come our enthroned reason.[14] Instead of a conquering hero, a political giant, or a philosophical genius who we could understand and judge to be worthy of our allegiance, Christ comes without authority or proof, into poverty, through a suspicious birth, and ultimately onto a cross as a criminal. In short, he comes in the very weakness and vulnerability that humankind fears. If this Christ is to be honestly judged according to human reason, he is a failure and the Pharisees are right in their Golgotha accusation: "He saved others but he cannot save himself! He's the king of Israel! Let him come down now from the cross and we will believe in him."[15] For Bonhoeffer, despite their vilified identity, the Pharisees have at least understood how Christ should be evaluated by our reason, and what we should demand of him before we will "believe."[16]

For Bonhoeffer, Christ has come in such a way that the only two responses to him are precisely the scorn of the Pharisees, or faith. But such a faith requires the submission of our reason. In his "Lectures on Christology" from 1933, Bonhoeffer argues that the reasonable "religious" evaluation of Christ begins with the questions "How?" and "What?" These are the questions of a mind evaluating an object. However, the only true question of Christology is "Who?" This is the question of absolute submission, of a mind that gives up its self-reliance and simply asks for its subject to freely speak and reveal itself. Only in this way can the effects of the fall be truly overcome, and we return to receiving all of reality—including our identities, security, and strength—once again from God. As Bonhoeffer states in *Discipleship*, "This weak Word, which suffers contradiction by sinners, is the only strong, merciful Word that can make sinners repent from the bottom of their hearts."[17]

---

14. Kierkegaard's understanding of Christ as paradox, incognito, and offense is most clearly articulated in *Concluding Unscientific Postscript* and *Practice in Christianity*. Bonhoeffer drew directly from these works in developing his own Christology. These thoughts are developed particularly in Bonhoeffer's 1932 article, "Concerning the Christian Idea of God," and his "Lectures on Christology" from 1933. However, they also underpin his understanding of Christ in *Discipleship* as the one who may only be recognized in faith. For more on Kierkegaard's influence on Bonhoeffer see Kirkpatrick, *Attacks on Christendom*.

15. Matt 27:42.

16. See here Bonhoeffer's evaluation of the Pharisees speaking on a completely different plane to Christ, making them unintelligible to one another, in Bonhoeffer, *Ethics*, 309–15.

17. Bonhoeffer, *Discipleship*, 173.

And so Christ also overcomes our inverted hearts. When the fabric of human relationships has been corrupted, so in the requirement of imitation Christ draws us back into the vulnerability of true sociality. In a letter to the philosopher, Theodor Litt, on January 22, 1939, Bonhoeffer wrote:

> Solely because God became a poor, wretched, unknown, unsuccessful human being, and because God wants to be found from now on solely in this poverty, in the cross, it is for this reason that we cannot get away from the human being and from the world, for this reason that we love our neighbors. Because the Christian faith is such that indeed the "unconditional is included in the conditional," the "hereafter" has entered the "this-worldliness" out of a sovereign freedom of grace, for that reason the believer is not torn apart, but rather finds in this single place in this world God and human being in one, and from now on the love of God and love for one's human neighbor are indissolubly united.[18]

In faith Christians take on the yoke of Christ, and through his power embody that same "vicarious representative action" (*Stellvertretung*) for others that defined his own life. Quite apart from a super-spiritual escape from the world that is associated with salvation through the all-powerful, transcendent God, it is through the imitation of Christ the failure that human beings are truly able to live in this world in community. But, such imitation can only be achieved when Christians recognize that our success *in* the world is not the success *of* the world. It is imitation of this "unsuccessful human being," and we can be no more victorious or glorious than Christ himself.

The Empowerment of Weakness

Bonhoeffer's portrayal of Christ's weakness has been a powerful resource in the development of liberation theology. Bonhoeffer's statement that "Only the suffering God can help" has become something of a battle cry for such thinkers as Jon Sobrino, Gustavo Gutierrez, and Leonardo Boff.[19] However, what is important is not simply that Christ's power is manifest

---

18. Bonhoeffer, *Theological Education Underground*, 111–12.

19. For more on Bonhoeffer's influence on liberation theology, see Kelly and Kirkpatrick, "Bonhoeffer and Liberation Theology."

through his solidarity with the weak and suffering, but that those who are like Christ in his weakness and suffering share in his power.

In 1943, Bonhoeffer wrote a short "reckoning" for his fellow conspirators, reflecting on what they had achieved and could understand from their experiences. Its final paragraph is entitled, "The view from below":

> It remains an experience of incomparable value that we have for once learned to see the great events of world history from below, from the perspective of the outcasts, the suspects, the maltreated, the powerless, the oppressed and reviled, in short from the perspective of the suffering. If only during this time bitterness and envy have not corroded the heart; that we come to see matters great and small, happiness and misfortune, strength and weakness with new eyes; that our sense for greatness, humanness, justice, and mercy has grown clearer, freer, more incorruptible; that we learn, indeed, that personal suffering is a more useful key, a more fruitful principle than personal happiness for exploring the meaning of the world in contemplation and action.[20]

If Christ is weak, then it is only those who stand alongside him who are able to interpret his words and life. When Gutierrez offers his famous description of a hermeneutics "from the underside of history'" he is directly referencing Bonhoeffer.[21] It isn't the powerful who can best understand God's intentions, but rather those who truly bear that image of Christ in suffering.

However, the weak aren't simply a channel of God's revelation because their form of life happens to bear similarity to that of Christ's, but also because God chooses them to be such. In 1934, Bonhoeffer preached a sermon in London on 2 Corinthians 12:9—"For my power is made perfect in weakness." Here he makes clear that Christianity has bought into fallen humankind's promotion of strength and success. While this may be most profoundly manifest in its image of the transcendent, impassive God, it can be witnessed even in the Christian virtue of charity, where the power of the strong over the weak is maintained. In contrast, Bonhoeffer writes,

---

20. Bonhoeffer, *Letters and Papers*, 52.
21. Cf. McAfee Brown, "Preface: After Ten Years," xv–xvi; Gutiérrez, *Power of the Poor*, 203.

> Christian love and help for the weak means humiliation of the strong before the weak, of the healthy before the suffering, of [the] mighty before the exploited. The Christian relation between the strong has to look *up* to the weak and never look down. Weakness is holy, therefore we devote ourselves to the weak. Weakness in the eyes of Christ is not the imperfect one against the perfect, rather is strength the imperfect and weakness the perfect. Not the weak has to serve the strong, but the strong has to serve the weak, and this not by benevolence but by care and reverence. Not the powerful is right, but ultimately the weak is always right. So Christianity means a devaluation of all human values and the establishment of a new order of values in the sight of Christ.[22]

In 1933, Bonhoeffer had visited Bethel, a community near Bielefeld, established to look after the disabled. Quite in contrast to the eugenics of the Nazi regime that represented the pinnacle of a cult of power and success, Bonhoeffer saw firsthand the extraordinary way in which God blessed and honored the weak as the ministers of his glory.[23] For Bonhoeffer it was not just Christ, but also the weak in the world, who fulfilled Paul's words at the start of 1 Corinthians: "God chose the foolish things of the world to shame the wise; God chose the weak things of the world to shame the strong. God chose the lowly things of this world and the despised things—and the things that are not—to nullify the things that are."[24]

For Bonhoeffer, therefore, what the world judges to be a failure has become the very source of God's power and glory. It is not just in the failure of Christ that this is true, but also in the lives that the world perceives to have failed and often seeks to eradicate.

Weakness, Power, and the Importance of Selfishness

The image of Christ the failure makes clear the stark difference between God's knowledge and values, and those created by humankind in separation from him—a difference that can only be rectified by the

---

22. Bonhoeffer, *London: 1933–1935*, 403.

23. For more on Bonhoeffer's direct engagement with disability, and its contrast to Nazi ideology, see Wannenwetsch, "Bonhoeffer and the War over Disabled Life."

24. 1 Cor 1:27–28. Cf. Bonhoeffer, *Barcelona, Berlin, New York*, 465; Bonhoeffer, *Fiction from Tegel Prison*, 107.

CHRIST THE FAILURE 103

transformation of the human heart and mind through faith alone. Bonhoeffer's theology therefore presents not just a profound critique of the fallen world and the pseudo-Christianity that had bought into it; he also challenges Christians to question whether their lives better imitate the failure of Christ or the success of the world. As he notes in *Discipleship*, "It can happen at any moment that pseudo-Christians are torn out of our midst, or that we ourselves are revealed as pseudo-Christians."[25]

But Bonhoeffer hasn't quite finished. Whilst in prison, Bonhoeffer wrote a poem entitled "Christians and Heathens," which is worth citing in full:

> People go to God when they're in need,
> plead for help, pray for blessing and bread,
> for rescue from their sickness, guilt, and death.
> So do they all, all of them, Christians and heathens.
>
> People go to God when God's in need,
> Find God poor, reviled, without shelter or bread,
> See God devoured by sin, weakness, and death.
> Christians stand by God in God's own pain.
>
> God goes to all people in their need,
> fills body and soul with God's own bread,
> goes for Christians and heathens to Calvary's death
> and forgives them both.[26]

The poem expresses the difference between a transcendent and a weak God. But it also goes much further.[27] The difference between a Christian and heathen is found not just in their recognition of who God is, but in their reaction to him. When heathens demand that God be a strong source of help, so true Christians "stand by God in God's own pain." In a letter to Eberhard Bethge on July 18, 1944, Bonhoeffer reflected on this line and commented, "'Could you not stay awake with me one hour?' Jesus asks in Gethsemane. That is the opposite of everything

---

25. Bonhoeffer, *Discipleship*, 178.
26. Bonhoeffer, *Letters and Papers*, 460–61.
27. For an excellent discussion of this poem, see Wannenwetsch, "'Christians and Pagans.'"

a religious person expects from God. The human being is called upon to share in God's suffering at the hands of the godless world."[28]

In imitation of Christ, Christians are called to embrace a vicarious suffering for the sake of others. However, in that same imitation we are also called to vulnerability and dependence. In the figure of Christ we find a being who chooses to be with us, who desires our companionship and help. In Gethsemane, Christ desired the encouragement, support, and protection of his disciples as he accepted the cup of suffering. Quite apart from describing a God who might actually suffer—a radical perspective in its own right, especially at that time—Bonhoeffer reveals to us a God who needs others. This is not a God who marches over human history to achieve his own ends, but a God who enters history and unites his history with that of humankind, desiring them, using them, needing them to achieve his aims.[29]

When we consider how Christians have often embraced the world's ideology of power and success, it is important to recognize how this has manifested itself theologically in an overemphasis on self-denial. Christians are those who give of themselves to others, who practice self-sacrifice, and dying to the self. And all this is indeed true. However, such a perspective has often become an edifice that removes our ability to receive, to be vulnerable to others, to ask of them, and to be the ones who seek out blessing. Such self-denial is, paradoxically, an act of self-establishment as it creates an invulnerability towards the other. The Christ of weakness is the one who is vulnerable to his disciples, who asks of them *for himself* (and not just for the world), who needs them. To be a Christian, therefore, is not just to serve but to be served. Bonhoeffer's Christology challenges us to ask what it would mean for the healthy,

---

28. Bonhoeffer, *Letters and Papers*, 480.

29. Bonhoeffer's prison theology influenced significantly Jürgen Moltmann and his understanding of the interrelation of the *pathos* of God and the consequent *sympatheia* of humankind. As Moltmann comments, "The divine pathos is reflected in man's participation, his hopes and his prayers. Sympathy is the openness of a person to the presence of another. It has the structure of dialogue. In the pathos of God, man is filled with the spirit of God. He becomes the friend of God, feels sympathy with God and for God. He does not enter into a mystical union but into a sympathetic union with God. He is angry with God's wrath. He suffers with God's suffering. He loves with God's love. He hopes with God's hope." Moltmann, *Crucified God*, 281. Bonhoeffer would not have gone so far as to affirm Moltmann's form of panentheism, but many of the central concerns are present. For more on Bonhoeffer's influence on Moltmann see Schliesser, "'Love of Life.'"

strong, and powerful to go to the weak and ask hopefully, humbly, "How can you help me today?"[30]

Bonhoeffer the Failure

So Bonhoeffer was a failure. And yet as he looked back over his life, it wasn't to the success of the world that he was drawn, but rather to the failure of God. To human reason, Christ is a failure, and must be recognized as such. When apologetics tries to overcome this contradiction it simply converts Christ into an idea and annihilates his power.[31] It is rather only once we have utterly reorientated ourselves to this weak God that our relationships can be transformed to become the body of Christ through vicarious suffering for others, and in recognizing the power of God manifest through the weak and suffering. Only in him do we find the image of giving but also receiving, or recognize our need for others and how they may minister to us and be Christ to us. It requires looking at lives that the world considers aren't worthy to be lived, even when this might be our own life, and to orientate ourselves to them with hope and expectation of God's power. It means believing that there is no meaningless life, but that it is precisely only when our life becomes weak, and perhaps seemingly meaningless, that God may truly let his power be manifest through it.

Bibliography

Bethge, Eberhard. *Dietrich Bonhoeffer: A Biography*. Rev. ed. Minneapolis: Fortress, 2000.

Bonhoeffer, Dietrich. *Barcelona, Berlin, New York: 1928–1931*. Minneapolis: Fortress, 2008.

———. *Conspiracy and Imprisonment: 1940–1945*. Minneapolis: Fortress, 2006.

———. *Creation and Fall*. Minneapolis: Fortress, 2004.

———. *Discipleship*. Minneapolis: Fortress, 2003.

---

30. For more on the nature of receiving from the weak, see Kirkpatrick, *How to Live a Good Death*.

31. Bonhoeffer would agree with Kierkegaard when he states, "One can see how extraordinarily . . . stupid it is to defend Christianity, how little knowledge of humanity it betrays, how it connives if only unconsciously with offense by making Christianity out to be some miserable object that in the end must be rescued by a defense. It is therefore certain and true that the person who first thought of defending Christianity in Christendom is *de facto* a Judas No. 2; he too betrays with a kiss, except his treason is that of stupidity. To defend something is always to discredit it." Kierkegaard, *Sickness*, 119.

———. *Ethics*. Minneapolis: Fortress, 2005.
———. *Fiction from Tegel Prison*. Minneapolis: Fortress, 2000.
———. *Letters and Papers from Prison*. Minneapolis: Fortress, 2009.
———. *London: 1933–1935*. Minneapolis: Fortress, 2007.
———. *Sanctorum Communio*. Minneapolis: Fortress, 1998.
———. *Theological Education Underground: 1937–1940*. Minneapolis: Fortress, 2012
Dramm, Sabine. *Dietrich Bonhoeffer and the Resistance*. Minneapolis: Fortress, 2009.
Gutierrez, Gustavo. *The Power of the Poor in History*. London: SCM, 1983.
Kelly, Geffrey B., and Matthew D. Kirkpatrick. "Bonhoeffer and Liberation Theology." In *Engaging Bonhoeffer: The Impact and Influence of Bonhoeffer's Life and Work*, edited by Matthew D. Kirkpatrick, 139–68. Minneapolis: Fortress, 2016.
Kierkegaard, Søren. *The Sickness Unto Death*. London: Penguin, 2004.
Kirkpatrick, Matthew D. *Attacks on Christendom in a World Come of Age: Kierkegaard, Bonhoeffer, and the Question of Religionless Christianity*. Eugene, OR: Pickwick, 2011.
———. *How to Live a Good Death*. Cambridge: Grove, 2016.
Kirkpatrick, Matthew D., ed. *Engaging Bonhoeffer: The Impact and Influence of Bonhoeffer's Life and Thought*. Minneapolis: Fortress, 2016.
McAfee Brown, Robert. "Preface: After Ten Years." In *The Power of the Poor in History*, by Gustavo Guttierez, vi–xvi. London: SCM, 1983.
Moltmann, Jürgen. *The Crucified God: The Cross of Christ as the Foundation and Criticism of Christian Theology*. London: SCM, 2008.
Pugh, Jeffrey C. *Religionless Christianity: Dietrich Bonhoeffer in Troubled Times*. New York: T&T Clark, 2008.
Rueter, Hans Richard. "Afterword." In Dietrich Bonhoeffer, *Act and Being*, 162–183. Minneapolis: Fortress, 1996.
Schliesser, Christine. "'Love of Life': The Impact and Influence of Dietrich Bonhoeffer's Life and Thought on Jürgen Moltmann." In *Engaging Bonhoeffer: The Impact and Influence of Bonhoeffer's Life and Thought*, edited by Matthew D. Kirkpatrick, 187–200. Minneapolis: Fortress, 2016.
Schlingensiepen, Ferdinand. *Dietrich Bonhoeffer 1906–1945*. Edinburgh: T&T Clark, 2010.
Wannenwetsch, Bernd. "Bonhoeffer and the War over Disabled Life." In *Disability in the Christian Tradition: A Reader*, edited by Brian Brock and John Swinton, 353–90. Grand Rapids: Eerdmans, 2012.
———. "'Christians and Pagans': Towards a Trans-Religious Second Naïveté or How to Be a Christological Creature." In *Who Am I? Bonhoeffer's Theology Through His Poetry*, edited by Bernd Wannenwetsch, 175–96. Edinburgh: T&T Clark, 2009.

9.

Orgasmic Failure
A Praxis Ethic for Adolescent Sexuality

Kate Ott

In the United States, one of the most fear-provoking subjects for parents, teachers, health providers, politicians, and religious leaders alike is adolescent sexuality.[1] This fear has generated cultural standards of "success" that are counter to healthy sexuality and relationship development. Public health often casts successful adolescent sexuality as avoidance of sexual behaviors that carry risk of pregnancy or sexually transmitted disease while religious communities promote success as virginity until heterosexual marriage. Both approaches rely on self-mastery of sexual behavior as the ethical standard to the exclusion of relationship quality and values, and in most cases perpetuate a heteronormative procreative definition of sex and sexuality. In response, I argue that failure as a praxis-based ethical approach to sexuality better serves adolescents than measurements of success based on restrictive behavior standards. I engage Jack Halberstam's proposal to replace self-mastery with failure as a

---

1. See Schalet, *Not Under My Roof* and her earlier piece "Must We Fear Adolescent Sexuality?" In these works Schalet compares the dramatization versus the normalization of adolescent sexuality and suggests that US culture and parents in particular consider teens to have raging, out-of-control hormones, frame sexuality as a battle between the sexes, and deny sexual relationships with a "not under my roof" response. This is over and against a response that educates about sexual desire as self-regulated, nurtures healthy and equal relationships between genders, and opens conversation discouraging secretive behavior.

key component of ethical action. Following failure as a praxis approach, I draw connections with Cristina Traina's retrieval of a developmentally nuanced view of sexual ethics and parenting to consider how erotic attunement, with its focuses on practice, attention to power relations, pleasurable touch, and justice, might replace our current sexual acts-based approach to adolescent sexuality.

Success as Self-Mastery

Public health and religious communities sexuality education approaches rely on self-mastery of sexual behavior, to avoid risk or the shame of soiling one's purity, as the ethical standard of success. Most major public health reports on adolescent sexuality begin with pregnancy rates and sexual transmitted disease statistics.[2] Sexuality education program success is primarily measured by prevention of these risk behaviors. Some may also include assessment of knowledge gained about safer sex practices, communication strategies, and follow-up use of contraception. Reducing the number of one's partners and practicing (serial) monogamy are often part of the risk-reduction message presented as a statistical variable. Youth learn that "successful" adolescent sexuality equals risk avoidance and little more.

Religious communities are no better, especially Christian communities, with two predominant approaches. The first is to deny that youth are sexual beings altogether by remaining completely silent, providing no education or actively silencing any discussion of sexuality concerns. This response speaks volumes about the shame and discomfort a religious community associates with the topic of sexuality. Second, many faith communities teach abstinence-only-until-marriage which suggests successful adolescent sexuality is defined as virginity. The definitions of virginity can be vague with regard to a variety of sexual behaviors, but certainly mean no penile-vaginal intercourse until marriage. They are often paired with a stringent message in favor of the complete avoidance of sexual desire, which is falsely seen as a slippery slope to uncontrollable sexual behaviors of all sorts.[3]

---

2. See the Alan Guttmacher Institute, the Center for Disease Control's Behavioral Risk Factor Surveillance System, and the Henry J. Kaiser Family Foundation as examples.

3. Ott, *Sex + Faith*. See the chapter on middle school and high school youth.

The confluence of shame and taboo that are generated by failure of self-mastery of sexual behaviors, in my view, leads to dysfunctional sexual self-concepts and relationships. Labeling most teen sexual expression as failures increases the likelihood of individuals lacking the confidence or knowledge to use prophylactics or contraception. It also contributes to youth using drugs and alcohol during sexual encounters to distract them from a range of feelings like nervousness, inadequacy, shame, guilt, and so on.[4] Sexual desire, connection, expression, and relationships are negatively cast as leading to distraction or destruction instead of healthy sexuality. My critique of the two dominant models of self-mastery for teens does not mean I am arguing for what is often seen as the opposite approach—hooking-up. The practice of hooking-up is often equally problematic in extending patriarchal heteronormativity into adolescent experiences of sexuality. Hooking-up in theory is very different from real life experience. In fact, research on hook-ups show a self-mastery logic at work that should be critiqued—encounters must be devoid of relational connection, show preference for male pleasure, involve limited communication, and perpetuate a limited view of sexuality as solely about specified sexual behaviors.[5]

If we look at data in the US, most adolescents are failing at self-mastery as a success measure.[6] Given trends throughout history, we will never prevent such failure. And, perhaps, that is a wrong-headed goal in the first place. An ethic of self-mastery of sexual behaviors has major consequences for healthy adult sexuality. Any act-based view of successful sexuality limits the fullness of sexual expression by valuing penile-vaginal intercourse as the primary, presumed, and prized sexual behavior. It consigns sexual pleasure to vice, as such desire is often considered uncontrollable, luring one away from the goal of self-mastery. Moreover, it perpetuates the limited notion that the only fruit or consequence of sexuality is procreation, which reinforces heteronormative

---

4. There are a variety of studies linking use of substances and sexually risky behavior. But fewer studies have focused on the specific link between shame, substance use, and sexuality. See, Rahim and Patton, "The association between shame and substance use in young people." This can be especially concerning for LGBTQ adolescents. See McDermott, Roen, and Scourfield, "Avoiding Shame," 815–29.

5. Freitas, *Sex and the Soul*.

6. See most recent "Factsheet: American Teen's Sexual and Reproductive Health," September 2016 by the Guttmacher Institute, at https://www.guttmacher.org/fact-sheet/american-teens-sexual-and-reproductive-health.

futurity. If diverse sexual behaviors, valuing sexual desire, and opening sexuality to multiple forms of generativity is failure, let's promote failure!

Practicing Failure

In *The Queer Art of Failure,* Halberstam suggests that embracing and engaging failure allows us to potentially "escape the punishing norms that discipline behavior and manage human development with the goal of delivering us from unruly childhoods to orderly and predictable adulthoods."[7] By turning to the subject of children, in this case specifically, teenagers, we begin to see limitations and deformations in the current notion of sexually successful development. Halberstam describes childhood as "a long lesson in humility, awkwardness, limitation," and quoting Kathryn Bond Stockton, a "growing sideways."[8] His description of childhood illustrates desires (perhaps latent in adults) to resist heteronormativity, capitalism, and to some extent speciesism. Halberstam wants the reader to disrupt idealized and saccharine myths about children, sexuality, and innocence and imagine new versions of maturation, *Bildung,* and growth that do not depend upon the logic of succession and success.[9]

A more accurate, even healthier view of adolescent sexual self-concept, relationships, and behaviors may lead us to embrace a sexual ethic of practical failure. In this sense, adults need to recognize the ways in which adolescents as desiring subjects live out ethical lives that contribute to, disrupt, reify, and provide alternatives to dominant and oppressive narratives (or cultural systems). Halberstam articulates three tactics for counter hegemonic knowledge production, what I would call the formation of a new ethical approach: (1) resist mastery, suggesting "we might read *failure* . . . as a refusal of mastery"; (2) privilege the naive or nonsensical, meaning "[t]he naive or the ignorant may in fact lead to a different set of knowledge practices" where "learning takes place independent of teaching"; and (3) hold memorialization suspect, transforming "a continuous narrative into one full of ruptures and contradictions" where forgetting is necessary.[10] Applying such tactics to adolescent sexual ethics suggests

---

7. Halberstam, *The Queer Art of Failure,* 3.
8. Ibid., 27.
9. Ibid., 119.
10. Ibid., 11–15.

that we can resist a goal of self-mastery of sexual behaviors especially as mastery is heteronormative and procreative in its teleology. Second, we can embrace a praxis-based approach that values experiential knowledge and unhinges "teaching" from particular centers of power. Third, we can release ourselves and our relationships from a linear developmental logic that views change or ending as a loss.

But, as some will say, this shift inevitably leads to harms, losses, and pain. Is it not the responsibility of adults to prevent such occurrences in the lives of youth? In relation to sexuality, youth already experience harms, losses, and pain, as well as benefits, fulfilled desires, and pleasure. This approach simply acknowledges such experiences and resists over-theorizing them. It also opens the possibility for adults as well as youth to recognize what Halberstam calls for: "While the relationship between sexuality and reproduction has never been much more than a theological fantasy, new technologies of reproduction and new rationales for nonreproductive behavior call for new languages of desire, embodiment, and the social relations between reproductive and nonreproductive bodies."[11] The call for new approaches is also reflected in the wisdom of teenagers like those chronicled in a recent sociological study of forty-eight African American young people from Genesee County in Michigan, discussing their experiences of sexuality education.[12]

These young people's responses complicate adult ideas of mastery, authority of educator, and a continuous linear sexual development. Young people suggest that sexuality education needs to include demonstrations (praxis), discussions of a variety of sexual behaviors, and relational aspects. Praxis as an ongoing process of practice and reflection requires personal experience be brought into the learning process. Youth can use their and peer experiences as a knowledge base that evidences trial and error, relational continuity and break-ups, and encourages a variety of sexual behaviors. Additionally, these narratives differ from stereotypical

11. Ibid., 37.
12. Here I turn to the voices of youth to provide a small amount of subjectivity to the objects of discussion. In the past, I have critiqued writings that discuss youth and children without incorporating their voices. The benefits of hearing directly from youth are numerous, not to mention an attempt at coherence between theory and practice. In particular, youth offer multifaceted and sometimes contradictory responses. This reinforces the shifts Halberstam calls for related to failure, privileging the naive, and learning through experience. On a near monthly basis I am with teenagers across the United States, welcomed into their youth groups to discuss sexuality, relationships, and faith. I hear very similar responses to the statements cited in this study.

hook-up culture as they embrace reflection, communication, and mutual pleasure.

Praxis is important: "As Amanda, 21, and Charlie, age unknown, said [respectively]: '. . . if we were taught how to use condoms, you know, that would be better. As far as size and lubrication and all that. I think we should be taught how to use it.' 'A demonstration period. . . . I have never seen a demonstration of a female condom.'" Some students also advocate for discussion of a multiplicity of sexual behaviors beyond penile-vaginal intercourse,

> . . . such as manual sex (fingering) and use of sex toys, as Jasmyn, 22, expressed: "Safe sex. You know, if you want to get your little groove on, they have little vibrators. . . . If he waitin' on test results, he can get down there and he can use that toy. You can sanitise that toy, you can put a condom on that toy. It's, you know, they always say don't have sex or use a condom. Throw other options out there."

These young people also want more conversations on emotional and relational aspects of sexuality including decision-making. For example, Kristin, age unknown, "said that she wanted to know about: '. . . what sex is or when to have sex or what sex is for.'" Tina, 23, "described: 'Not only abstinence, but a lot of us learn by experience that after you have sex you have this emotional attachment with that person and that's not taught in, no where . . . that emotional attachment with that person, that is a big factor in sex and why people keep on having it with that person, even though she know he might have sex with twelve other girls.'"[13] These anecdotal responses show that youth practice failure in a way that embraces praxis, inclusion of a variety of sexual behaviors, and the centrality of relational and decision-making experiences. If we are to follow the lead of young people, there springs forth a need for a new languages of desire, embodiment, and social relations, as Halberstam suggests.

Erotic Attunement

Here I want to offer one example of new language, erotic attunement, a concept defined by Christian ethicist Cristina Traina. Attunement, Traina says, is "perceptive attention and adjustment to feelings, needs,

---

13. Kimmel et al., "'I make sure I am safe . . .,'" 172–85. Citations from page 177.

and desires—both one's own and others."[14] The ongoing nature of attunement, which one might get better at but never masters, provides a relational approach rather than a behavioral goal when considering how sexuality functions across relationships. It reclaims the pleasure of touch, "Not only permits but demands that we truly enjoy the goodness of touch."[15] Erotic attunement does not seek to confine sexual desire and pleasure or even to temper it by fulfilling it with a directedness toward a good measure like marriage or procreation. Traina's proposal thus diverges from the historical tradition of procreative ethics originally tied to the writings of St. Augustine of Hippo and still largely promoted by Roman Catholic doctrine today. Augustine's ideal of self-mastery has promoted a tradition of Christian sexual ethics that treats others as an object, considers male desire as dangerous, overpowering to the will and reason, and sets up women as the objects upon whom sex is enacted. She also points to the fact that the procreative ethic "drains much of the ethics of relationship from the ethics of sexuality."[16] Instead, Traina wants us to acknowledge desire and see, feel, and know its loves from a wholly and perhaps holy realistic and aware disposition. Of course, such a practice eschews manageable assessment features like reduction of risk behaviors or specific behavioral do's and don'ts leading to a different set of knowledge practices.

Erotic attunement is not a relativistic ethical stance. Traina's use of the erotic is attentive to power relations and justice demands.[17] She notes that attunement requires a "constant motion between self-awareness and attentiveness to the other."[18] She looks to other feminist and womanist theologians who have reclaimed the erotic suggesting that erotic love or *eros* does not objectify or instrumentalize the other. Rather, erotic love "desires the person not as we fantasize her to be but as she is"[19] neither seeking possession or control of her.[20] It "recognizes and pursues the beautiful as a kind of catalyst that brings forth the creative potential that already resides inside the lover."[21]

14. Traina, *Professional Sexual Ethics*, 44.
15. Traina, *Erotic Attunement*, 241.
16. Ibid., 88.
17. Ibid., 242.
18. Ibid., 141.
19. Traina, "Erotic Attunement," 47.
20. Traina, *Erotic Attunement*, 180.
21. Ibid., 203.

These claims echo major shifts in theologies of sexuality developed in the late twentieth century into the twenty-first century. Womanist, feminist, and queer studies in religion usher in four major insights in theology that have influenced sexual ethics.[22] First, theological anthropology is autonomous and rational as well as relational and embodied, disrupting a gendered codification of human creation at work for centuries in Christian theology. In other words, we are individuals to be treated as ends in and of ourselves and we are equally defined by our relationships with others and God. As embodied beings, we come to know not through abstract rational thought but experiential, emotional, and critical awareness. These states of being are part of our createdness regardless of gender. That is to say, men are not autonomous, rational beings, while women are reduced to relational, emotionally supportive care-givers. Ignoring relational and embodied aspects of personhood detrimentally affects our relationship with self, other and God.[23]

Second, we are sexual beings from birth until death. Sexuality is not an object separate from the self that can be given to someone on a wedding night, controlled by doctrines, or eradicated by law. Our sexuality is formed and informed by much more than sexual behaviors. There are innate features of sexuality as well as experiences related to sensuality, intimacy, and growth and development that shape our sexuality.[24] These experiences take place in relationships on individual, communal, and societal levels. This leads to the third major shift. Our sexual self-concept or sexual health/disease is directly influenced by the inter-structuring of oppressions in the form of systemic sin including racism, ableism, and

---

22. In this section I provide an overview of major writings in sexual theology and ethics. Neither I, nor most of the authors cited in the next few paragraphs, submit to a strong distinction between ethics and theology. Most fit within broad liberationist traditions. They are presented here for the reader as sort of a short bibliographic list to capture major thinkers in the field of Christian sexual theology and ethics. Inevitably, there are influential thinkers missing. I recognize the lack of biblical scholars and social theorists who are conversation partners for the theologians and ethicists named. I also strongly feel that many of the shifts named are, thankfully, readily integrated into today's writings on sexuality from academic Christian perspectives, and thus am not footnoting every aspect of this discussion.

23. Cahill, *Sex, Gender, and Christian Ethics*; Nelson, *Embodiment*.

24. For specific chapters on sexual self-concept and to broaden our definition of sexuality see, Thorson-Smith, "Becoming 'Possessed.'" See also editors Ellison and Douglas, *Sexuality and the Sacred*, 2d ed., 2010, in addition to essays in the 1994 edition.

political, economic, and ecological disparities.[25] In the United States, we need only consider for a moment the history of legal regulations grounded in Christian nationalism that socially construct experiences of sexuality via marriage law that preferenced heterosexual, single race coupling, and codified financial and property rights;[26] welfare policy, which disproportionately affects young black and brown women's reproductive healthcare options;[27] or racism and homophobia imbued in HIV/AIDS policy and education, which lead to stereotyping and misinformation preventing public health response in the United States and globally (which continues today).[28]

Lastly, and perhaps most influentially for this essay, *eros* as a key aspect of sexual desire is reclaimed from a denigrated third love status among agape and philia for its generative and creative power. In *Erotic Justice: A Liberating Ethic of Sexuality*, Marvin Ellison writes,

> Sexuality is a mode of communication, the giving and receiving of recognition and regard. The erotic desire for knowledge—to know and be known by another—goes far beyond the need of the intellect or the genitals. The whole self becomes engaged. We long for an embodied response from another who confirms our individuality, knows us subject-to-subject, and responds to us as a person fully alive. Sexuality infuses personal and social life with energy for connection and mutual recognition.[29]

Sexuality is an aspect of self and a social force. The erotic animates sexuality. In the move away from act-based or even relationship driven sexual ethics, Christian ethicists have moved to a value-centered approach to sexual ethics. Some Christian ethicists have claimed that sexual pleasure, the embodied erotic, should be the guiding norm for sexual ethics.[30] Others suggest a combination of norms working in concert such as do no unjust harm, free consent, mutuality, equality, commitment, and social justice.[31]

---

25. Douglass, *Sexuality and the Black Church*, and Althaus-Reid, *Indecent Theology*.
26. Reuther, *Christianity and the Making of the Modern Family*.
27. West, *Disruptive Christian Ethics*.
28. Townes, *Breaking the Fine Rain of Death*, and Phiri and Nadar, *African Women, Religion, and Health*.
29. Ellison, *Erotic Justice*, 79.
30. Gudorf, *Body, Sex, and Pleasure*.
31. Farley, *Just Love*.

Each of these normative approaches, similar to Ellison's explanation of the erotic, presume a somewhat equal power relationship between adults. Traina, on the other hand, articulates erotic attunement as a virtuous practice that can be lived out across unequal power relationships like parent and child. When discussing adolescent sexuality, we presume power differentials, even to the point of considering adolescent moral agency partially formed and thus incapable of moral decision-making. In this sense, Traina's argument impacts not only how we theologically define sexuality and ethically address power dynamics across relationships, but also upends developmental configurations of moral agency.[32]

Regardless of age, Traina argues that attunement to the erotic requires practice as it "combines perception, imagination, and experimentation in an endless, partnered dance"—a dance that partakes in a self-correcting process.[33] Those with more power, whether that be based on age, economics, physique and so on, take on a greater responsibility and accountability for attunement. As well, the way in which sexuality has been socially constructed and the erotic denigrated requires a process of reclamation and resistance to dominant forces like heterosexism, racism, abelism, ageism, and economic and legal forces, as we have seen. Traina discusses attunement as a virtue we strive toward, not something we achieve and never have to revisit. Referring to the work of T. J. Gorringe in *Toward the Education of Desire*, Traina suggests, "we must do 'imaginative work on the appetite,' educating embodied desire through 'training and exercise,' above all by becoming aware of desire and then by constantly questioning it and the influences that have shaped it."[34] For Traina, awareness of and education related to embodied desire fits within the larger feminist and queer movement to unblock erotic power as part of demystifying systemic social disorders. She argues throughout her book that intimate relationships evidence patterns of vice and virtue expressed in the wider community.[35] Thus such relationships are a microcosm, not a distinct, privatized realm separate from social injustices. She writes, "If we really wish to reduce the irruption of violent, addictive,

---

32. See specifically Traina's chapters 7 and 8 in *Erotic Attunement*. For more on issues of moral agency and childhood see Wall, *Ethics in Light of Childhood*, and my own essay that brings the two into conversation, "Children as An/other Subject."

33. Traina, *Erotic Attunement*, 217.

34. Ibid., 180.

35. Traina, *Erotic Attunement*, 180 and 193.

and depersonalized expressions of sexuality we must self-consciously cultivate just, relaxed, open, erotic sensuality."[36]

Attunement, Failure, and Praxis

Teenagers, even children, need to begin early to develop erotic attunement. It begins, as Traina suggests, between parents and children, and is nurtured, practiced, and revised through failure. As children grow into friendships and later sexual partnerships, erotic attunement serves as an ethical guide related to various intimate behaviors as well as everyday interactions and communication needed to strengthen just relationships. Teen sexual ethics based on self-mastery of sexual behaviors compartmentalizes sexuality, valorizes penile-vaginal intercourse, and reinforces patriarchal heteronormativity. Teen sexual ethics grounded in erotic attunement and embrace of failure promote praxis-based learning from intentional experimentation, critical reflection on wider social dynamics that constrain and liberate sexuality, and mutual revision of relationships and behaviors. Erotic attunement assumes process and failure are essential aspects of sexuality.

Bibliography

Althaus-Reid, Marcella. *Indecent Theology: Theological Perversions in Sex, Gender, and Politics*. New York: Routledge, 2000.

Cahill, Lisa Sowle. *Sex, Gender, and Christian Ethics*. New York: Cambridge University Press, 1996.

Douglass, Kelly Brown. *Sexuality and the Black Church: A Womanist Perspective*. Maryknoll, NY: Orbis, 1999.

Ellison, Marvin. *Erotic Justice: A Liberating Ethic of Sexuality*. Louisville, KY: Westminster John Knox, 1996.

Ellison, Marvin M., and Kelly Brown Douglas, eds. *Sexuality and the Sacred: Sources for Theological Reflection*. 2nd ed. Louisville, KY: Westminster John Knox, 2010.

Farley, Margaret. *Just Love: A Framework for Christian Sexual Ethics*. New York: Continuum, 2006.

Freitas, Donna. *Sex and the Soul: Juggling Sexuality, Spirituality, Romance, and Religion on America's College Campuses*. Updated ed. New York: Oxford University Press, 2015.

Gudorf, Christine E. *Body, Sex, and Pleasure: Reconstructing Christian Sexual Ethics*. Cleveland: Pilgrim, 1994.

---

36. Ibid., 243.

Halberstam, Judith. *The Queer Art of Failure*. Durham, NC: Duke University Press, 2011.

Kimmel, Terrinieka T., Tiffany C. Williams, Bettina Campbell Veinot, Terrance R. Campbell, Mark Valacak, and Daniel J. Kruger. "'I make sure I am safe and I make sure I have myself in every way possible': African-American youth perspectives on sexuality education." *Sex Education*, vol. 13, no.2 (2013) 172–85.

McDermott, Elizabeth, Katrina Roen, and Jonathan Scourfield. "Avoiding Shame: Young LGBT people, homophobia and self-destructive behaviours." *Culture, Health and Sexuality*, vol. 10, no. 8 (2008) 814–29.

Nelson, James B. *Embodiment: An Approach to Sexuality and Christian Theology*. Minneapolis: Augsburg, 1978.

Ott, Kate. "Children as An/other Subject: Redefining Moral Agency in a Postcolonial Context." *Journal of Childhood and Religion*, volume 5, Issue 2 (2014). http://childhoodandreligion.com/wp-content/uploads/2015/03/Ott-May-2014.pdf.

———. *Sex + Faith: Talking to Your Child from Birth to Adolescence*. Louisville, KY: Westminster John Knox, 2013.

Phiri, Isabel Apawo, and Sarojini Nadar, eds. *African Women, Religion, And Health: Essays in Honor of Mercy Amba Ewudzi Oduyoye*. Ossining, NY: Orbis, 2006.

Reuther, Rosemary Radford. *Christianity and the Making of the Modern Family*. Boston: Beacon, 2000.

Rahim, Masuma, and Robert Patton. "The association between shame and substance use in young people: a systematic review." *PeerJ.*, vol, 3 (2015). https://www.ncbi.nlm.nih.gov/pmc/articles/PMC4312064/.

Schalet, Amy T. *Not Under My Roof: Parents, Teens, and the Culture of Sex*. Chicago: University of Chicago Press, 2011.

———. "Must We Fear Adolescent Sexuality?" Medscape General Medicine 6.4 (2004) 44.

Thorson-Smith, Sylvia. "Becoming 'Possessed'": Toward Sexual Health and Well-being." In *Body and Soul: Rethinking Sexuality as Justice-Love*, edited by Marvin M. Ellison and Sylvia Thorson-Smith, 232–50. Cleveland: Pilgrim, 2003.

Townes, Emilie M. *Breaking the Fine Rain of Death: African American Health Issues and a Womanist Ethic of Care*. Eugene, OR: Wipf and Stock, 2006.

Traina, Cristina. "Erotic Attunement." In *Professional Sexual Ethics: A Holistic Ministry Approach*, edited by Patricia Jung and Darryl Stephens, 45–53. Minneapolis: Fortress, 2013.

———. *Erotic Attunement: Parenthood and the Ethics of Sensuality between Unequals*. Chicago, IL: University of Chicago Press, 2011.

Wall, John. *Ethics in Light of Childhood*. Washington, DC: Georgetown University Press, 2010.

West, Traci. *Disruptive Christian Ethics: When Racism and Women's Lives Matter*. Louisville, KY: Westminster John Knox, 2006.

10.

Please Don't Go Out and Change the World
An Interview with William Cavanaugh

WILLIAM T. CAVANAUGH,
Interviewed by ROBERTO SIRVENT

Roberto Sirvent: You were the first theologian to come to mind when I started thinking about theology and failure. I had read an interview where you said you would never be invited to give a commencement address, since your advice would be "Please *don't* go out and change the world." Can you explain what you mean by this?

William T. Cavanaugh: First of all, I'm just so honored that when you thought of failure you thought of me.

RS: (Laughs.)

WTC: "Let's see: theology and *failure* . . . Cavanaugh!" (Laughs.) I did say that about commencement speeches. All universities seem to be advertising these days, "Come here and we will help you change the world." My alma mater Notre Dame has a really bad case of "change-the-world-itis" too. What I said in that interview is that the world has had enough of well-meaning Americans trying to change it. Part of what happens in universities is that we try to train our students to become universal subjects. They come and we take them from their small towns in Iowa and we turn them from parochial into universal subjects as the name "university" indicates. And so we train them to look down upon the world and see the world from a kind of "God's eye" point of view. And this creeps into the way we do things so easily. We train students to imagine that they're entitled to an opinion on what's going in Syria and so on. Even if they don't know too much about it, they need to develop an idea of what to do about it. And I just think there's a real danger in that. There's something good about that, of course, because there are bad things out in the world that needs to be changed, and it's good to try to empathize with people out there. But we assume too quickly that *we* can do it. When I teach my course on World Catholicism, we kind of "drop in" on people all over the world. My students and I—I'm not immune to this—immediately think that we can empathize with people, so we read about a Guatemalan peasant woman and we immediately think, "Oh, we're on her side!" And the story, of course, is much more difficult that that. The act of reading about her is a kind of consumption of her experience. And the historical fact is that most of us are on the side, in that story, of the oppressors rather than the oppressed. We need to recognize that. I think it would be really helpful if we started from the idea that we don't have the slightest idea what it's like to be a Guatemalan peasant woman, and then work from there instead of this automatic assumption that we can empathize with anybody.

RS: I often hear commencement speakers tell students "You're special!" or "You're unique!" I get the feeling you're not one of these commencement speakers. Do you think this type of encouragement feeds into the idea that students can and should go out and change the world?

WTC: Yeah, I remember watching an episode of Barney with my kids when they were little and Barney was singing "Everybody's special!" and I thought, "Oh Lord, if that doesn't make you feel special then I don't know what does" (laughs). Yeah, kids get too much encouragement these days and universities encourage us to think that we know enough and we're good enough and we're powerful enough to change the world. And I think all three of those things need to be questioned. We need to have a little bit more humility about those things. Universities are not very good about teaching humility. The idea that we know enough—there's all these ways of looking at the world from the top-down that put us into this position of having to have an opinion on everything. I think about the political campaign last year where Gary Johnson was asked about Aleppo and he said, "What is Aleppo?" He didn't know what Aleppo was. It's the second largest city in Syria. Nevertheless, he went on to explain his policy on Syria and what we should do about Syria, and I thought, I'm going to vote for the first person who says, "I don't have the slightest idea what we should do about Syria." But we're trained not to say things like that. We're trained to believe that we know enough about that and we're trained to think that we're *good enough* to make these kinds of changes too. You can just look at the national sins of the United States over the past couple of centuries and think this is also something that needs to be questioned. And of course the idea that we're *powerful* enough so that if we *do* intervene we're going to change things for the better. We think the next war is always going to fix what the last war broke. That's why we're dealing with ISIS these days; it's a side effect of the last time we tried to fix the Middle East. So I think we need to step down from that kind of encouragement and take a more sober look at our own capacities.

RS: When I first approached you about doing this interview, you said that failure is "ripe for theological reflection." How so?

WTC: There's so much of political theology and ethics that is about trying to rearrange the world. And I do think there needs to be a different kind of discourse. I guess it's the kind of discourse that you might find in somebody like Gustavo Gutierrez, who moved from larger ideas about changing the structures of society to more of an appreciation of the life of the poor and the inherent dignity of those who are not successful—those who live in subsistence situations and so on. I don't think it's something that hasn't been done in some ways, but I do think that it has a certain kind of affinity with this option for the poor as being an appreciation for the life of the poor and a call to live with poor people, rather than simply trying to figure out how to fix them. Theologically, it's a really rich place to think about these things. In terms of other theological loci that are ripe for this, you might look at theodicy: the idea that God does not simply fix the evils of the world. I think that might be a fruitful place for reflecting on this theology of failure. God does not simply just come in and sort the world out but allows us to make our own mistakes and do evil. The way Gerhard Lohfink explains this is that God is a revolutionary but God is nonviolent. Rather than Marxist revolution where you change everything in one grand gesture of violence, God calls the chosen people, asks them to live a different way, and then invites people to join this movement. Which is why God tries to change the world in such a strange way, by calling a goatherd from Ur to get things rolling, rather than one grand powerful gesture. So I think those are just a few areas of theology that can be enriched by thinking about this question of failure.

RS: I remember watching a video of a lecture you did in Australia where you discussed the concept of incarnation and excarnation. Do you think that discussion fits into the topic of failure, in the sense of trying to avoid these grand gestures to fix everything, and instead—I forgot who you quote—"entering into the chaos of others"?[1]

WTC: Yes, I think it's Jim Keenan's line about mercy, which can be defined as "the willingness to enter into the chaos of another." I like that a lot because so much of what we do is excarnated—the term *excarnation* comes from Charles Taylor.[2] When we want to care for one another it's kicked up the ladder to a bureaucracy or we expect the state to do it, and again it's this dominating sort of top-down way of looking at things. It removes us from our bodily existence and bodily contact that we have with one another. It's what Ivan Illich talks about in terms of the parable of the Good Samaritan.[3] The Good Samaritan parable is not about our neighbor being *everybody* but that our neighbor is *anybody*—anybody that contingency throws in our path. And so it's a direct flesh-to-flesh arrangement rather than an attempt to deal in abstractions and bureaucracies and so on.

RS: I know you're a fan of James Scott's *Seeing Like a State*.[4] What do you think the church can learn from his observations on peasant resistance?

WTC: I think it's really interesting that he frames it in terms of "seeing"—our optics on the matter. Again, it's this sort of top-down way of looking at the world that if you want to manage a large space then you have to be above it, far above it. And you have to rearrange it so that it's readable, so that it's not just a matter of reading from high above, but you have

---

1. Keenan, "The Scandal of Mercy Excludes No One."
2. See Taylor, *A Secular Age*.
3. See Cavanaugh, *Field Hospital*, 117.
4. Scott, *Seeing Like a State*.

to arrange things so that they're legible. And that can create all kinds of chaos on the ground. You need to simplify complex realities, which inevitably is a kind of violent process. So Scott goes through and shows in case after case after case that these kinds of large-scale attempts to better the human condition go wrong precisely because you need to disrupt people's lives on the ground. And this applies to large state-led projects like Soviet collectivization or the Ujamaa villages in Tanzania, but it also applies to capitalist projects. "Creative destruction" is what [Joseph] Schumpeter called it[5] and what both the foes and the boosters of capitalism call it. The Koch brothers use this term of creative destruction all the time, and it can have tremendously disruptive effects on the ground and that's what Scott is trying to call attention to. So he advocates listening to local people, favoring projects that are small, favoring projects that are reversible, and being prepared for surprises. And I think there's a lot of wisdom in that. That's a kind of nonviolent way. Unfortunately, we tend to think exactly the opposite. So we expect the World Bank to come in and tell farmers "Get big or get out," that you have to scale up agriculture, and subsistence agriculture is looked at as unworthy of a human being. So we take people's autonomy away from them, we take their control away from them, and we substitute their *dignified* subsistence with a kind of *undignified* poverty: wage slavery.

RS: You've written a lot about ecclesiology. What would be the first steps in imagining an ecclesiology of failure? In other words, what should the church be good at failing at?

WTC: I suppose what that would mean is something like an option for the failures. I think this is what Pope Francis is really trying to do—to have a poor church for the poor, to be closer to the failures of society than to the successes of society. For so long the church has tried to ingratiate itself with the "powers that be" in an attempt to better society, and I think what Pope Francis is calling us to is a church that's much closer to the poor. I suppose a kind of "anti-prosperity gospel" would be one of the manifestations of that. There's this church growth idea that you need to get big in order to attract more people and be a successful church where you have bowling alleys and food courts and things like that. But there's an opposite sort of temptation that equally goes off the rails. It's this idea

---

5. See Schumpeter, *Capitalism, Socialism, and Democracy*, 81–86.

that the shrinkage of the church is a sign that you're doing something right, that you are the faithful remnant that has held on—the pure. And I think both of those things are misguided. So I'm certainly not advocating for a church of the pure. And I think this is what Pope Francis wants us to do as well—to be open to all the messiness that people bring to the church. That's the kind of ecclesiology that I would be in favor of, too.

RS: What about the church's failures in the past? I'm thinking primarily about its complicity in violence, colonialism, and oppression. What does it look like for the church to be a site of penitence and repair?

WTC: I think the sins of the past—and they're not only the past but the present as well—come mostly from that impulse to try to ingratiate the church to the structures of power, and it's sometimes good intentioned and sometimes not. The idea is that if you have control and if you have power, then you can reform society in the image that you think it ought to be in. I'm teaching a section of a course right now on Latin American history and this of course is very prevalent there. You want to control education, you want to control marriage, and you want to be friendly with the government so that the government will allow the church to evangelize the society. And of course the church ends up being corrupted by these kinds of practices. So the kind of penitence and repair that you mention are really important. I think of John Paul II apologizing to the indigenous peoples of the Americas. I think the way forward then is making a church that's *of* and *for* the indigenous. For example, what's going on in Chiapas where you have a really kind of inculturated theology and inculturated church where people on the ground are empowered to make a life for themselves. That, I think, is the way forward to penitence and repair.

RS: Our conversation reminds me of one of the many ways I struggle when coaching my students when it comes to career and vocation. I hear students with the best of intentions say they want to seek those positions of power—they want to be a Senator, or President, or CEO, or run their own NGO one day—because they think it will actually help people on the ground. How would you go about coaching students to rethink that paradigm?

WTC: I wouldn't want to dismiss it too quickly, but I think one of the questions that students—and not just students—don't ask enough is "How is this going to change *me* if I am to gain these positions of power?" And that's a really important question. Especially when we're young we assume that we know who we are and we know what our ideals are and nothing's going to change us. But I just don't think that's true. It's like Stanley Hauerwas used to say, "The church went to Washington to change Washington, and Washington changed the church." And I think that's true on a personal level as well. What do you have to do to become CEO of Exxon? If you're an environmental crusader, then to have you as CEO of Exxon, you could do an immense amount of good. But would they have you as CEO of Exxon if you were an environmental crusader? Asking realistic questions like that is important. Also, never to, first of all, discourage what's good or altruistic about the way students tend to think about these matters. And never to say that "business is bad" or "government is bad"—these are silly overgeneralizations—but always to be thinking on what scale is it possible to live out your ideals. That question of scale I think is really important. And instead of thinking about these questions in abstract terms, ask students to identify people that they really think are doing what they want to do. So make it concrete: "Find me an executive of a company that is running their business in a way that you think a business ought to be run for the benefit of the common good." And they're out there. There are business people that are doing that. But then look and see what they all have in common. Do they tend to be CEO's of Fortune 500 companies or do they tend to be smaller companies? How do they operate? And help students gain realistic goals and see what's actually possible and what's not.

RS: That reminds me of an essay you wrote called, "Actually, You *Can't* Be Anything You Want (And It's a Good Thing, Too)."[6] Can you tell us more about that essay and how it might fit into the topic of failure?

WTC: I wrote that for a volume on vocation. I tried to just do a history of the political economy and how we got to this place where we have these tremendous choices that face students, which some students find very paralyzing—the idea that you need to decide what kind of life you're going to have. Most people throughout most of history just did what their

---

6. Cavanaugh, "Actually, You *Can't* Be Anything You Want."

parents did. They didn't have this incredible array of choices. So I do a little bit of an analysis of how we got to this point in history and show that it has to do, basically, with the rise of modern capitalism. People are freed up, so-called, from subsistence farming and thrown out into the labor market, and for the lucky ones we have this incredible array of choices. But all of the traditional markers for how to make choices have been taken away. And that's why we can experience it as so coercive and so non-liberating and anxiety-producing at the same time. So we're marinated in this cultural messaging that you can be whatever you want and do whatever you want. First of all, that's not true. There are all kinds of limits. And the deeper question is, how do we even know what we want? So you have to do a deeper theological analysis of what are good wants and what are bad wants, and how do you discern them. You need to discern them in conversation with people who will make demands upon you: your family and your community, and so on. And think of these things in terms of "What do people need from me?" rather than just "What do I want?"

RS: In what ways do you think Christ failed? And how should we go about discerning which of these failures we're called to imitate and which failures were unique to his mission and calling?

WTC: I was thinking about this question yesterday during the Gospel reading, in the episode in Mark, chapter 8, in Caesarea Philippi, where Jesus asks, "Who do you say that I am?" and Peter answers correctly, "You are the Messiah." Jesus orders them not to tell anybody about it and says, "But the Messiah is going to get killed." Peter says, of course, like we all want to say, "No! No, that's not going to happen. This is all going to be a tremendous success!" And Jesus says, "Get behind me, Satan," because of course it's not going to be a tremendous success. It's going to end in failure. He's going to be tortured to death and all of the disciples are going to scatter. So that's a clear way in which Christ redefines success. That's not the end of the story of course. There's resurrection. But he doesn't come back like Arnold Schwarzenegger comes back, like he's going to come back and get revenge, in the sense that "Jesus is back and he's mad as hell!" (laughs). So the whole notion of the cross is at the center of this. You have to "take up your cross and follow me," Jesus says; "Lose your life for my sake" [Matt 16:24–26]. All of these are signs of failure but there's always a kind of transposition of what failure means, and what failure accomplishes in that way. But it's clearly something that's very different. One of the things, of course, that it does is it chastens our ambitions. When Paul says that Christ became sin for our sake, that's a sign of tremendous failure in one sense [1 Cor 5:21]. But it means that we need to be realistic that we take on the sins of one another, that we all participate in the body of Christ in such a way that we take on both the joys and the sorrows, and even the sins of one another. We're born into this world of interconnection, where we're already tainted by sin. This is how Karl Rahner explained original sin: it was through a banana. You eat a banana for breakfast and it comes from Central America where people are being exploited. And you realize you've become sin, too. You've taken on sin, too, just by being born into this world. So there's this sort of chastening there. I also thought about the woman caught in adultery and what Jesus does there. He doesn't explain much. He doesn't really do or say much in that incident at all. And he neither harangues the woman nor does he harangue the crowd. He just draws on the sand until one by one they go away. And there's something in that incident that struck me as being really interesting—that he doesn't gather a crowd around him but instead disperses this lynch mob. So there's a way in which we're not called to create these successful movements but to dispel the sort of violence people do when they gather in these kinds of mobs.

A bunch of different episodes came to mind when thinking about this: what it means to think of Jesus as a failure. But the second part of your question: which of these failures are we called to imitate and which failures were unique to his mission and calling? I'm not sure that there are any of these that were unique to Christ's mission and calling. I think in a lot of ways when he says, "Take up your cross and follow me," I don't think there's anything we're not meant to participate in. Obviously we're not God, but this idea that Christ absorbs the violence of the world and doesn't give it back and therefore is a failure in the world's terms—this is the kind of thing we're supposed to participate in.

RS: In an online review of Ted Smith's book, you briefly discuss how despairing it is for the church to embrace the popular hymn's lyric that "God has no hands but ours."[7] How do we avoid this kind of despair? And how can failure help us in the process?

---

7. Cavanaugh, "The Blurred Line between Law and Violence." Reviewing Smith, *Weird John Brown*.

WTC: I think that's a line from Teresa of Ávila, "God has no hands but ours." I love Teresa of Ávila but there's a certain danger of Pelagianism there in idea that *we* have to save the world because God doesn't. Ultimately, the idea that God has no hands but ours is like not believing in God. It's not believing that God actually acts in the world, that God is actually real, but we have to do the heavy lifting because God won't get off his chair and do anything. How do we avoid that kind of despair? I think we just need to relax and remember that God is in charge, that God is God. And if God is God then we can relax a little bit since we're not in charge of history. God is in charge of history. So the trick is seeing how God is in charge of history. I saw the movie *Silence* recently. I've taught the novel[8] for years and so I was really excited to see the movie. The title, of course, comes from this idea that the main character, Rodrigues, thinks that God is not in charge; that God is not doing anything. All of these people are suffering—the persecution of Christians in sixteenth-century Japan—and yet God does nothing to help them. God is silent. But in the climactic point in the novel and the film he hears Jesus' voice telling him to go ahead and apostatize by trampling on an image of Jesus and Jesus says, "It is to be trampled on that I came into this world." And that's the precise point at which God breaks God's silence and identifies with the failures of the mission and the failures of the people. "It is to be trampled on that I came into this world." There's no happy ending. The Christians are persecuted and the church is extinguished in Japan and yet 400 years later we're reading this and we come away convinced that the truth is on the side not of the persecutors but the persecuted. There's a sense there that we want God to act now, and there's a way that God is acting that's not very satisfying in an immediate sort of way. It's not going to be a very popular movie for one thing. But there's a way in which this is ultimately what's true; that God changes the world through humility because humility is what a changed world looks like. It's not a means to an end. Humility *is* the end. And that's a really hard thing to grasp, because what that means is that in order to change the world we have to give up our pretensions to change the world. This is a very weird God that we're following here.

RS: Do you see a lack of humility in the way theologians study and talk about God?

---

8. Endo, *Silence*.

WTC: Yeah, but not any more than any other area I suppose. We're all doing our best. There's a certain sort of style of theology—like political theology and social ethics—that wants to fix the world. And I think it would be helpful if we backed away from that a little bit.

RS: One last question. I know you're working on a book about idolatry. I was wondering how you think failure can help us understand idolatry and how it can even help us resist idolatry.

WTC: I guess the root of idolatry is the root of all sin, which is Genesis 3:5: "Eat of this and you will be like God." So idolatry is wanting to take God's place. It's wanting to substitute something else for God, which is something that is more satisfying to our own desires. It's the replacement of the real God with a fake one that usually looks an awful lot like us. So to acknowledge that that's the kind of root of idolatry and the root of sin might have a certain kind of humbling effect—that the recognition that we're not God is the beginning of a good life. And this recognition that we're not God, I suppose, is at the root of what you're calling failure.

Bibliography

Cavanaugh, William T. "Actually, You *Can't* Be Anything You Want (And It's a Good Thing, Too)." In *At This Time and in This Place: Vocation and Higher Education*, edited by David S. Cunningham, 25–46. New York: Oxford University Press, 2016.

———. "The Blurred Line between Law and Violence." *Marginalia: Los Angeles Review of Books,* February 20, 2015. https://marginalia.lareviewofbooks.org/blurred-line-law-violence-william-cavanaugh/.

Field Hospital: The Church's Engagement with a Wounded World. Grand Rapids: Eerdmans, 2016.

Endo, Shusaku. *Silence*. Translated by William Johnston. New York: Picador, 1969.

Keenan, James. "The Scandal of Mercy Excludes No One." *Thinking Faith*. https://www.thinkingfaith.org/articles/scandal-mercy-excludes-no-one.

Schumpeter, Joseph A. *Capitalism, Socialism, and Democracy*. London: Routledge, 2003.

Scott, James C. *Seeing Like a State*. New Haven, CT: Yale University Press, 1999.

Smith, Ted A. *Weird John Brown: Divine Violence and the Limits of Ethics*. Stanford, CA: Stanford University Press, 2014.

Taylor, Charles. *A Secular Age*. Cambridge, MA: Harvard University Press, 2007.

Part 3

Failure as Resistance

11.

"A Strange Kind of Slavery"
David Foster Wallace's Enslaved Self

Dennis F. Kinlaw III

For a body of work enamored by the infinite, David Foster Wallace's encyclopedic corpus encircles a very basic observation: American individuals are desperate to escape the confines of being finite creatures. From the grotesque gluttony of characters convinced they can swell to universal size to those who simply "kneel and revere the double S,"[1] such "aspirations to be infinite" disclose a certain discomfort with the day-to-day demands of reality.[2] While the motivation varies from character to character, the need to give one's self away remains a unifying force in Wallace's work. "We're absolutely dying to give ourselves away to something," Wallace explains, "to run, to escape, somehow."[3] The task of deciding what to commit one's self to in a contemporary setting that idolizes pleasure, success, and power pushes Wallace's characters into an impasse—what should I worship? Wallace lays out the theological character of this conundrum in his 2005 commencement address at Kenyon College:

> In the day-to-day trenches of adult life, there is actually no such thing as atheism. There is no such thing as not worshipping. Everybody worships. The only choice we get is what to worship.

---

1. Wallace, *Infinite Jest*, 1072.
2. Wallace, *The Broom of the System*, 135.
3. Quoted in Lipsky, *Although Of Course You End Up Becoming Yourself,* 81.

> And the compelling reason for maybe choosing some sort of god or spiritual-type thing to worship—be it JC or Allah, be it YHWH or the Wiccan Mother Goddess, or the Four Noble Truths, or some inviolable set of ethical principles—is that pretty much anything else you worship will eat you alive.[4]

Identifying the impulse to worship as a "default" setting, Wallace attends to these "trenches of adult life" in his fiction as a means of detailing the ways unmindful modes of worship produce a kind of self-encagement.[5] Whether the object of adoration is entertainment, drugs, or tennis, there unfolds in such forms of escape a loss of meaningful connection between the world and Wallace's characters. Yet by inhabiting the cages of his characters Wallace illuminates the possibility of freedom from idolatrous pursuits. That such freedom is characterized by an awareness of one's finitude—an awareness that exposes the limits of self-centered pursuits and arrives in moments of failure—opens Wallace's characters to more mindful modes of worship on the far side of idols. Achieving this freedom, however, requires us to become conscious of our cages.

America, a country celebrated as the "Land of the Free," is populated primarily in Wallace's work by alienated individuals, isolated in the emptiness of their own pursuits. Born into a landscape governed by economic interest, people are forced to find some sense of purpose amidst profit margins. Even time is open to economic development in Wallace's view, with the calendar year of *Infinite Jest* subsidized by sponsors such as Burger King, Maytag, and Glad. But as the furthest reaches of human experience are gradually incorporated into this economy, the possibility of choosing an alternative model of meaning is lost altogether. The erasure of any sense of purpose beyond profit narrows the self's purview considerably. As the French saboteur Rémy Marathe remarks in *Infinite Jest*, "'You U.S.A.'s do not seem to believe you may each choose what to die for.'" While the elevation of economics to a life-or-death affair may seem the overbearing diagnosis of an outsider, Marathe's foreignness in fact provides the estranged perspective needed to sufficiently measure the stakes of such day-to-day American ideals. In Marathe's reasoning, "Our attachments are our temple, what we worship, no? What we give ourselves to, what we invest with faith."[6]

---

4. Wallace, *This is Water*, 98–102.
5. Ibid., 82.
6. Wallace, *Infinite Jest*, 107.

Even as Marathe's inquiries are met with smug dismissal within the text, they nevertheless succeed in calling into question the automatic nature of so many American allegiances. Committing oneself to economic success within a cultural system that fails to recognize the significance of other models of meaning is one such unconscious allegiance. "It's a very American illness," Wallace explains, "the idea of giving yourself away entirely to the idea of working in order to achieve some sort of brass ring."[7] The unreflective submission that economically oriented systems demand of their inhabitants produces "a strange kind of slavery" within American culture.[8] Though we remain free to choose how to brandish the success we achieve, we still remain bound by this original submission to an economically determined model of success. Once this model of success has been given in to, reality recedes and the self is enshrined at the center of its own facsimile of freedom. The "so-called real world of men and money and power" closes its temple doors behind us as we wade blindly into "a pool of fear and anger and frustration and craving and worship of self."[9]

To be sure, the freedom that follows can be fun. No other American writer has depicted scenes of such uninhibited and ultimately deadly fun as David Foster Wallace. Faces are nearly frozen in a "rictus of pleasure" from the ceaseless indulgences provided by a culture committed to profiting off our pleasure. The range of self-pampering services supplied by a luxury cruise line and itemized in Wallace's "A Supposedly Fun Thing I'll Never Do Again" offers one of many narrative homages to the excessiveness of American tastes. Aboard a pleasure cruise whose service personnel are paid to ensure you are never in need of a refill, the contemporary self is temporarily free from the "consciousness of death and decay" that hovers around poverty-stricken ports.[10] Yet the serene isolation of this scene—the self marooned in the mid-Atlantic—intimates the alienating aspect of any freedom in which the self sits at the center. For here we are given only the freedom "to be lords of our tiny skull-sized kingdoms, alone at the center of all creation."[11] Certainly the image of a single man

---

7. Miller, "The Salon Interview," 64.
8. Global Informer, "David Foster Wallace on the Slavery Impulse."
9. Wallace, *This is Water*, 115.
10. Wallace, "A Supposedly Fun Thing," 263–64.
11. Wallace, *This is Water*, 117.

receiving endless room service in a subterranean cabin captures the type of alienated lordship imagined in Wallace's commencement speech.

But if Wallace's comedic analysis of cruise ships confronts the surreal character of a consumer-based culture, more perceptive still is his sensitivity to the *aloneness* that looms beneath these systems of self-worship. One's vocation just as much as one's vacation provides a place in which this "idolatry of uniqueness" comes to isolate the individual.[12] As an affirmation of autonomy and embrace of the ultimate sovereignty of self, one's sense of uniqueness marks the individual's continued descent into his own private kingdom, according to Wallace. The capacity to learn from others is replaced here by an unflagging sense of self-sufficiency. As Wallace explains, the belief that we are "fundamentally different from the common run of man, unique and in certain crucial ways superior" makes possible the self-narcotizing myth that we "will make a difference in [our] chosen field simply by the fact of [our] unique and central presence in it."[13] The temptation to position oneself above and apart from one's peers extends naturally from the type of success-driven outlook assumed in much of contemporary society. An individual's uniqueness is simply a given: "What else could explain the fact that they themselves have been at the exact center of all they've experienced for the whole 20 years of their conscious lives?" Wallace inquires.[14] The self-idolatrous logic of such musings creates something like an echo chamber within the recesses of so many skull-sized kingdoms across Wallace's work.

For all of his narrative debts to the self-reflexive techniques of postmodern writers, Wallace's commitment to creating self-conscious characters owes more to his interest in illuminating the value of vulnerability, humility, and the help of others lost in a landscape of empty idols. But the recovery of such values remains fenced off and fissured by the incessant chatter of self-consciousness. The pursuit of success proceeds like an unending loop in Wallace's work whereby the need to succeed is coupled with a growing awareness of the emptiness of such a need. The exhaustion that follows from self-consciousness creates a kind of paralysis that marks the misguidedness of one's pursuits. No character captures this self-reflexive realization as convincingly as Neal, the advertising executive and eventual suicide in the short story "Good Old Neon." Neal's singular desire to be "admired, approved of" and "applauded" leads only

12. Wallace, *Infinite Jest*, 604.
13. Wallace, "Mister Squishy," 30.
14. Ibid.

to the feeling of fraudulence.[15] The onset of this feeling inspires Neal to develop his own logical paradox—the "fraudulence paradox"—during a logic course:

> The fraudulence paradox was that the more time and effort you put into trying to appear impressive or attractive to other people, the less impressive or attractive you felt inside—you were a fraud. And the more of a fraud you felt like, the harder you tried to convey an impressive or likable image of yourself so that other people wouldn't find out what a hollow, fraudulent person you really were.

Neal's desire to appear successful generates here only a heightened awareness of his failings. The "viscous infinite regress" set in motion by his ambition to be applauded is intensified by a self-consciousness that perceives no escape.[16] The possibility that failure itself might provide a breach of sorts whereby the self may be let out of this paralysis is ignored in the endless pursuit of success. Indeed, the threat of failure initiates in the "inbent" minds of Wallace's characters only an additional loop of fear.[17] "Knowing some internal stress could cause failure," one character notes, "merely set up internal stress about the prospect of internal stress." These recursive structures of thought compound to create a "neurology of failure" that plagues those in pursuit of success with an ever-present fear that such success is fleeting.[18]

At least partially awoken to the meaningless of their self-centered endeavors, many of Wallace's characters nevertheless double down their effort to avoid failure and so consign themselves to utter isolation. The result of this redoubled effort to avoid failure is devastating. It is at this moment that one's idol "has devoured or replaced and become *you*" rather than an ever-receding object of pursuit. "You become a citizen of nothing," Marathe concludes, "You are by yourself and alone, kneeling to yourself."[19] Yet the realization that this idolatry of self comes at the cost of one's self provides the possibility for surrender as well. If such acts of surrender are rare within Wallace's work, they offer still a significant

---

15. Wallace, "Good Old Neon," 141.
16. Ibid., 147.
17. Wallace, *Infinite Jest*, 138.
18. Wallace, *The Pale King*, 17.
19. Wallace, *Infinite Jest*, 347, 90.

opening in which the sovereignty of self is overturned and a type of living informed by failure comes into being.

Don Gately, the twenty-nine-year-old former burglar and recovering Demerol addict at the center of *Infinite Jest*, offers an unlikely yet convicting account of the transformative capacity of failure. Arrested for a botched burglary and forced into sobriety during his time behind bars, Gately is faced with the decision of whether to return to substances or abandon his idol of addiction entirely. At last, he is "in the kind of a hell of a mess that either ends lives or turns them around."[20] By choosing to discard his idol and confront the consequences of a self-consuming life, Gately opens himself to a model of living informed by failure. Faced with the "chilled conviction that you have no faith whatsoever left in yourself," the encaged self slowly emerges from its cycle of self-serving and begins to be made anew. As a result, the sense of uniqueness supporting the anemic kingdom of self begins to buckle under the weight of an awareness of what connects individuals together.

"You are not unique," Gately realizes during one of his first Alcoholics Anonymous meetings, but enjoined by an "initial hopelessness [that] unites every soul." If hopelessness seems a fragile form of union to turn to in the wake of self-worship, it signals still the vulnerable condition of a self that recognizes the limits of its abilities in the light of failure. It is through this purgative power of failure that an alternative sense of self comes into view. Failure "has to happen," Gately reasons, in order "to like upset the idolatry" that we are self-sufficient or superior individuals.[21]

The importance of failure as a catalyst whereby characters like Gately are liberated from the myth of self-sufficiency extends across American literature. As Gavin Jones notes in *Failure and the American Writer: A Literary History*, "modern subjectivity emerges from an encounter with failure" as the idea of the autonomous self is irreparably called into question.[22] For Wallace, the self that emerges from this crisis affirms the critical importance of finding "something bigger than the self" to serve and so ultimately turns to others as a source of help as well as a means of self-sacrifice.[23] "Try to learn from everybody," one character advises, "especially those who fail. This is hard."[24] Indeed, the ability to listen and

20. Ibid., 347.
21. Ibid., 349.
22. Jones, *Failure*, 48.
23. Wallace, *Infinite Jest*, 107.
24. Ibid., 176.

learn—as simple as such tasks may seem—represents the central struggle for those facing failure. Among the many "new facts" Gately learns during his time in a half-way house, the realization that "it takes great personal courage to let yourself appear weak" stands out as a vital indicator of this struggle.[25] But rather than confronting failure with a "total bitter impotent Job-type rage" that leads one to "[fall] back and up inside himself," Wallace's characters are challenged to open themselves to the significance of others for the first time in their lives. By persisting though this challenge, an attenuated model of self is recuperated that finds a certain freedom in accepting its finitude. Unlike the illusory freedom that seeks to escape finitude through the idolatrous pursuit of success, the freedom that follows from failure is one that exposes the emptiness of idols and highlights the importance of other people. "[R]eal freedom," Wallace argues, involves "being able truly to care about other people and to sacrifice for them over and over in myriad petty, unsexy ways every day."[26] If such a self-sacrificial model of living is obscured by the encaged perspectives of those committed to success at all costs, its importance comes into view in those rare moments of rupture afforded by failure.

It is in this sense that "everything that is a failure is always a victory," as Wallace explains in one of his final interviews, for in accepting the emptiness of one form of living we become receptive to those containing some secret fullness.[27] The rarity of such moments of receptivity, however, is compounded by a culture that elevates economic and self-centered models of success to an idolatrous status. But even as these models excel "in terms of selling people products and keeping the economy thriving," as Wallace concedes, they fall short in "helping us help each other know how to live and to be happy."[28] Creating narratives which succeed in illuminating more fulfilling modes of living through their depiction of failure provides an important critical lens through which to view Wallace's narrative ambition. Like the characters he created whose "interest in grand-scale failure was unflagging,"[29] Wallace perceives in failure a rare possibility of renewal and constructs his fictional worlds that fail in crucial ways so that they too might "shake the reader awake" from

25. Ibid., 204.
26. Ibid., *This is Water*, 120–121.
27. Dazzle Communication, "Le Conversazioni 2006."
28. Wallace, "David Foster Wallace on the Slavery Impulse."
29. Wallace, *Infinite Jest*, 994.

their alienated slumber.[30] That *Infinite Jest* was originally entitled *A Failed Entertainment* signals one way Wallace seeks to *fail* his reader. By failing to entertain us fully—forcing us to read hundreds of footnotes and familiarize ourselves with arcane topics like pharmacology—Wallace pushes his reader to become conscious of their own limits. For those who failed to make it through *Infinite Jest* in its entirety—the breaking point of one's narrative endurance brought painfully into view—perhaps another attempt will clarify the significance of even this failure. For those turning to Wallace for the first time, "if you sit up front and listen hard, all the speakers' stories of decline and fall and surrender are basically alike, and like your own": so long as you run from failure, you remain a slave to yourself.[31]

Bibliography

Dazzle Communication. "Le Conversazioni 2006." YouTube video, 2:52. https://www.youtube.com/watch?v=mVzhhvCRTCo.

Global Informer. "David Foster Wallace on the Slavery Impulse." YouTube video, 1:53. https://www.youtube.com/watch?v=idjos2cCz7Y.

Jones, Gavin. *Failure and the American Writer: A Literary History.* Cambridge: Cambridge University Press, 2014.

Lipsky, David. *Although Of Course You End Up Becoming Yourself: A Road Trip With David Foster Wallace.* New York: Broadway, 2010.

Manufacturing Intellect. "David Foster Wallace uncut interview." YouTube video, 1:24:01. https://www.youtube.com/watch?v=cdUXCdfBOjA.

Miller, Laura. "The Salon Interview: David Foster Wallace." In *Conversations with David Foster Wallace*, edited by Stephen Burn, 58–65. Jackson, MS: University of Mississippi Press, 2012.

Wallace, David Foster. "Good Old Neon." In *Oblivion*, 141–81. New York: Little, Brown and Company, 2004.

———. *Infinite Jest.* New York: Back Bay, 2016.

———. "Mister Squishy." In *Oblivion*, 3–66. New York: Little, Brown and Company, 2004.

———. "A Supposedly Fun Thing I'll Never do Again." In *A Supposedly Fun Thing I'll Never Do Again: Essays and Arguments*, 256–90. New York: Little, Brown and Company, 1997.

———. *The Broom of the System.* New York: Penguin, 1987.

———. *The Pale King: An Unfinished Novel.* London: Penguin, 2012.

———. *This is Water: Some Thoughts, Delivered on a Significant Occasion, about Living a Compassionate Life.* Boston: Little, Brown and Company, 2009.

30. Lipsky, *Although Of Course You End Up Becoming Yourself*, 79.
31. Wallace, *Infinite Jest*, 345.

12.

Blessed Are the Failures
Leaning into the Beatitudes

Rebekah Eklund

IT IS RELATIVELY COMMONPLACE to observe that the beatitudes espouse countercultural values and disrupt conventional notions of success. As early as the fourth century, John Chrysostom noted that all the things Christ blesses are "the very things which all others avoid" and are "so contrary to the accustomed ways of men."[1]

This seems sensible: after all, people who are meek and mourning, or hungry and thirsty and poor, do not appear to be the kind of people the world admires as successful. The beatitudes have genuine liberative potential to disrupt patterns of consumerism ("blessed are the poor"), vengeance ("blessed are the merciful"), and violence ("blessed are the peacemakers"). Press a little closer, though, and this judgment appears less than stable. Is the Matthean blessing on the "poor in spirit" (Matt 5:3) less subversive than the Lukan blessing on the "poor" (Luke 6:20)? And some of the values represented by the beatitudes are not so countercultural at all. Take the peacemakers, for example: we award Nobel prizes to those folks.

Even more telling is Chrysostom's reference to the "accustomed ways of men." In fact, it is the English translator who has supplied "men";

---

1. Chrysostom, Homily 15, 95.

Chrysostom wrote (lit.) "the accustomed ways of the many [*pollōn*]."[2] Nonetheless, it is worth asking if the beatitudes are likewise contrary to the accustomed ways of women. If a woman is meek and in mourning, is she considered a success or a failure—or simply a stereotypical woman? That is, it is worth asking for whom and in what contexts the beatitudes are liberative or countercultural. They appear to be most countercultural, most subversive, when viewed from positions of privilege. For those who are poor or mourning, the beatitudes are a description of their current situation, not a challenge to it. Conversely, the beatitudes issue implicit judgments to the rich (the not-poor), the arrogant (the not-meek), and the persecutors or the accommodators (the not-persecuted).

It is tempting to admire the beatitudes from a distance, for those who do not find themselves described there. For example, comparatively wealthy Western Christians have sometimes praised the benefits of poverty (the poor are closer to God, are more grateful, etc.) without being compelled to adopt such states of deprivation themselves. Others have emphasized the spiritual aspect of the beatitudes, sometimes at the expense of their material function: by the third century, some Christian theologians were arguing that Jesus' blessing on the poor (and/or the poor in spirit) applies to the rich so long as the rich are humble and generous.[3]

Liberation theologians, on the other hand, speaking from contexts of oppression and poverty, typically read the blessing on the poor not as a recommendation to stay poor, nor as a blessing on spiritual humility detached from material conditions, but as a signal of God's identification with them—and, paradoxically, God's determination to put to an end the very state declared blessed. Gustavo Gutiérrez, for example, finds in the beatitudes a clear expression of God's preferential option for the poor.[4] Elsa Tamez describes poverty as "not a virtue but an evil that reflects the socioeconomic conditions of inequality in which people live." For Tamez, the poor in Latin America are not blessed because they have embraced poverty but "because the reign of God is at hand and because

---

2. Field, *Joannis Chrysostomi Homiliae in Mattheum*, vol. 1.

3. E.g., Clement, "Who Is the Rich Man that Shall Be Saved?," vol. 2, 595.

4. Gutiérrez, *The God of Life*, 121–22. While many scholars accuse Matthew of spiritualizing Luke's concrete beatitudes, Gutiérrez observes that "Matthew is especially insistent on the need of concrete, 'material' actions toward others and especially the poor" (ibid., 119).

the eschatological promise of justice is drawing ever nearer to fulfillment and, with it, the end of poverty."[5]

All this suggests that context matters—that the location from which one reads the beatitudes affects the force and function of the beatitudes with respect to each particular set of readers. The blessing on the pure in heart "means" differently to those who are pure in heart and to those who are impure in heart. To the former, it functions as a promise (you will see God); to the latter, it functions as either invitation (if you want to see God, become pure in heart), or indictment (because you are not pure in heart, you will not see God).

This returns us to Chrysostom's observation about the accustomed ways of men. The beatitudes present a particular problem for feminist theology, since the attitudes or actions they represent are not all obviously liberating for women. Might they, in fact, reinforce the victimization of women?[6] For feminist theology, the problem is not *merely* a hermeneutic one. As Sandra Schneiders writes, Scripture is andocentric, patriarchal, and at times sexist: "the problem is in the text."[7] Yet feminist scholars like Schneiders still want to claim the text as *revelatory*, as a text that bears witness to God's revelation and self-gift in Jesus Christ.[8]

In the case of the beatitudes, *is* the problem in the text? On the one hand, feminist scholarship has been relatively quiet toward the beatitudes. In the words of Mary Ann Hinsdale, "Interestingly, feminist theology does not seem to explicitly treat the beatitudes or the Sermon on the Mount."[9] She notes Elsa Tamez as an exception,[10] but also observes that Tamez addresses Matthew's first beatitude in relation to the poor, not specifically poor women.[11]

On the other hand, several women, including Hinsdale herself, have recently engaged the beatitudes by wondering if they are genuinely good news for women.[12] Hinsdale specifically addresses the blessings on the

5. Tamez, *Bible of the Oppressed*, 74.
6. Hinsdale, "Blessed are the Persecuted," 178.
7. Schneiders, *Beyond Patching*, 38.
8. Ibid., 51.
9. Hinsdale, "Blessed are the Persecuted," 176.
10. Tamez, *Bible of the Oppressed*, 72–74.
11. Hinsdale, "Blessed are the Persecuted," 176. Tamez herself points out that there are "differences between reading the Bible from the point of view of the poor and reading it from a woman's perspective"; see Tamez, "Women's Rereading of the Bible," 174.
12. Hinsdale, "Blessed are the Persecuted," 176–79. See D'Angelo, "Blessed the One

persecuted and on those who hunger and thirst for justice, concluding that the fourth Matthean beatitude is indeed good news for women, since women are "clearly among those who 'hunger and thirst for justice'"; but that the blessings on the persecuted are more ambiguous for women. Hinsdale reluctantly accepts that persecution may be blessed, but only if it resists victimization.[13] Like poverty, "[p]ersecution itself is not to be sought after, or glorified, but the pursuit of justice demands the breaking of boundaries which cause persecution in the first place."[14]

The observation that liberation theology has often embraced the beatitudes whereas feminist theology has not represents a form of critique often called intersectionality, a term coined by law professor Kimberlé Crenshaw. In the words of Crenshaw, "Intersectionality is an analytic sensibility, a way of thinking about identity and its relationship to power. Originally articulated on behalf of black women, the term brought to light the invisibility of many constituents within groups that claim them as members, but often fail to represent them."[15] So women might ask male liberation theologians if the beatitudes are as liberating for poor women as they are for poor men.

The same type of analysis has been applied to another recent strand of feminism: the "Lean In" movement rooted in Sheryl Sandberg's 2010 TED Talk, "Why We Have Too Few Woman Leaders." While some have lauded the Lean In movement for empowering a certain group of women, others have critiqued it for its uncritical acceptance of neoliberal capitalism and its lack of attention to issues of class and race, whereby a select group of wealthy and usually white women are able to "have it all" by paying other women (often poor women of color) to take on the traditionally female tasks of cooking, cleaning, and raising children.[16] If it is difficult to imagine "leaning in" while embodying the beatitudes, this is perhaps because—to invoke Chrysostom once more—the virtues of leaning in adopt the accustomed ways of men, the traditionally masculine values of the capitalist workplace.

The beatitudes, then, have no *single* (or simple) message regarding success and failure even in light of feminist theory. They alternately may

---

Who Reads," 71–73, 77–78.

13. Hinsdale, "Blessed are the Persecuted," 179.
14. Ibid., 182.
15. Crenshaw, "Why Intersectionality Can't Wait."
16. Gutting, "A Feminism Where 'Lean In' Means Leaning on Others."

assure, convict, console, and unsettle. As Rowan Williams suggests, "The sacred text thus enacts its sacred character not by its transparency but by its nature as unresolved, unfinished, self-reflexive or self-questioning. It is through these things that its 'excess' appears . . ."[17] The beatitudes likewise have no single "meaning" shorn of context. Like the parables, their simplicity is deceptive, even destabilizing. "Christ's confusing teachings, according to Williams, are *generatively*, perhaps even *deliberately*, underdetermined."[18]

Still, constraints remain: because the central message of the gospel is "profoundly liberating," an interpretation that victimizes women is invalid; it fails the test of being true to the good news.[19] Within certain roomy limits, we may consider different options for embodying the beatitudes in a variety of contexts, based on what Schneiders calls the "fruitfulness" of the interpretation: "an interpretation, even if new or startling, that 'makes the text speak,' that, for example, exploits the potentiality of the text to illuminate the faith of the community without violating the canons of good exegetical and critical method, should be taken seriously."[20] Two case studies will test this point by exploring how the rubric of success and failure might apply to women in relation to the blessings on the mourners and the meek.

Mary D'Angelo points out that the one beatitude "exemplified most fully by women" is the blessing on those who mourn. "To some extent," she writes, "this is not surprising; mourning is a female role, in fact, a woman's profession, in antiquity."[21] Seen from one angle, this is positive: Jesus lauds women who are the typical mourners of a society, elevating their status and promising them comfort, which Scripture often links to God's favor and vindication (Isa 61:1–3). Less positively, commending women for the stereotypically "womanly" act of mourning has the danger of reinscribing the harmful caricature of women as more emotional (read: unreliable, silly, etc.) beings. Public mourning is certainly more countercultural, and likely more liberating, when performed by certain men than by women.

---

17. Williams, "Historical Criticism and Sacred Text," 227.

18. Quash, *Found Theology*, 75.

19. Schneiders, *The Revelatory Text*, 176. For her discussion of criteria for valid interpretations, see 163–68.

20. Ibid., 165.

21. D'Angelo, "Blessed the One Who Reads," 72.

Second, however, what is mourning? Is it sorrow over loss? Is it sorrow over sin? Is it an expression of lament, a powerful form of prayer that intertwines protest at injustice and a longing for God's presence in the midst of pain?[22] Laura James's paintings inspired by the Matthean beatitudes, *A Sermon for our Ancestors*, depict Jesus preaching the beatitudes to African slaves in chains. The panel "Blessed are the mourners" shows a black man being lynched while two well-dressed white men look on and a large group of black slaves huddles together mourning in the background.[23] The panel links the act of mourning not only to deep personal grief but also to an act of evil that cries out for God's justice. The beatitude becomes, in this context, a cry of pain that is also a protest, a demand—and the promise of comfort hints not only at the vindication of the black slaves but issues a warning to the white onlookers (*woe to those who laugh now*). So mourning has layers of potential interpretation; can the same be said for meekness?

It is hard to see how being meek could be countercultural for the non-privileged, given the associations of the English word *meek* with timidity and submission. For centuries, however, Christian interpreters understood meekness not as passivity but as a form of disciplined self-restraint exemplified in the command not to return evil for evil.[24] The Greek word for meek (*praüs*) may also be rendered "gentle"; but Jesus describes himself as "gentle" (*praüs*, Matt 11:29) in a Gospel in which he is also capable of overturning tables and describing the religious leaders as a brood of vipers (Matt 21:12; 23:13–36). D'Angelo draws on Matthew's wider context to argue that the blessing on the meek does not entail submission; rather, in Matthew, "meekness is clearly embodied in nonviolence, in peacemaking and forgiveness," and in the Canaanite women's "unassuming, but unflinching, assertiveness and persistence." D'Angelo concludes that for early Christianity, "the meekness that was blessed had an attitude."[25]

Yet the translation (or even function) of *praüs* is not the *whole* problem. At stake is the larger emphasis in the Christian tradition on

---

22. Eklund, *Jesus Wept*, 10–17, 56–66.

23. Laura James, *A Sermon for our Ancestors* 2006 (acrylic on canvas), inspired by Matt 5:1–14. The images are included in Jennings, "Overcoming Racial Faith," 4–9.

24. So Augustine, *Commentary on the Lord's Sermon on the Mount*, 14; *Incomplete Commentary on Matthew*, 86; Leo the Great, "Letters and Sermons," 204. Gregory of Nyssa, *The Lord's Prayer* and *The Beatitudes*, 101–3.

25. D'Angelo, "Blessed the One Who Reads," 73.

self-giving love, self-sacrifice, and humble service. Feminist scholars have argued that the Christian tradition has long had "a *theoretical* one-sided emphasis upon charity, meekness, obedience, humility, self-abnegation, sacrifice, service," but that this emphasis "became accepted not by men, but by women, who hardly have been helped by an ethic which reinforces the abject female situation."[26] To refer again to constraints on interpretation, elements in Matthew's wider context disrupt this one-sided emphasis, as D'Angelo demonstrates, while reception history likewise insists that "meekness" has not been a stable or consistent concept throughout history. But we are still left with the challenge of how to reconfigure what meekness "means" or what it looks like, say, for an educated white woman in a male-dominated field in twenty-first-century Baltimore—and whether embodying meekness might lead to a liberating form of failure vis-à-vis worldly conceptions, rather than a form of failure with which women in male-dominated fields are all too familiar.

In order to address this conundrum, allow me to recruit Johann Baptist Metz as a witness. Lauren Winner quotes Metz to muse on the gendered act of kneeling in prayer: "Who can't stand upright can't really kneel."[27] Initially, Winner suggests that "perhaps the Church is called to be a place where women learn to stand and men learn to kneel."[28] She then complicates this point in two ways: first, she observes that "many enslaved Christians in antebellum America 'really' kneeled in prayer," despite their oppression. She concludes, "It is precisely from the witness of their bodies in the communion of saints that I may yet learn what kneeling means."[29] Second, Winner invokes the common visual trope of the kneeling black slave and the standing free white man or woman in order to interrogate the intersection of her gender with her whiteness. "As someone who has been taught to identify with the helpful, powerful, and upright white woman in the abolitionist icon," writes Winner, "kneeling in church may prove, for me, a decidedly fruitful practice of humility."[30]

This raises the question of not only the potential rewards but also the potential cost of practicing the beatitudes. It is not impossible to

---

26. Daly, *Beyond God the Father*, 100, quoted in Andolsen, "Agape in Feminist Ethics," 152.

27. Winner, "Interceding," 273, 275.

28. Ibid., 274.

29. Ibid., 275.

30. Ibid.

imagine a scenario in which being poor in spirit or pure in heart may not line up precisely with advancing an ambitious career. Would I be willing to hunger and thirst for justice if I thought it might cost me tenure? This makes the academy a difficult context in which to admire the countercultural force of the beatitudes, where mercy and meekness are not typically rewarded with promotion and prestigious book contracts—and where women and people of color are often already at a disadvantage.[31]

When I teach the beatitudes in one of my classes, many students are especially drawn to the observation that the beatitudes are fundamentally intended to shape the life of a community, not an individual. They are not postures, actions, or attitudes to be practiced in isolation. Thus we may learn what they look like from others, especially others who are different from us. Nor are they achieved instantaneously (for those of us who do not find that the beatitudes already describe us in every way). Rather, one of the insights of the early Christians was that they describe transformations brought about by God's grace, and, yes, practice over time. Thus, we may have to be willing to fail even at the beatitudes. But better to accept their challenge and seek, creatively and haltingly, to lean into them, to explore their potential as liberative resistance, than to admire them from a distance and not to try them at all.

Bibliography

Andolsen, Barbara Hilkert. "Agape in Feminist Ethics." In *Feminist Theological Ethics: A Reader*, edited by Lois Daly, 149–59. Louisville, KY: Westminster John Knox, 1994.

Augustine. *Commentary on the Lord's Sermon on the Mount: With Seventeen Related Sermons*. Fathers of the Church, vol. 11. Washington, DC: Catholic University of America Press, 2001. 1.2.4.

Chrysostom, John. "Homily 15." In *Homilies on the Gospel of Saint Matthew*, vol. 10, *Nicene and Post-Nicene Fathers*, edited by Philip Schaff. Ebook. Grand Rapids: Eerdmans, 1978.

Clement of Alexandria. *"Who Is the Rich Man that Shall Be Saved?"* In *Ante-Nicene Fathers*, vol. 2, 591–604. Peabody, MA: Hendrickson, 1994.

Crenshaw, Kimberlé. "Why Intersectionality Can't Wait." In Theory column, *The Washington Post*, September 24, 2015. https://www.washingtonpost.com/news/in-theory/wp/2015/09/24/why-intersectionality-cant-wait/?utm_term=.57d0384a6d96.

Daly, Mary. *Beyond God the Father: Toward a Philosophy of Women's Liberation*. Boston: Beacon, 1973.

---

31. Lilienfeld, "How Student Evaluations are Skewed," and Jaschik, "Unintended Help for Male Professors."

D'Angelo, Mary R. "Blessed the One Who Reads and Those Who Hear: The Beatitudes in their Biblical Contexts." In *New Perspectives on the Beatitudes*, edited by Francis A. Eigo, 45–92. Villanova, PA: Villanova University Press, 1995.

Eklund, Rebekah. *Jesus Wept: The Significance of Jesus' Laments in the New Testament*. Library of New Testament Studies. London: Bloomsbury T&T Clark, 2015.

Field, Frederick. *Joannis Chrysostomi Homiliae in Mattheum*, vol. 1. Cambridge, 1839.

Gregory of Nyssa. *The Lord's Prayer; The Beatitudes*. Ancient Christian Writers. Translated by Hilda C. Graef. Mahwah, NJ: Paulist, 1954.

Gutiérrez, Gustavo. *The God of Life*. Maryknoll, NY: Orbis, 1991.

Gutting, Gary. "A Feminism Where 'Lean In' Means Leaning on Others: An Interview with Nancy Fraser." The Stone (blog). *Opinionator*. October 15, 2015. http://opinionator.blogs.nytimes.com/2015/10/15/a-feminism-where-leaning-in-means-leaning-on-others/?_r=1.

Hinsdale, Mary Ann. "Blessed are the Persecuted . . . Hungering and Thirsting for Justice: Blessings for Those Breaking Boundaries." In *New Perspectives on the Beatitudes*, edited by Francis A. Eigo, 161–89. Villanova, PA: Villanova University Press, 1995.

Incomplete Commentary on Matthew (Opus imperfectum). Ancient Christian Texts, vol. 1. Edited by Thomas C. Oden. Downers Grove, IL: IVP Academic, 2010.

James, Laura. *A Sermon for our Ancestors* 2006 (acrylic on canvas), inspired by Matt 5:1–14 (Laura James/private collection/Bridgeman Images). The images are included in Willie James Jennings, "Overcoming Racial Faith," *Divinity Magazine*, Spring 2015, 4–9.

Jaschik, Scott. "Unintended Help for Male Professors." *Inside Higher Ed*, June 27 2016. https://www.insidehighered.com/news/2016/06/27/stopping-tenure-clock-may-help-male-professors-more-female-study-finds.

Leo the Great. "Letters and Sermons: Sermon 95.5." In *Nicene and Post-Nicene Fathers*, 2nd ser., vol. 12, edited by Philipp Schaff and Henry Wace. Ebook. Peabody, MA: Hendrickson, 1994.

Lilienfeld, Eva. "How Student Evaluations Are Skewed against Women and Minority Professors." *The Century Foundation*, June 10, 2016. https://tcf.org/content/commentary/student-evaluations-skewed-women-minority-professors/.

Quash, Ben. *Found Theology: History, Imagination and the Holy Spirit*. London: Bloomsbury, 2013.

Schneiders, Sandra M. *Beyond Patching: Faith and Feminism in the Catholic Church*, revd. ed. Mahwah, NJ: Paulist, 2004.

———. *The Revelatory Text: Interpreting the New Testament as Sacred Scripture*. Collegeville, MN: Liturgical, 1999.

Tamez, Elsa. *Bible of the Oppressed*. Maryknoll, NY: Orbis, 1982.

———. "Women's Rereading of the Bible." In *With Passion and Compassion: Third World Women Doing Theology*, edited by Virginia Fabella and Mercy Amba Oduyoye, 173–80. Maryknoll, NY: Orbis, 1994.

Williams, Rowan. "Historical Criticism and Sacred Text." In *Reading Texts, Seeking Wisdom*, edited by David F. Ford and Graham Stanton, 217–28. Grand Rapids: Eerdmans, 2003.

Winner, Lauren F. "Interceding: Standing, Kneeling, and Gender." In *The Blackwell Companion to Christian Ethics*, 2d ed, edited by Stanley Hauerwas and Samuel Wells, 264–76. Malden, MA: Wiley-Blackwell, 2011.

13.

The Uselessness of God: Failure as Political Resistance

SILAS MORGAN

Introduction

IN THE SPRING OF 2010, something quite remarkable happened. The world stood up for philosophy. At the end of April 2010, the University of Middlesex (UK) announced it was shuttering the entire Philosophy department because it made no "measurable" contribution to the university. This was an example of a trend of closing down, contracting, or suspending humanities provisions by the university management. This effort was met by a thunderous global response: a massive wave of public support and student protest, accompanied by letters of support by notable academic voices around the world. It became a touchpoint for a variety of struggles, most importantly the reception of the austerity movement in Europe after the global economic crash of 2008, and the conflict between university management who are trying to ditch the humanities for more vocational and practical training in the STEM fields, where the university believed they could make more money.

By choosing to close what was, by all metrics, a successful department, the university ostensibly claimed that the study of philosophy could not be properly monetized and so was of no practical use to the university or its students. Rather than defending the department by touting its economic successes, its utility to its students or by making the case for its usefulness to the university, the SAVE MDX PHIL campaign insisted that the cardinal virtue of philosophy and the humanities disciplines more broadly—the reason why they must be studied by students and protected by the broader public—was that they were indeed useless to industry, that they could not be monetized, and did not conform to the logics of competition and market forces—that they did not belong in a factory. The global campaign to save the Middlesex philosophy department ended in a partial victory. It was relocated to Kingston University in July 2010.

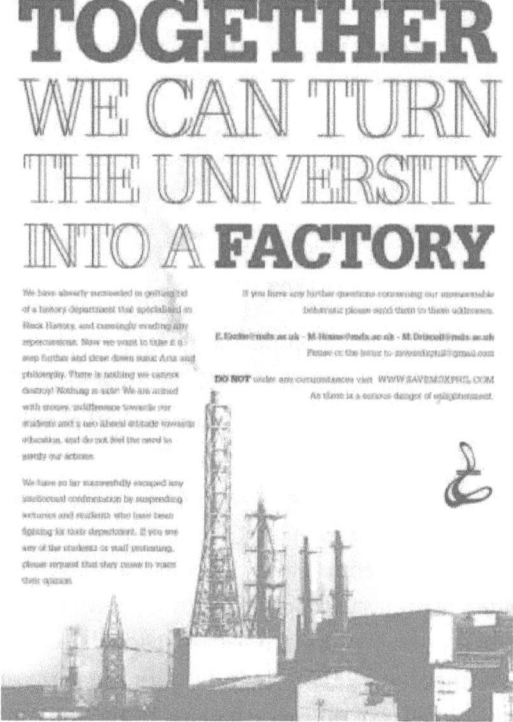

In recent years, it has become commonplace (almost to the point of being cliché) for theology (and theologians who write it) to emphasise its usefulness, to insist that theology is at its best when it is put to work. Whether in reference to shaping cultural norms, motivating social action, or interpreting aesthetic experiences, the adequacy of theology is judged by its ability to be useful, not only within communities of faith, but also in public. What makes theology good for something is its ability to be put to work.

Emphasizing the "publicness" of theology is one such example of this trend. In order to place theology firmly in the center of everyday life, theologians work very hard to convince whoever may be watching or reading that theology is not *that* strange, that its ideas and formulations deserve their rightful place in public discourse, perhaps even in political decision-making, and as such has great practical value. This is an important trajectory, not only in contemporary theology but also in contemporary political thought, as theorists and philosophers have consistently weighed in on how best to approach the function and use of theology when it goes public, at times speaking in terms of the *power* of religion in the public sphere (as Cornel West does[1]) and at others exploring the semantic *value* of theology when translated into the norms of the democratic constitutional state and its conception of human rights (in Jürgen Habermas's recent work on the subject).[2]

All this talk of power, use, and value takes place in the context of neoliberalism as the economic and social system, which determines what is possible and what makes sense—what registers as real in our world. Neoliberalism is not just a set of ideas that make up the driving force of our global economic matters; rather, it is that which defines political possibility. It sets the parameters, the paradigms in which all political actions are intelligible. It makes public acts sensible; it allows discourse to work, to fit, to count in the first place. Against this backdrop, I offer an apology for the uselessness of theology, the pointlessness of its substantive offerings to the world—namely, I suggest that the benefit of theology—what theology may be good for in these neoliberal times—is that it fails, it loses, it falls short. By not fitting within the coordinates set for it by neoliberalism, it sheds light on a different way, an alternative set of possibilities for human thinking, living, and relating outside the norms of use and function—the scripts of "having a point." The virtue of such a useless position should not be lost, for when the public context of theology is neoliberalism, when this force plays such a dominant role that it shapes human values, behaviors, tastes, and so on, failure is a gift to the discourse and the communities and institutions that use theology to structure their practices and give meaning to their lives.

1. West, "Prophetic Religion," 92–101.

2. This turn was first seen in Habermas, "Notes on Post-Secular Society," 17–29, with further developments in Habermas, "An Awareness of What Is Missing," 15–24.

Michel Foucault, whose own relationship to neoliberalism is debated, spoke of "governmentality" as that technique of discursive regimes that operationalize particular values, normalizing them into the very symbolic systems through which human beings form and act out (of) their subjectivity.³ Put differently, these symbolic systems are the very things that human beings rely on to make sense of themselves as selves-among-others, to position themselves in the arrangements and attachments that confer recognition and bestow responsibility. It is these attachments and arrangements that comprise the political and so the great risk—the central drama of the case—lies in the inability of thought, theological or otherwise, to escape it, to do that which it best to do, to think outside of power: to be useless.

I believe that "uselessness" or "pointlessness" is the paradigmatic form of failure in a neoliberal context, and so I want to argue that, in such a context, the highest form of resistance and dissent is to embrace failure, and thus find ways to encourage and sustain the political subject, and also help generate the social habits and political practices necessary for the publics and communities of faith who support these subjects in their failing, losing, inefficient, and noncompetitive ways.

Neoliberalism—"It's the Market, Stupid."

The turn to political theology in North America was born out of global crisis: the aftermath of industrialized war in Europe and the Asian Pacific (1950s), the rise of right-wing military dictatorships in Central and Latin America funded by the US (1960s), and the threat of nuclear war with the USSR (1960s–the late 1980s). With the fresh memories of Christian silence about genocide, and complicity in ethnic, military, and state-sponsored violence, political theology has emphasized divine solidarity with the victims of history, the moral demand to advocate for the socially and politically marginalized, and attention to the contexts of human experience and historical nature of reality. This emphasis has put pressure on the tension within binaries that have long existed at the center of Christian thought: the relationship between the active and

---

3. Foucault, *Security, Territory, Population*, 1.

contemplative,[4] between leisure and labor,[5] between the mystical[6] and the political.[7] While there have been attempts to combine or reconcile these binaries, their tensions within political theology as a whole have persisted, leading to a strong emphasis on social justice, political activism, and attention to specific public policy goals, such as homelessness,[8] mass incarceration,[9] and environmental conservation.[10] Good theology is *useful* theology—words and ideas, beliefs and practices that *work*, that agents can use to *do* something. What does the failure of theology mean in a context of mounting pressure on theologies to be useful, to shape our social world, to be meaningful in public and political spheres? Answer to these questions are complicated by the fact that theology must also contend with neoliberalism, the dominant ideology at work in our world today.

The critical humanities, as an approach to disciplinary struggles of the liberal arts, must reckon with the forces most at work in its context. Political theorists such as Noam Chomsky and David Harvey[11] have argued that the conditions that shape human life and work are most shaped by the forces of neoliberalism, a frequently cited term that is rarely understood, but nevertheless determines the structure and function of success and failure in our time.

Harvey insists that with all its focus on economics, neoliberalism is a fully political project, aimed at recovering the wealth and power of the capitalist class, lost in the advance of social movements in the 1960s and 1970s, not only in the US but around the world.[12] One of the major victories of these movements was the success of worker organizations

---

4. Coakley, *God, Sexuality, and the Self*.

5. Pieper, *Leisure, the Basis of Culture*.

6. This is best represented by a trajectory of conservative US Catholic theology that finds inspiration from a *ressourcement* of patristic and medieval theologies. Cf. Griffiths, "Theological Disagreement," 23–36; Hütter, *Suffering Divine Things*; McIntosh, *Discernment and Truth*.

7. Here I am thinking of the two or three classic figures in European political theology, Johann Baptist Metz, Dorothee Sölle, and Jürgen Moltmann. See Metz, *Faith in History and Society*; Sölle, *Political Theology*; *Suffering*; Moltmann, *The Crucified God*.

8. For example, see Bouma-Prediger and Walsh, *Beyond Homelessness*.

9. Levad, *Redeeming a Prison Society*; Taylor, *The Executed God*.

10. McFague, *The Body of God*; Keller, *Face of the Deep*; Kim and Koster, eds., *Planetary Solidarity*.

11. Touraine, *Beyond Neoliberalism*; Chomsky, *Profit over People*.

12. Harvey, *A Brief History of Neoliberalism*, 19.

and labor unions in securing collective bargaining and profit sharing agreements that effectively redistributed capital to workers, creating stability and mobility for working class and middle class communities. Neoliberalism was, in effect, the product of a strategic development to curtail these developments and use the global crises of the 1970s as tactical occasions to set in motion waves of privatization, deregulation, and cuts to social programs aimed at the common good. Neoliberalism valorizes the Market above all else, and considers competition the best mode by which to reward economic and political power.[13] If one wins in a neoliberal world, it must be because one deserves to; those who lose or fall behind do so as a result of their weakness and inefficiency. This supposed meritocracy, of course, assumes a number of things about social reality and global economic life that are just quite simply false: not everyone starts at the same place or has access to the same set of resources, and the system is not set up to give everyone equal access to the same tools and opportunities.

Naomi Klein offers a trenchant account of neoliberal tactics in her *The Shock Doctrine*, in which she describes the series of crises—some manufactured, others used to their advantage—used by neoliberal powers to install massive changes and shifts in times during which people are afraid and distracted by pain and bewilderment.[14] She gives examples like tax cuts for the rich, outsourcing, privatization of education and prison systems, and the redistribution of wealth to the already rich at the expense of the poor. This "disaster capitalism"—a tactic developed and perfected by Milton Friedman and the Chicago school—follows a predictable "depatterning" strategy.[15] It starts with the original disaster: a coup, terrorist attack, an extreme weather event, or violent military conflict that creates massive instability, a breakdown and resetting of legal and ethical boundaries, and a reshuffling of political priorities. The social fabric of the state is broken, "softened up" by the catastrophic blows of objective violence, and the terror and fear that comes in the aftermath. Neoliberal forces use this disaster as a fog to obscure their actions from view.[16] While people

13. Ibid., 65.
14. Klein, *The Shock Doctrine*, 6–15.
15. Ibid., 32ff.
16. What makes neoliberalism challenging is its shadowy character; talking about neoliberalism makes one appear conspiratorial and paranoid because, as an ideological structure, neoliberalism rarely is identified or "seen" in public as itself, but rather takes the shape of various forces and forms which, by their nature, are abstract and

are distracted and overwhelmed, governments institute massive deregulation in favor of profiteering, sell public assets to private corporations, and drastically cut funding for social programs aimed at the economic and social advancement of working and middle classes.[17]

Once the population recovers from the original event, all of this shifting has been normalized, and most people do not object because they either are unaware or because they have more pressing matters to attend to: rebuilding after environmental disaster, protecting "homeland security," or social reconstruction after a civil war. Examples of this economic shock treatment are plentiful: the NATO attack on Belgrade in 1999 cleared the way for rapid series of privatizations of public goods and resources in the former Yugoslavia. The terrorist attack on New York and the Pentagon on 11 September 2001 launched the global "War on Terror", which has been almost completely for-profit enterprise, in which the global "homeland security industry" ensures the near constant flow of money and political power. After the 2004 Tsunami in South East Asia, as many communities were still reeling from the enormous human and economic loss, their seaside fishing villages in Sri Lanka were quickly turned into fancy seaside resorts before the people had the strength to resist or organize protests.

What is most instructive about Klein's account of how neoliberalism works is that while it valorizes competition and trusts fully in the aggressive apparatus of the Market to regulate itself and ensure that only the best ideas win, it is most effective when it works in secret, when it takes advantage of disasters—when no one is watching. This does not mean that no one actually believes in neoliberalism. Most of us do, we just do not know that we do. We are unconscious of how the way we live, relate, and consume sustains it and keeps its effects intact in our world.

---

hard to identify. They are akin to what Walter Wink famously termed, the "Powers-that-Be." To critique the Powers, one must first name them: identifying our experience of the pervasive ways they dominate our lives. Cf. Wink, *Naming the Powers*. It is important to note that Wink's trilogy was written in the immediate context of his experiences in Pinochet's Chile in the early 1980s, after which he attempted to name the Powers at work in what he saw and experienced in the lives of the oppressed and their oppressors.

17. Klein, *The Shock Doctrine*, 9.

"Simply for the Love and Delight of It"—Theology as a Critique of Instrumental Reason

The primary feature of neoliberalism is its ideological quality.[18] Ideology works insofar as its presence is excessive and transgressive to the point that it remains shadowy, anonymous, and undiscernible in public. Capitalist class solidarity finds its most explicit expression in the subjectivization processes by which it naturalizes "the Market" as social and political activity. For neoliberals, the most seductive aspect of the market is the way that it shapes the identity and agency of human beings. Not only does it regulate social and political possibilities, its real power lies in the way it determines the kind of persons that human beings become.

The bio-political nature of neoliberal power was prefigured in Michel Foucault's theory of "governmentality", in which he emphasized the managing, assessing, and monitoring of human beings as the central technology of discipline—the attempt to regulate society through the institutionalization of freedom, namely for market economies. The freedom of the individual is thus secured through the regulation and policing of the *demos*, for their own economic and political good. The most efficient way for a struggling economy to become great again is to allow for the state to become "governmental"—the collective must submit to some regulation, even if this means we lost a bit of personal liberty through debt, low wages, rising housing costs, loss of collective labor bargaining, loss of working class solidarity, and so on. The remaking of the world happens best through competition because the paradigms of the market stress test the social world, weeding out the weak and rewarding the strong, the effective, the efficient, the adaptive.

There are many ethical and political problems with neoliberalism: cuts to social spending, redistribution of wealth to the already rich at the expensive of the poor and vulnerable, devastating effects of deregulation on planetary health, the erosion of democratic politics. But the problem with neoliberalism from a theological perspective is that it sets up a theology of success based purely on competition and instrumental reason, with no sense of values like love, justice, or solidarity, all of which I see as

18. By ideology, I do not follow the Marxist contention that ideology is "false consciousness," but rather that ideology is yet another form of consciousness, the defining feature of which is that it is so ubiquitous so as to be hidden from view. This conception of ideology as "the Big Other" is mostly attributable to Slavoj Žižek, who borrows this term from the psychoanalytic theory of Jacques Lacan. See Žižek, *The Sublime Object of Ideology*.

the hallmark commitments of Christian theological ethics. It appears in our social space, not a set of beliefs that can be objected to or opposed, but as a pseudonymous force that disguises itself through a set of abstract names, none of which get to the heart of the theological problem: "economic inequality," "globalism," "the decline of American manufacturing," "free trade," personal liberty," and the worse of all, "usefulness"—or what the Frankfurt School called "instrumental reason."

In the early 1930's, the theorists of the early the Frankfurt School put forward their infamous critique of the Enlightenment, which they saw as responsible for the "irrationality" of instrumental reason. The Enlightenment turned reason against itself, allowing it to become instrumentalized and, in so doing, created the opportunity for domination, the structure of which is based on the privilege of the instrumentally useful versus the Inherently Valuable. The latter—the site of critique itself—became eclipsed by the accompany culture industry, so much so that "anyone who resists can survive only by being incorporated. Once registered as diverging from the culture industry, they belong to it as the land reformer does to capitalism."[19]

Max Horkheimer names the wide spread influence of instrumental reason, noting that even "the average man will say that reasonable things are things that are obviously useful." The techniques of "classification, inference, and deduction . . . the abstract functioning of the thinking mechanism," are used to determine what is reasonable[20], rather than the exploration of what helps human persons thrive, or what ideas best serve the values that keep human beings free, equal, and linked by community. Instrumental reason elevates usefulness because it is equated with one's self-preservation; it divides human persons, qualitatively shifting identities and relations as factors in competitive relations, fully oriented to the survival of the individual *tout court*.

The Uselessness of Religion, the Pointlessness of Theology

Concerning the role that religious traditions and practices have in fostering resistance, womanist theologian and ethicist Keri Day points out that neoliberalism is not merely an analytic category, or a "really existing"

---

19. Horkheimer and Adorno, *Dialectic of Enlightenment*, 104.
20. Horkheimer, *Eclipse of Reason*, 3.

set of economic conditions, but it is most importantly, "a rationality that structures and governs human conduct and behaviour within societies that employ markets."[21] Central to this rationality is competition and so it has an invested interest in seeing human persons understand themselves and their relations as instrumentalities that are useful for accumulating material goods and social power; it all about gaining leverage in a competitive environment of scarcity, a scarcity that is generated by the market for the sake of increasing the stakes of enterprise participation.

The notable way that Keri Day sets up the link between theology and religion and neoliberalism is not the idea that neoliberalism shows itself to be religious rationality, an argument that would follow along the lines of Walter Benjamin's forceful diagnosis about capitalism. Thankfully, she instead focuses on "neoliberalism as a type of rationality and governmentality that reshapes and transforms the human subject within our modern global context."[22] Neoliberalism is more than a set of ideas about how markets run or an economic value system. What is most dangerous about neoliberalism, Day writes, is that, as a "normative rationality," "it aims to create a different community of persons,"[23] guided and governed by competition and individual freedom instead of cooperation, social responsibility, and solidarity across difference.

How might theology resist neoliberalism's hold on modern democracies and their political subjects? How might theology offer an alternative narrative by which human beings might be able to see a different way forward for themselves other than capitulation to neoliberalism? Day is eager to caution us that religion (much less theology) does not have a stellar record of resistance against hegemonic forces. Its history is ambiguous: it has both disrupted and legitimated neoliberal values. If we are to look to theology as a form of resistance against neoliberalism, theology must be able to counter neoliberalism in its attempt to make cooperation or collaboration appear impossible or unrealistic, to make ethnic, religious, and political difference appear as obstacles, not catalysts, to human well-being and social justice. What religion can do in this context is to set forth alternative possibilities, to ender creative and imaginative

---

21. Day, *Religious Resistance to Neoliberalism*, 8.
22. Ibid.
23. Ibid., 9.

futures, to think the human, its social world, and its affective relations otherwise.[24]

I agree. But I do wonder if this goes far enough. Theology, in Day's account, is useful insofar as it engages in the "art of the possible" by setting forth new visions of living, caring, and relating outside the economy of competition and radical self-interest. Such visions gain purchase when they are able to, indeed, compete with neoliberalism in the race to become central, organizing principles of social life. It seems to me that theology, if it hopes to properly counter neoliberalism, must decouple itself from the syntax of usefulness, and so give up on having a point, indeed, empty itself of all claims to do anything at all. It must recapture what the early theorists of the Frankfurt school called the "inherently valuable," which was opposed to the "instrumentally useful." Theology needs to become "good for nothing," if it hopes to fail, and to do so properly. It is not sufficient to defend uselessness as a mode of failure that is the opposite of success. In order to be immanently critical of usefulness, failure must open up conceptual and practical spaces outside and beyond the dialectic of success and failure, and so speak to the possibilities that failure opens up for thinking of God beyond instrumental reason.

To speak of the uselessness of God leads to obvious implication: the pointlessness of theology; that is, if God has no point, then theology—the discipline tasked with the responsibility of speaking about God—has no point. If it is pointless, it has no status in a neoliberal system, it gains no advantage, it does not compete within an institutional apparatus. It has no power, it has no prestige, it has no legitimacy. In a word, theology fails, and, in the process of this failure, it frees itself. By never being realized, by never having a point, it gains an ability to offer conspiratorial resources for resistance. Resistant thought, ideas outside the discursive regime of governmentality, is thought that declares itself useless to such a system and so is discarded and left behind.

Proud defences of theology's pointlessness come from the strangest of places. Terry Eagleton, the British Marxist literary critic, turns out to also be an apologist for Christianity. This may seem scandalous, but it's also true. Eagleton, in an effort to fend off the ill-spirited invectives of the New Atheist critique of religion, has attempted to recast Christianity not in an effort to save it, but rather to correct their misrepresentation of it, and to give his readers a chance to consider a Christianity that is worth

24. Ibid., 12.

rejecting. Central to Eagleton's political reading of Christianity is to highlight the pointlessness of God and how it issues a resounding critique of modern secular culture and its levelling. "God, in short, is every bit as gloriously pointless as Ditchkins tells us he is," Eagleton writes. "He is a kind of perpetual critique of instrumental reason."[25] God is dangerous because it counters the neoliberal idea that instrumental use of something for competitive advantage in the marketplace replaces inherent value: "God the Creator is not a celestial engineer at work on a superbly rational design that will impress his research grant body [to] no end, but an artist and an aesthete to boot, who made the world with no functional end in view, but simply for the love and delight of it."[26] God has no need for anything else other than God. "If we are God's creatures, it is in the first place because, like him, we exist (or should exist) purely for the pleasure of it."[27] With such a pointless God as its primary subject, theology is freed to embrace its uselessness and so take up with playful abandon its task of using the logics of God and God's love for the world to counter the leveling and dominating irrationality of neoliberalism's desire to instrumentalize relations and affections for competitive advantage, all towards success in the "marketplace" (financial security, social status, personal branding). Eagleton waxes on:

> To see God as completely pointless, and the moral life as much the same, is not to deny that instrumental reason has its place. There would, for example, be no emancipatory politics without it, and no science and technology either. Aesthetics are seduced by the beauty and sensuous particularity of things, theologians by the fact that their existence is so mind-bendingly contingent, while scientists and technologists have to press these things into the knowledge and service of humankind, and so cannot afford to spend all their time emitting grunts of pleasure or shouts of astonishments. Even so, on this theological view, morality is quite as pointless as the universe itself. . . . This self-delighting energy, which is entirely without point or function, stands in no need of justification before some grim-faced tribunal of History, Duty, Geist, Production, Utility or Teleology."[28]

---

25. Eagleton, *Reason, Faith, and Revolution*, 10.
26. Ibid., 8.
27. Ibid., 10.
28. Ibid., 13–14.

The implication here is that if theology is pointless, then it is also useless—it is good for nothing. And while this offends the neoliberal sensibilities that instrumentalizes reality for the sake of putting it to work, this is what makes theology *theo*-logical. Theology speaks of—gives words to—the sure gratuity of God's presence in the world that has no intelligibility within human reason or language. The apophatic tradition has always struggled to maintain this balance: humans desire to give expression to their experiences of desire for God, and then the very nature of God always transcends and confounds human attempts to instrumentalize it; language—indeed even reason—is a failure of representation, that it quickly becomes ideological in its tendency to take language and put it to work, to try to use it to render God useable, to give God a point, to make God do something for us. While this tendency is as old as human language, it takes a distinctly post-Enlightenment political turn, one identified by the early Frankfurt theorists as an irrationality which in itself turns reason into a force of domination and oppression.

Critical Theory Strikes Back

The modality by which uselessness is made political is *failure*, a pejorative rendering of theology as pointless by a neoliberal framework that highly values the competitive edge that ideas (that have a point, that are made to be an instrument) give those who wield them. Luckily, failure has a theory, and all the more fortunate still, it is a queer one. The predominant theorist of failure is Jack Halberstam, whose *The Queer Art of Failure* offers something of a manifesto on the subject.[29]

Halberstam's primary thesis in *The Queer Art of Failure* that there is something peculiar about failure that coincides with queer existence as a way of being in the world that opens up new relationships and attachments to knowledge, memory, affectivity, and so on. This retheorization of failure calls upon acts of stupidity, silliness, and forgetfulness as negative ways of being, unknowing, and anti-sociality that resist and mock predominant logics of success, power, (re)production, and power. And so, to fail is to affirm oneself entirely outside the aura of neoliberal legitimacy: it is to have no point, it is to no longer count, to not matter. It is Halberstam's goal to reframe failure as

---

29. Halberstam, *The Queer Art of Failure*.

a way of refusing to acquiesce to dominant logics of power and discipline and as a form of critique. As a practice, failure recognizes that alternatives are embedded already in the dominant and that power is never total or consistent; indeed failure can exploit the unpredictability of ideology and its indeterminate qualities.[30]

Furthermore, Halberstam presents failure as a queer strategy for life and persistence, amidst cultural formulations and dominative social forces that constrain and regulate all forms of knowing, acting, and being according to conventional logics of success, such as neoliberalism, heteronormativity, and advanced market capitalism. Failure emerges as a queer "art of existence" that is uniquely capable of incubating and generating *critical* forms of thought and knowledge that clear space for alternative ways of life. These political formulations take a dark turn: they are antisocial, antihumanist, and negative forms of life, modeled on relational dynamics of atemporality, disjunction, dissensus, and unbecoming. This kind of unplugging is necessary to counter the dominative logics of success, many of which run along disciplinary, generational, and reproductive lines, and have often been the obstacles to the persistence and survival of queer life.[31]

If failure is the way forward, this queer art of existence, all beware! For Halberstam, failing, losing, or getting lost is not to be celebrated or lifted up as this hidden, hopeful path of redemption or liberation.[32] To fail is to stutter, to fall, to stumble; it is the way of bleakness, of futility, of emptiness, and of loss.[33] The affective register for failed thought is defeat, sterility, and vacuity: "to fail [is] to make a mess, to fuck shit up, to be loud, unruly, impolite, to breed resentment, to back, to speak up and out, to disrupt, assassinate, shock, and annihilate."[34] To mistake failure for a kind of 'mystical nihilism'[35] is to miss the point about what is important about how the ways of knowing and living that failing generates and losing sustains work to (trans)form the queer political subject. Childish and pointless, acts of failure and of losing may indeed transgress and exceed the common-sense boundary of the sober 'grown up', but the thesis here

30. Ibid., 88.
31. Ibid., 70–74, 124–125.
32. Ibid., 120–121.
33. Ibid., 23.
34. Ibid., 110.
35. Critchley, *Faith of the Faithless*, 103–155.

is that the space opened up by the anarchy of stupidity, of forgetfulness, of silliness helps us get beyond the regulative norms and use negative affects to undermine and expose the fallacies and false promises in the toxic positivity and optimism of contemporary life.[36] And so, acts of failing and losing are rude, disorderly, and uncivil events that question whether disciplinarity, legibility, mastery, and memory as strategies of success really provide the best avenue for queer ways of life. When neoliberalism sets the standards for success, perhaps we are all better off as failures.

It is true that looking to failure to open up an alternative way of being may be read as both utopian *and* nihilist. Halberstam counters this by refusing to counter: failure is a decisively *queer* art, one that comes out of the concrete bodily experience of queer life, struggle, and persistence. We are reminded by the queer art of failure that queer theory has never sought to be a program, that, in all its agonist hybridities and multiplicities, it has consistently eschewed anything like official recognition, establishment, or institutionalization. It has never tried to be normal, or, in a word: to be successful. Embracing the naive, the nonsensical, and incivility arises from the subjugated knowledge of queer persons and bodies who have persisted nevertheless in a world that has been constructed specifically to make their lives unlivable.[37] It is clearly discernible, then, how failure also entails a particularly queer form of politics. Beside the antisocial, anti-humanist, and anarchist aspects, failure introduces a ruptural politics of negativity that does not seek anything resembling a revolutionary politics, but rather one of critical resignation. What might a theology look like that has taken up failure as a critical category for thinking the political and the theological together in a such a way that eschews political praxis for something much more inaugural and interventionary?

Failing as a queer way of life commits oneself to "not being taken seriously", and "losing one's way."[38] This directly confronts the regulatory and formatives tactics of institutions, guilds, and disciplines, all of whom depend on the normalizing standards of legitimacy and respectability. For queer folk, existing outside the domain of the normal is both the contested site of struggle and for flourishing. Edelman reminds us that, "queerness can never define an identity; it can only ever disturb one."[39] It

---

36. Halberstam, *The Queer Art of Failure*, 186.
37. Butler, *Precarious Life*, 146.
38. Halberstam, *The Queer Art of Failure*, 6.
39. Edelman, *No Future*, 17.

is this way that we can think about queer, not as a marker of identity or even of sexuality, but as that which names a specific relation to power:

> "Queer"... acquires its meaning from its oppositional relation to the norm. Queer is by definition whatever is at odds with the normal, the legitimate, the dominant. There is nothing in particular to which it necessarily refers. It is an identity without an essence. "Queer," then, demarcates not a positivity but a positionality vis-a`-vis the normative—a positionality that is not restricted to lesbians and gay men but... available to anyone... marginalized because of her or his sexual practices.[40]

As a liberatory act, failure is a queer art of existence because it is a position of resistance and non-obeisance to that which is deemed right and successful. It can become a queer theological art by likewise refusing respectability and civility, actively calling to question the kind of regulatory, normalizing, and exclusionary practices that mark the life of our faith communities, our academic institutions, and our disciplinary guilds. By refusing order, and legibility, failure as a queer theological art takes up the affective register of rage, impoliteness, and disrespect in an effort to liberate itself from the toxic power of competition and the seductive pose of the normal which are required to satisfy the script expected for belonging or commendation. It must no longer try to be taken seriously, but instead must present itself as a stupid alternative, an alien threat to the conventional logics of the guilded, the powerful, and the disciplinary. Failure and our failings also shifts us away from actionist political projects by depriving theology of any self-satisfaction or moral sentimentality. Such failings are not desirable by any means (failure cannot merely be success by another name), but are nevertheless generative because they move us to do things differently, to take a breath and do something again, to sustain our protest and dissent in all its anxiety-provoking, and fear-inducing beauty.

Conclusion

So, if theology hopes to be a resource for resistant thought—useless thought that has as its object "that which has no point"—it must succeed at failure, namely that it must fail to be successful. But what does it mean for theology to be successful today? Of course, it depends on who you

---

40. Halperin, *Saint Foucault*, 62.

ask, but there is notable consensus that theology must somehow contribute to establishing justice, peace, reconciliation, nonviolence, equality, and order. Theology must be practical, and by that I mean, that it must generate actual praxis. It must address the tram lines of "race, sex, class, and gender" and actively confront concrete challenges in practical and actionable ways. *Theology must do work*. Theology must be praxis, and in absence of this, it is at best empty, and at worst, insidious. To counter this, a *critical* political theology embraces the idea of failing at praxis as a *Refusenik* stance towards its disciplinary policing of theological scripts. A theological account of failure, I argue, inaugurates a queer theological discourse that eschews outlining practical consequences or proposing actionist programs, based on itself, but is nevertheless thoroughly political in that it recognizes the critical-theoretical aspect of its work. It follows Theodor Adorno, for whom the refusal to translate critical theory into a program for political action often led to the improper charge of political passivity and resignation.[41] Yet, for Adorno, as for Jack Halberstam, it is indeed the call to practical activity that was most apathetic, most resigned to the current configuration of political possibilities.[42] It displays the inherent belief that the options before us are the best, or only ones, that we could think of, and that any suspension of action was not worth it; nothing really could ever change.

Yet, insofar as human emancipation is the common interest between queer theory, political theology, and critical theory, the real problem is that political theology all too often presumes to know exactly what human emancipation is and how to accomplish it. Learning failure as a queer theological art may help a critical political theology inhabit a more immanently critical posture of negativity (as Halberstam explains) so as to discover something we cannot (yet) know and a future we have not pretended to have already mastered. I think the problem is that useful theologies buy into the positivity of emancipation without recognizing their complicity in the toxic logic of success, dependent and reliant on

41. Adorno and Horkheimer's critical theory was often critiqued from the left for their "bourgeois idealist" refusal to involve themselves in active revolutionary struggles. Described as "the Grand Hotel Abyss" by Georg Lukacs in his indicting phrase, their theory consists "of nothing, of absurdity." This is *precisely* the point, says Halberstam. This is what it means for theory, and so too, for theology, to fail. For more on this, see Adorno, "Resignation," 165–68, and Adorno, "Critique," 281–88. Brittain connects this directly to political and liberation theology in his excellent *Adorno and Theology*, 114–39.

42. Adorno, "Resignation," 167.

the demands and configurations of the present. Useful theologies succeed by acting as if they know what ought to come and are unable to embrace justice, peace, and reconciliation (for example) for what they are: failed projects.[43]

The critical distance that a theological account of failure takes from praxis comes from a thoroughgoing distrust for political immediacy that would constrain or otherwise impinge upon the autonomy of theory. Rather than acquiesce to a fusion of theory and praxis that would try to guide and inspire a revolutionary politics, a *critical* political theology questions the dominant role of practicality that guides modern theological thought, disavowing any kind of purchase it may have on the present for the sake of unencumbered, free, and opening thinking that is unconstrained by current demands of actionable immediacy.

Making failure both a critical and theological art will, perhaps, better position theology to be able to respond to the inherent violence of the normal, to actualize a critical political theology that takes up a subversive posture of radical protest, eschewing hopeful and optimistic calls for a redemptive futurity, and opt instead for a "tearing down," a critical iconoclasm that reclaims the abnormal as a site of possibility for being and living. We might realize that our options for engaging the world theologically can move beyond doctrinal formulas, the (generational logic of) the history of ideas, and positive political agendas which seem all too sure what justice looks like and that reconciliation is always desirable. Instead, the queer art of failure might teach us theologians not only how to disrespectfully dissent from prevailing logics of success, but also how to fail, and to do so by becoming uselessness to a neoliberal regime eager to put us to work.

Bibliography

Adorno, Theodor W. "Resignation." *Telos* 1978, 165–168.

———. "Critique." in *Critical Models: Interventions and Catchwords*, 281–288. New York: Columbia University Press, 1998.

Brittain Christopher. *Adorno and Theology*. London: T&T Clark, 2010.

Bouma-Prediger, Steven, and Brian J. Walsh. *Beyond Homelessness: Christian Faith in a Culture of Displacement*. Grand Rapids: William B. Eerdmans, 2008.

Butler, Judith. *Precarious Life: The Powers of Mourning and Violence*. London: Verso, 2003.

---

43. These ideas have been shaped in large part thanks to conversations with Dr. Timothy McGee. I am grateful to him for his generosity of word and spirit.

Chomsky, Noam. *Profit over People: Neoliberalism and Global Order.* New York: Seven Stories, 1999.
Coakley, Sarah. *God, Sexuality, and the Self.* Cambridge: Cambridge University Press, 2013.
Critchley, Simon. *Faith of the Faithless.* London: Verso, 2012.
Day, Keri. *Religious Resistance to Neoliberalism: Womanist and Black Feminist Perspectives.* New York: NY: Palgrave Macmillian, 2015.
Eagleton, Terry. *Reason, Faith, and Revolution: Reflections on the God Debate.* New Haven, CT: Yale University Press, 2009.
Edelman, Lee. *No Future: Queer Theory and the Death Drive.* Durham, NC: Duke University Press, 2004.
Foucault, Michel. *Security, Territory, Population: Lectures at the College de France, 1977-1978,* ed. Michel Senellart. New York, NY: Palgrave MacMillian, 2004.
Griffiths, Paul "Theological Disagreement: What It is and How To Do It." CTSA Proceedings 69. 2014. https://ejournals.bc.edu/ojs/index.php/ctsa/article/view/5502/4984.
Hütter, Reinhard. *Suffering Divine Things: Theology as Church Practice.* Grand Rapids, MI: Eerdmans, 2010.
McIntosh, Mark A. *Discernment and Truth: The Spirituality and Theology of Knowledge.* New York: Crossroad/Herder, 2004.
Habermas, Jürgen. "Notes on Post-Secular Society." *New Perspectives Quarterly* 25.4 (2008) 17–29.
———. "An Awareness of What Is Missing." In *An Awareness of What Is Missing: Faith and Reason in a Post-Secular Age,* 15–23. Cambridge: Polity, 2010.
Halberstam, Judith. *The Queer Art of Failure.* Durham, NC: Duke University Press, 2011.
Halperin, David. *Saint Foucault: Towards a Gay Hagiography.* New York: Oxford University Press, 1995.
Harvey, David. *A Brief History of Neoliberalism.* New York: Oxford University Press, 2005.
Horkheimer, Max, and Theodor W. Adorno. *Dialectic of Enlightenment,* ed. Gunselin Schmid Noerr, trans. Edmund Jephcott. Stanford, CA: Stanford University Press, 2002.
Horkheimer, Max. *Eclipse of Reason.* New York: Oxford University Press, 1947.
Keller, Catherine. *Face of the Deep: A Theology of Becoming.* London: Routledge, 2003.
Kim, Grace Ji-Sun, and Hilda P. Koster, eds. *Planetary Solidarity: Global Women's Voices on Christian Doctrine and Climate Justice.* Minneapolis: Fortress, 2017.
Klein, Naomi. *The Shock Doctrine: The Rise of Disaster Capitalism.* New York: Metropolitan, 2014.
Levad, Amy. *Redeeming a Prison Society: A Liturgical and Sacramental Response to Mass Incarceration.* Minneapolis: Fortress, 2014.
McFague, Sallie. *The Body of God: An Ecological Theology.* Minneapolis: Fortress, 1993.
Metz, Johann Baptist. *Faith in History and Society: Toward a Foundational Political Theology.* New York: Seabury, 1979.
Moltmann, Jürgen. *The Crucified God: The Cross of Christ As the Foundation and Criticism of Christian Theology.* Minneapolis: Fortress, 1993.
Pieper, Josef. *Leisure, the Basis of Culture.* Translated by Alexander Dru. London: Faber and Faber, 1952.

Sölle, Dorothee. *Political Theology.* Translated by John Shelley. Philadelphia: Fortress, 1974.
———. *Suffering.* Philadelphia: Fortress, 1984.
Taylor, Mark L. *The Executed God: The Way of the Cross in Lockdown America*, 2nd edition. Minneapolis: Fortress, 2015.
Touraine, Alain. *Beyond Neoliberalism.* Cambridge: Polity, 2001.
West, Cornel. "Prophetic Religion and the Future of Capitalist Civilization." In *The Power of Religion in the Public Sphere*, ed. Eduardo Mendieta, 92–100. Columbia: Columbia University Press, 2011.
Wink, Walter. *Naming the Powers: The Language of Power in the New Testament.* Philadelphia: Fortress, 1984.
Žižek, Slavoj. *The Sublime Object of Ideology.* London: Verso, 1989.

14.

Pink Blankets, Sexual Violence, Moral Paralysis, and Christian Vocation

Elisabeth T. Vasko

Introduction

The box arrived on my birthday. Inside was a soft pink blanket tied with a silver ribbon.[1] Delighted, I sorted through the packing material for information about its sender. Finding nothing, I called my sisters. I posted a message on social media. The next morning, I crept downstairs to take another look. Perhaps the gift tag was *inside* the blanket and I had simply missed it. As I untied the ribbon, folds of soft pink material tumbled down around my feet. Instinctively, I wrapped my body in its warmth and was flooded with memories of childhood and my own daughter's infancy. Moments later, my five-year-old daughter woke up, ran downstairs, and cuddled me.

In the days that followed, the anonymity of this gift bothered me. I asked myself: was this gift really intended for me? Perhaps the postal carrier delivered it to the wrong house. I even entertained the possibility that the blanket was not a gift at all. Maybe it was a lice-infested present from a disgruntled student! (I washed it just in case.) One afternoon, upon waking from a deep slumber wrapped in the blanket's warmth, it dawned on me: my own discomfort with the gift had very little to do with this

1. This essay is dedicated to my goddaughter.

marvelous piece of pink fleece. I was frustrated because I could not mitigate the gift's gratuitousness by offering something in return. I could not thank the giver. I could not return it. All I could do was try to accept it. Yet, somehow, I felt I could only keep it if I could repay its sender. In this way, the blanket, while a small gesture within the contours of my history, pointed toward a much larger issue involving the triangulation of debt, love, and self-worth. In order to claim this gift as my own, I felt a need to experience myself as a person valuable enough to receive it. Further complicating my own acceptance of this gift are notions of love involving payment and obedience. As a victim-survivor of sexual violence, my capacity for embracing the Christian praxis of self-love continues to be haunted by ghosts, both personal and social.

In this essay, I begin to unpack the ways in which theoretical accounts of self-love have not fully attended to the practical effects and intergenerational impact of moral paralysis and self-hatred (the internalization of oppression). Drawing insight from the work of James Alison in *On Being Liked* and the biblical narrative in Acts 10:1–48, I draw out key markers for ecclesial identity and Christian vocation in the context of sexual violence.[2] I argue that Christian churches and the theological academy have a responsibility to shape future generations in the praxis of self-love. Love of self, when rightly ordered, holds the potential to break open cycles of violence. Yet, before doing so, it is important to get clear a few terms.

Key Terms: Love, Victim-Survivor, and the Collective We

First, *love*: At the heart of Christian vocation is a call to grow in love in the world. In its most basic sense, this call is rooted in the gospel imperative to love God, self, and neighbor (Mark 12:30–31).[3] As James Keenan explains, within Christian tradition, these three loves are interwoven: "love of God makes possible the love of self. And these together make possible the love of neighbor."[4] Yet, for many Christians, love of self drops out of the equation. As Edward Vacek points out, when asked, most Christians describe love in terms a loss of self for the sake of another, pointing to

---

2. Alison, *On Being Liked*, 100–113.

3. In this passage, Jesus also recalls Deuteronomy 6:4–5 and Leviticus 19:18. See Keenan, *Moral Wisdom*, 16.

4. Keenan, *Moral Wisdom*, 16.

Jesus' death on the cross as the exemplar for human expression.[5] Many have rightly critiqued this theological and ethical paradigm, drawing attention to the ways in which it fails to account for the lived experiences of women and minorities.[6] While we may have gotten the critique right, I am not convinced we know what the praxis looks like. This is important because authentic Christian love is relational and particular. We do not love abstract beings. We love people *in* their particularity, *because of* their particularity, and sometimes, *despite* their particularity.[7] The same is true for love of self and love of God. General sentiments—I love all black people, I love all queer people, I love all feminists—ring hollow apart from the work of real relationships.

Victim-survivor. The question of how one compassionately refers to those who have experienced sexual trauma is important. Many have argued that the language of *victim* removes agency from who have been violated. Yet, the exclusive use the term *survivor* not only places pressure on those who have survived sexual assault to always be models of strength and resilience, but it also plays into Western tendencies to "get past" the problem of sexual violence too quickly. Those of us who have experienced sexual trauma are survivors. We are not frail. We are strong and we are resilient. But, at the same, tremendous harm has been done to us—harm that has not always been recognized and continues to be silenced. For these reasons, I choose to adopt Traci C. West's term *victim-survivor* throughout this essay.[8]

Finally, my use of the collective *we* is intended as a signifier of solidarity within an academy and church that continues to call into question the credibility, rationality, sanity, and morality of those of us who speak out. As Susan J. Brinson suggests, "We need not speak *for* other survivors of trauma in order to speak *with* them."[9] What I present here should not

---

5. Vacek, *Love, Human and Divine*, 198.

6. A few examples include: Saiving, "The Human Situation"; Kamitsuka, "Toward a Feminist Postmodern and Postcolonial Interpretation of Sin"; Wimberly, *Moving from Shame to Self-Worth*; Townes, *A Troubling in My Soul*; and Weaver, *Self-love and Christian Ethics*.

7. In other words, my reference to Christian love throughout this essay is not in legalistic sense, but should be understand as a relational embodied praxis oriented toward the flourishing of the lover and the loved (self, other, the divine), in a particular social context. For more, see the sources cited in notes 4–6 above.

8. West, *Wounds of Spirit*, 5.

9. Brinson, *Aftermath*, 30. Another approach would also be Alcoff's "The Problem of Speaking for Others."

be taken as a standard for all members of a group. I think we need to get away from the all-or-nothing approach to contextual theologies and contextual spiritualties. Such a tendency is tied to the "deep suspicion of 'advocates' speaking out of their particular moral struggles, especially anyone who appears self-interested in making moral claims."[10] Within such a framework, where a "disinterested, 'pure' ethic above the rancor of social divisions and untainted by particular biases or interests" reigns supreme, competition instead of cooperation drives discourse.[11]

Sexual Violence and Community Trauma

Sexual violence is a global phenomenon. The World Health Organization estimates that one in three women worldwide will experience either physical and/or sexual intimate partner violence at some point in their lives.[12] Ethnicity, disability, and orientation increases the likelihood of victimization.[13] In the United States, surveys from the National Coalition Against Domestic Violence estimate that approximately one in five women will be raped in her lifetime. Contrary to common perception, one of the most dangerous places for women and children is the home, as seven out of ten instances of sexual assault are committed by someone known to the victim-survivor and 44 percent of victim-survivors are under the age of eighteen.[14] Sexual violence has lasting economic, emotional, and spiritual consequences.[15]

Jennifer Beste explains: "Trauma shatters persons' key assumptions regarding the self and one's relations to others in the world, including a sense of self-protection, personal invulnerability, and safety and

10. Ellison, *Making Love Just*, 5.

11. Ibid.

12. World Health Organization, Department of Reproductive Health and Research, London School of Hygiene and Tropical Medicine, South African Medical Research Council, *Global and Regional Estimates of Violence Against Women: Prevalence and Health Effects of Intimate Partner Violence and Non-Partner Sexual Violence* (2013), 2. See more at: http://www.unwomen.org/en/what-we-do/ending-violence-against-women/facts-and-figures#notes.

13. See European Union Agency for Fundamental Rights (2014). *Violence Against Women: An EU-Wide Survey*, Annex 3, 184–88. See more at: http://www.unwomen.org/en/what-we-do/ending-violence-against-women/facts-and-figures#notes.

14. "Perpetrators of Sexual Violence: Statistics."

15. For more on trauma and sexual violence see: Beste, *God and the Victim*; Copeland, *Enfleshing Freedom*; and Shoop, *Let the Bones Dance*.

predictability in the world."[16] Theologically speaking, sexual trauma can fracture the soul, rendering one silent before the cries of a compassionate God. In this way, sexual violence pushes up against the failures of God and the human community, occupying the space where God's heart stands still.

While sexual violence is a public health problem, it is not an infectious disease of the contagious kind, whose healing requires sterile environments, or sterilization. The silence and fear that leaves Christian communities tiptoeing around sexual violence is tied to systemic unknowing in racist heteropatriarchy. This is the kind of unknowing that asks safe questions in order to hear familiar answers. We cannot trick ourselves in believing that such silence stands on neutral grounds. In the absence of an ongoing praxis of truth-telling, such silence creates the perception of communal agreement. Silence is performative, giving shape to the stories we tell about ourselves, others, and the divine.

Despite increased awareness about the prevalence of sexual violence, there remains little substantive discussion about the moral challenges of racism, homophobia, and sexism, and other related social problems within religious communions and the academy. Sexual assault and domestic abuse continue to be understood as the problems of unfortunate individuals, whom we feel sorry for.[17] Even well-intended statements about God's unconditional love can appear illogical, connoting hypocrisy or benevolent paternalism, when uttered apart from a practical reckoning about the ways in which the body of Christ has participated in sexual injustices. This is for multiple reasons, two of which I highlight here. The first is tied to the question of a practical theodicy. As Traci C. West explains, "the abusive situation sets up a dynamic whereby the victim-survivor feels that 'love' can only be received it if is earned" via perfect obedience.[18] These feelings can be validated and replicated by patriarchal theological messaging that describes God as distant and punitive.[19] In such a model, love is painful and abuse falls easily within the paradigm of one's life.

Compounding this reality is gender socialization and the privileging of hegemonic masculinity in Western Christendom. Ellison explains,

---

16. Beste, "Receiving and Responding to God's Grace," 6.
17. Ellison, *Making Love Just*, 90.
18. West, *Wounds of the Spirit*, 61.
19. Ibid.

"men are regularly socialized to dominate in their interactions with women" and women are regularly socialized to be submissive in their interactions with men.[20] Drawing upon the work of Diana Scully, Ellison argues that rape is culturally constructed purposeful behavior that has a policing effect, punishing women who step out of line and teaching young girls to "recognize their own lack of worth."[21] In this way, sexual violence is a community problem.[22] It is a method of social control that continues to inform the self-image of women and men, girls and boys.

Most caregivers want their children to grow up knowing that they are loved and learning to love themselves. In a world marked by misogyny, xenophobia, and homophobia, we cannot assume this is the case. This point came to fore as I watched Hilary Clinton's 2016 presidential concession speech. As she spoke about the reality, failure, and pain of losing, I recalled an instance where I caught my daughter imitating my behavior in front of a mirror. In that moment, I felt scandalized—almost paralyzed. A self-actualized feminist would not pull her shoulders back and tuck her stomach in front of the mirror. By such standards, I would be declared negligent, vain, or both. These two ideological constructs are consonant with other instances in my life. A glance back further into my own social history places me in an impossible bind due to sexual violence, namely, how does a self-identified feminist end up in a situation, much less an intimate relationship, where she gets raped? How did she let heteropatriarchy get the best of her? My point is that even in progressive circles there continues to be a straight-and-narrow path for talking about sexual violence. And my silence is only partially indicative of the problem as I identify as a straight, white woman. Silence compounds moral paralysis and self-hatred on individual, intergenerational, and societal levels, and this precludes potent opportunities for community building, healing, and social transformation.

Moral Paralysis and Self-Hatred in a Violent World

In "Unbinding the Gay Conscience," James Alison makes a parallel point as he contextualizes the Roman Catholic Church's stance on same-sex relationships and gender-variant behavior in view of Peter's hesitation in

---

20. Ellison, *Making Love Just*, 84.
21. Ibid.; West, *Wounds of the Spirit*, 76.
22. West, *Wounds of the Spirit*, 55.

Acts 10 to include the Gentiles.²³ Peter's first response is marked by what Alison terms a double-bind: "You yourselves know that it is unlawful for a Jew to associate with or to visit a Gentile; but God has shown me that I should not call anyone profane or unclean."²⁴ According to Alison, a double-bind follows the basic formula of "I love you, but I do not love you," or "I can only love you if you become someone else." At issue, in Acts 10, is sociocultural and religious exclusion based upon purity codes. As Alison points out, today this translates into religious justifications for sexual and gender-based stigma. Contemporary examples might look like: "My command is that you should love, but your love is sick," or "You should just go away and die, but it is forbidden to kill yourself," . . . or "You cannot be gay, but you must be honest."²⁵ "I respect you, but you must obey to me," or "All persons are created *imago Dei*, but the question on women's ordination is closed," or "What you have to say is important, but you need to stop being so emotional," or "I believe you, but weren't you drinking that night?"

Double-binds, which are often conveyed through symbol systems and communal practices, produce situations in which the self has been formed by two contradictory desires. This process creates a trap, or catch-22, binding the conscience and constraining moral agency in the world.²⁶ Alison explains, "A bound conscience is one which cannot go this way or that, forwards or backwards, it is paralysed, scandalized. In that sense it is a form of living death."²⁷ To speak of a bound conscience is to speak of moral paralysis, trauma, and self-hatred in a violent world:

> The sort of person with the bound conscience is not able to stand up and be who they are. . . . The sort of person who labours instead in a world of half-truths, any belonging being a half belonging, because always "if they knew" then "I wouldn't really be allowed here."²⁸

---

23. Alison, *On Being Liked*, 100–13.
24. Acts 10:28. All biblical passages are from the NRSV unless otherwise specified.
25. Alison, *On Being Liked*, 103.
26. By the term *moral agency*, I mean realizing Christian love through the choices one makes. See Keenan, *Moral Wisdom*, 121.
27. Alison, *On Being Liked*, 103.
28. Ibid., 100.

This is what the Gospel writers refer to as *skandalon*—a scandal or stumbling block.²⁹ To question whether you belong every time you enter a room or to look in the mirror and wonder whether God made a mistake is to wrestle with the doctrine of the *imago Dei* at a practical level. This is to exist in the space of the cross, in spaces where God's heart stands still.

Christian Moralisms, Sexual Violence, and Silence: A.K.A. Teenage Sexual Ethics

Historically, heteropatriarchal Christianity has conceptualized the world in mutually exclusive and oppositional dualistic categories (i.e., good and bad, male and female, white and black).³⁰ Within the context of Christian sexual ethics, such a framework is generative of what Ellison calls moral minimalisms (or what I term teenage sexual ethics) insofar as "people become focused on compliance to a narrow, rules-based moral framework."³¹ Similar to Adam and Eve's hiding in the garden, the goal becomes figuring how to not get caught—or alternatively how to pass without garnering too much social attention. Ellison explains: Christian moralisms foster "a stunted ethical dependency on external authority (God, the bible, church authorities), which alone defines what is right. Within such a paradigm, the good Christian is expected to conform and to not outwardly complain."³² Simply put, Christian moralisms foster cultures of silence about sexual injustice on multiples planes. As Ellison argues, when "people are not expected to stretch their moral imaginations 'beyond the rules,' [they are] much less [likely] to tolerate in themselves or others the ambiguity and complex messiness of everyday life."³³

The capacity to embrace ambiguity is vital to loving and to the enactment sexual justice in society and in the church. As Ellison suggests, stigma "is often invoked around sex and sexuality such that a purity/pollution dichotomy differentiates those who are considered normal/good/clean from the spoiled/dangerous/and dirty."³⁴ It therefore matters a great deal who has the power to judge persons as morally good. While

---

29. Ibid., 103.
30. Ellison, *Making Love Just*, 30–31.
31. Ibid., 30.
32. Ibid.
33. Ibid., 31.
34. Ibid.

some groups are pushed to the outskirts of the community, labeled as hypersexual and therefore as "out of control," "others claim moral and spiritual superiority and the entitlement to enforce the rules."[35] This kind of sexual and spiritual hierarchy often appears in the form commonsense knowledge, but is very rarely named explicitly.

Teenage sexual ethics and double-binds lend toward scapegoating violence and the internalization of oppression. The call to discipleship is a call to grow in love. It is not a call to perfection nor is it a call to blind obedience.[36] Therefore, the fundamental question is whether we are courageous enough to become conduits of radical love. In contemporary society, this is an invitation to accompany in the spaces of trauma.

Sexual Trauma and Christian Vocation

At the end of Acts 10, in a quasi-redemptive move, Peter declares: "Can anyone withhold the water for baptizing these people [the Gentiles] who have received the Holy Spirit just as we have?"[37] In view of sexual trauma, this scriptural narrative points toward three key moments that prove to be fruitful starting points for shaping contemporary Christian responses at a practical level:

1. We must begin with a public acknowledgment that it is not only possible to preach *skandalon*, but, in heteropatriarchal contexts, it is highly probable. James Alison has illustrated that it is possible to preach the gospel in a way that represents a double-bind.[38] He reasons that "any presentation of the Christian faith which says 'I love you but I do not love you' or 'I don't love you as you are, but if you become someone different I will love you,' is preaching a double bind, a stumbling block, a pathway to paralysis."[39] Christians are morally responsible for the ways in which we proclaim the gospel in word and in deed. To be clear, Alison is not arguing that malappropriations of the Christian faith are solely responsible for sexual violence, violence against LGBTQ persons, white supremacy, and the internalization of these forms of hate. To proclaim a double-bind, unchecked, is to proclaim a failure of love. It is to suggest that a particular

---

35. Ibid.
36. Keenan, *Moral Wisdom*, 31.
37. Acts 10:47.
38. Alison, *On Being Liked*, 103–4.
39. Ibid., 104.

being or group has fallen between the cracks of God's all-encompassing embrace.

Double-binds also present pastoral and practical challenges for the well-intentioned. Often fear of failure prevents ecclesial and theological bodies from addressing sexual violence in public. Given the high prevalence of sexual and domestic violence, such silence it is morally irresponsible. However, justice is not an abstract reality. In a parallel fashion, neither is theological reflection. The most reliable way to discern if one is proclaiming a scandal is through relationship with others. Like Peter, everyone must risk making a mistake to ascertain whether they are preaching and reinforcing a double-bind.

2. We need to tell the truth about the cyclical nature of violence and our own participation in cycles of violence. Peter, the one who denied Jesus out of fear of being crucified himself, is reluctant to include the Gentiles (Acts 10:16, 36–43). In this way, Scripture memorializes trauma's capacity to fracture memory as it gives shape to communal identity. Under imperial reign, the cycle of violence continues, as the formerly scapegoated seek their own protection by ostracizing others, providing a poignant reminder that very rarely in history, religious or otherwise, are the lines between innocence and guilt starkly drawn. At times we all live and breathe in the space of what Alison terms the "Petrine backsliding from the Gospel."[40] Namely, we forget where we come from and who we are called to be.

Practically speaking, in the contemporary contexts marked by sexual violence, the narrative functions as a poignant call to join the conversation. All too often, sexual violence is relegated to the realm of white feminist concerns.[41] Yet, sexual violence is an intersectional reality. Narrow definitions and narrow conversations not only preclude those who have been victimized from recognizing harm done, but they also allow false notions of moral innocence to prevail within society. It is time to start talking about intersectional sexual justice with greater purpose and intentionality. The task at hand is "making the connections [explicit] between people's personal pain and larger social ills," including anti-gay oppression, male violence, and white supremacy.[42] Doing so requires privileged persons to tell the truth about the ways we have benefited from

---

40. Alison, *On Being Liked*, 102.

41. A similar thing could be said about LGBTQ violence being relegated to queer concerns and racism to the concerns of black and brown bodies.

42. Ellison, *Making Love Just*, 91.

the eroticization of power as dominance. For many, such is a harrowing task. On a personal level, it is painful to come to terms with the ways in which my body participates in the eroticization of violence against black and brown bodies and queer bodies, historical and present.[43] Yet, social reticence to engage these painful truths in my own community does little to facilitate healing at personal and societal levels.

Given the ways in which sexual violence continues to be hidden under the guise of social norms, truth-telling will not be the result of happenstance. Rather, it must be the result of a conscious decision, in which the sense of certainty that couches privileged persons' view of the world is exposed. From the kinds of "knowing" that privileged people consider credible, to unjust religio-cultural structures and symbol systems that we are willing to accept simply because they "do no harm to us," we must become vigilant about our own presumption of innocence. We are all called to be on the lookout for the ways in which our cravings for certainty crop up, tempting us to trade in image for truth-telling, and anxiety for justice. It is precisely for this reason that white heterosexual women cannot be left alone to theorize on sexual morality, nor the enactment of sexual justice in the church.

3. Failure is a vital part of compassionate and creative love. What Peter does is quite remarkable. He admits he was wrong, publicly (Acts 10:46–47). While Peter's context is different than that of contemporary Western culture, to admit a mistake or sin is to display weakness. In contemporary culture, displays of vulnerability are contrary to notions of hegemonic masculinity. In a highly competitive society, we are too quick to equate failure with a person's identity or being. In a hegemonic capitalistic system, children are taught that another's vulnerability is an opportunity for their own advancement. The term *weak* is quickly replaced with *failure*, becoming grounds for ostracization. At a young age, we begin to focus our attention on the failures of others, thus normalizing insecurity and denial of complicity in social problems. Such a framework translates into a very shallow definition of community, self, and identity.

Namely, in a climate marked by constant activity and social tolerance, it is easy to execute the moral imperative to love God, self, and

---

43. I am referring to the sociocultural and religious complexities of white guilt and the shame that many victim-survivors of sexual assault experience. The brevity of this essay prevents me from unpacking this important topic further. It deserves an essay of its own so as to allow for the necessary nuances in human experience, historical and present.

neighbor without ever taking the time to get know God, self, or neighbor. Frankly, "love at a distance" is easier and less risky than love that requires intimacy. We place constraints on our love so as to protect ourselves from getting hurt or rejected. Self-protection is important. Yet, this kind of love is too easily twisted into a lie.[44] This kind of love risks distortion into self-sacrifice unto the point of death. This kind of love can mean obedience to ideals that are unattainable.

When we love someone, we get to know them. This means acquiring the capacity for appropriate vulnerability. Appropriate vulnerability does not mean relinquishing bodily integrity or emotional safety. Appropriate vulnerability refuses to allow ones' self-expression (moral agency broadly construed) in the world to be bound by a politics of fear, guilt, and shame.[45] In a world where sins are not permissible or at least in one where they are equated with failure, truth-telling is stunted and moral innocence is encouraged. This is not to diminish the harm done. Rather, it is a call for a cultural shift in which we slow down and take time to get to know ourselves, our histories, and those who are around us. For when we are known and we know ourselves, accepting new challenges no longer appears as risky.[46]

History has always been full of change-makers, risk-takers, and people who have failed egregiously. Yet, many of us have been too busy to take notice and to learn from those who are living right beside us, past and present. The gifts of compassion and creativity take time. Compassion is often found in the life's unexpected, often inconvenient, but most beautiful pauses. Creativity requires idle time and play. When we become so focused on getting to the top or getting things done, we lose sight of who we are and who we are called to be.

Bibliography

Alcoff, Linda. "The Problem of Speaking for Others." *Cultural Critique* 20 (Winter 1991–1992) 5–32.
Alison, James. *On Being Liked*. New York: Continuum, 2003.
Beste, Jennifer. *God and the Victim: Traumatic Intrusions on Grace and Freedom*. New York: Oxford University Press, 2007.

---

44. Alison, *On Being Liked*, 107.

45. For some, this form of resistance will be surviving violence itself. For others, it will extend beyond this. For more, see West, *Wounds of the Spirit*, chapters 5 and 6.

46. Alison makes a similar point in *On Being Liked*, 108.

———. "Receiving and Responding to God's Grace: A Re-examination in Light of Trauma Theory." *Journal of the Society of Christian Ethics* 23.1 (2003) 3–20.

Brinson, Susan J. *Aftermath: The Remaking of A Self*. Princeton, NJ: Princeton University Press, 2002.

Brown, Joanne Carlson, and Rebecca Parker. "For God So Loved the World?" In *Violence Again Women and Children: A Christian Theological Sourcebook*, edited by Carol J. Adams and Marie M. Fortune, 36–59. New York: Continuum, 1995.

Copeland, M. Shawn. *Enfleshing Freedom: Body, Race, and Being*. Minneapolis: Fortress, 2009.

Ellison, Marvin. *Making Love Just: Sexual Ethics for Perplexing Times*. Minneapolis: Fortress, 2012.

European Union Agency for Fundamental Rights (2014). *Violence Against Women: An EU-Wide Survey*, Annex 3.

Kamitsuka, Margaret D. "Toward a Feminist Postmodern and Postcolonial Interpretation of Sin." *Journal of Religion* 84.2 (2004) 179–211.

Keenan, James. *Moral Wisdom: Lessons and Texts: From the Catholic Tradition*. 3rd ed. Lanham, MD: Rowman and Littlefield, 2017.

"Perpetrators of Sexual Violence: Statistics." https://www.rainn.org/statistics/perpetrators-sexual-violence.

Saiving, Valerie. "The Human Situation: A Feminine View." *Journal of Religion* 40.2 (1960) 100–12.

Shoop, Marcia Mount. *Let the Bones Dance: Embodiment and the Body of Christ*. Louisville, KY: Westminster John Knox, 2010.

Townes, Emilie, ed. *A Troubling in My Soul: Womanist Perspectives on Evil & Suffering*. Maryknoll, NY: Orbis, 1993.

Vacek, Edward Collins. *Love, Human and Divine: The Heart of Christian Ethics*. Washington DC: Georgetown University Press, 1994.

Weaver, Darlene. *Self-love and Christian Ethics*. Cambridge: Cambridge University Press, 2002.

West, Traci C. *Wounds of Spirit: Black Women, Violence, and Resistance Ethics*. New York: New York University Press, 1999.

Wimberly, Edward P. *Moving from Shame to Self-Worth: Preaching and Pastoral Care*. Nashville, TN: Abingdon, 1999.

15.

Failure and the Modern Academy

Elizabeth Newman

What does it mean to be an excellent college or university? George Bernard Shaw once famously said that a Catholic university is an oxymoron. He meant that "Catholic" negated the very idea of a university since Catholics had to acknowledge the authority of the church over academic freedom. Protestants only escaped such criticism because the ties between church and academy had already been minimized if not entirely severed. In most cases, the qualifier "Christian" had come to refer to campus ministry, service opportunities, religion courses, or denominational representation on certain boards. The excellent academy, one assumed, must move beyond the backwaters of Christian denominationalism, and instead embrace academic freedom and the pursuit of knowledge wherever it may be found.[1]

In what follows, I argue that this now dominant story is ultimately one of failure. Such a claim might seem ludicrous since quasi-Christian or formerly Christian institutions appear to be wildly successful, i.e., training future doctors, lawyers, business leaders, teachers, and so forth. The failure, however, lies in the conviction that faith is extrinsic to the true university. I argue that this framework, essentially gnostic, fails to register how communion is intrinsic to all being.

---

1. While there are exceptions to this narrative of Christians and higher education, the story that has captured the academic imagination by far is one of disengagement between the academy/disciplinary knowledge and church/faith. Especially helpful for analyzing this narrative are Burtchaell, *The Dying of the Light*; Marsden, *The Soul of the University;* and Sloan, *Faith and Knowledge*.

The Excellent University: A Case Study

Catholic educators understandably responded to the kind of criticism leveled by Shaw. In the 1960s, most notably, a prominent group of North American Catholics, led by Fr. Theodore Hesburgh, CSC, then president of Notre Dame, gathered to reassess the Catholic university, especially its relation to the church. Catholic universities, they emphasized, were first and foremost places of excellence:

> The Catholic university today must be a university in the full modern sense of the word, with a strong commitment to and concern for academic excellence. To perform its teaching and research functions effectively the Catholic university must have a true autonomy and academic freedom in the face of authority of whatever kind, lay or clerical, external to the academic community itself . . . The Catholic university adds to the basic idea of a modern university distinctive characteristics which round out and fulfill that idea.[2]

Such a statement sought to dispel any notion that Catholic education contributed to a "ghetto mentality."[3] As Hesburgh emphasized, "the church does not have to be present in the modern world of the university, but if it is to enter, the reality and terms of this world are well established and must be observed."[4] The university terms that Hesburgh identifies—recognized "throughout the world"—are 1) an emphasis on teaching and research, 2) a new function of service to humankind, 3) freedom and autonomy, and 4) a system of governance that involves "diverse layers of power and decision." Descriptions such as "Catholic or Protestant, British or American" qualify but do not supplant the idea of an excellent university.[5]

---

2. This passage, from what became known as the Land O'Lakes statement, can be found at http://www.catholichistory.net/Events/LandOLakesStatement.htm. Philip Gleason identifies at least two causes leading to its development: the need for lay experience on university boards and the worry that "sectarian" institutions might not receive government aid, in *Contending with Modernity*, 315–16. David O'Brien positively evaluates this statement 1) as an extension of Vatican II and 2) as a necessary endorsement of "Americanism." See O'Brien, "A Catholic Academic Revolution."

3. For an excellent analysis of this history, see Gleason, *Contending with Modernity*.

4. Hesburgh, *Challenge and Promise*, 4.

5. Ibid., 3–4.

Excellence Revisited

Such assumptions are commonplace today. Being "Methodist" or "Baptist," for example, has little to do with the university-wide excellence of a Duke or Wake Forest. In such institutions, Methodist or Baptist identity, etc., is sometimes located in a divinity school. Edward Farley points out, however, that "the clerical paradigm and the correlation of theology with clergy preparation" has only exacerbated the location of theology "outside the university's circle of sciences."[6]

Yet, as I will argue more fully, theology never really moves outside the inner university circle. It is rather always a matter of other theologies coming to dominate. As Alasdair MacIntyre observes in his lecture, "Catholic Instead Of What?,"[7] Augustine was a Catholic rather than a Manichean or Platonist. The same applies to the university. Some set of theological convictions determine the university and its understanding of excellence.

David L. Schindler, in his evaluation of Hesburgh's educational vision, argues that the idea of the university that Hesburgh and company promote is itself not value neutral. Schindler identifies their understanding more explicitly with liberalism, central to which is the claim of neutrality. "As operative in the university, [liberalism] stands for a certain priority of method over content ... [The] precise intention is to avoid any *a priori* assumption of content which would, *ipso facto*, prejudice the (putative) pure openness of the methods. The burden of critical methods, so conceived, is that they are, of their inner logic, equally open to, and thus neutral toward, all potential contents."[8] Schindler identifies this stance with "proceduralism": the deflection of any debate about substance into a debate about freedom. Such formal methodological procedures, however, import content already in their very form. In this case, Schindler emphasizes that the content is a Cartesian mechanizing of the intellect (in the order of facts) and a voluntarizing of the will (in the order of values).[9] That is, one engages reality through its various parts but with

---

6. Farley, *Theologia*, 197. Farley adds, "In the religious studies movement, as in the European Enlightenment, theology's legitimacy in the university and even in the study of religion is highly suspect."

7. This lecture can be found at https://www.youtube.com/watch?v=j7WWMkIOlsw.

8. Schindler, *Heart of the World*, 153.

9. Ibid., 163. As Schindler elaborates, "Descartes wishes to devise a method which leaves one initially neutral with respect to any possible content drawn from objects"

little sense of how the parts relate to each another or to a larger purpose and whole. At the same time, values come to be regarded as matters of the will. However unwittingly, a neutral objective versus value subjective framework informs this view which it not neutral but "weighted against authentic Catholicism."[10]

As an example of how this voluntarizing of the will is often enshrined in the modern college or university today, we can turn to the common focus on "core values." These typically include such values as learning, diversity, excellence, or community. Some institutions might list "faith/spirituality." Yet such values usually remain abstract ways to protect neutrality. Thus diversity comes to mean "commitments to celebrate, embrace, value..." or diversity is embraced "for diversity's sake."[11] The underlying assumption is not that we are "beings toward good"[12] but that values are matters of the will. A key reason for this, as George Grant observes, is that the modern paradigm of knowledge empties the conception of good into uncertainty. In the last century, Grant notes, "'good' has largely been replaced in our ethical discourse by the word 'value'. The modern emptying of 'good' can indeed be seen in the emptiness of its replacement... The vagueness has resulted in the word generally being used only in the plural—our 'values.'"[13]

In the academy, this separation between knowledge and value—and the equation of the former with various disciplines and the latter with choice—has had at least four dire consequences. First, religious faith itself is interpreted as a set of values rather than as truth or knowledge. Thus, as Stanley Hauerwas puts it,

> students take course after course in which there [is] no discernible connection to Christian claims about the way things are... [This] surely [creates] the conditions that [make] the conclusion that Christianity is at best irrelevant, and at worst false, hard to avoid... At best they assume the church may be important for spiritual or moral issues, but those spheres of life are not assumed to be about truth.[14]

---

(162).

10. Ibid., 161.

11. The first clause is taken from the University of Notre Dame's core values; the second is from a 2001 faculty proposal from Saint Mary's College, Notre Dame.

12. Grant, *Technology and Justice*, 43.

13. Ibid., 41

14. Hauerwas, *State of the University*, 47.

So understood, Christianity comes to pertain to a sphere of life outside the classroom. Secondly, and related to the first, the idea that Christian convictions are irrelevant to all of life educates students out of the church. As Robert Wuthnow suggests, one of the best "indicator[s] of whether as a person ages they will be identified with a church is determined by their having gone to a college or a university."[15] Thirdly, for all the lip service paid to diverse values and the encouraging of critical thinking, the modern academy serves one purpose: to prepare the student to compete. This is true not merely for those who must publish or perish. It applies equally to those who must take part in the global economy as lawyers, MBAs, or software engineers. Those in the "multiversity," as Grant calls it, who come "from some tired tradition may not be much concerned with any discussion of 'faith and the multiversity.' They can accept the dominant paradigm with open arms because it is their ticket to professionalism and that is the name of the game."[16] Fourthly, and related to the third point, the implicit academic formation—into a market society—is one where human bonds are reduced to contract and self-interest, and where concepts such as the "common good" become simply incomprehensible. Indeed "the dominant language of 'choice' legitimates the extension of free-market mechanisms (aided and abetted by the regulatory state) into virtually all areas of socio-economic and cultural life—including education, health, the family, and sex."[17]

A Gnostic Impulse

Let us identify more fully the theology that shapes this dominant framework. It is one in which the world in and of itself is valueless. Values, rather, have to do either with what we impose on the world or with self-determination. Such an approach cannot affirm that being *is* intrinsically good. That is, the heavens cannot declare the glory of God (which is at best merely poetic speech). Rather nature itself is devoid of purpose: our bonds to the created world, to the particularities of time and place more

---

15. Ibid. Hauerwas is engaging Robert Wuthnow's *The Restructuring of American Religion*, particularly his study of a growing trend beginning in the 1950s of laity receiving college education. Hauerwas notes that Wuthnow's study indicates that the college educated who do stay in church are "less likely to identify with Christian orthodoxy."

16. Grant, *Technology and Justice*, 68.

17. Pabst, *Crisis of Global Capitalism*, 19.

often than not interpreted as bondage.[18] Such an understanding is essentially gnostic.

While it might seem that gnosticism is an ancient myth that only a minority today explicitly endorse, William H. Poteat argues that gnostic patterns dominate modern sensibilities.

> The impulse to destroy everything that is given and fashion a new heaven and a new earth is the impulse of pure spirit subject only to its own self-assertion, culminating in Dostoyevski's Kirilov who declares himself to be God and suicide the earnest of his Godhood. Its influence is now so ubiquitous, so commonplace, not to say, domesticated, that a feat of extraordinary perspicacity is required to see that it pervades the institutions of this culture and is rampant in the academy. In the academy it is the rage that gives it away.[19]

Such a claim might sound extreme. "The impulse to destroy everything . . ." is surely an overstatement. Yet, if being is not intrinsically good, then the gnostic alternative lies close at hand: we, as pure spirits, create *ourselves* out of nothing. As MacIntyre concisely puts it, "I am what my choices make me."[20] So understood, the gnostic sentiment "I'm spiritual but not religious" applies not only to individuals such as Sheila Larsen[21] but to the academy as well. By isolating the "spiritual" and placing it in a separate sphere, the modern academy is reenacting a gnostic script. The spirit floats free, having little to do with the institutional body. True gnosis migrates from common folk to superior souls who have moved "from mere 'faith' to real, enlightened 'knowledge.'"[22] Gnosticism, so understood, is a thoroughly rationalistic movement, its mirror image surviving in a pluralism of values.[23]

---

18. Poteat, *Recovering the Ground*, 210. One thus seeks to escape the particularities of time and place, rather than receive these as gift.

19. Ibid., xii.

20. Alasdair MacIntyre, lecture, Culture of Death Conference, University of Notre Dame, October 13, 2000. A video tape of this lecture is available from the Notre Dame Center for Ethics and Culture.

21. Bellah, et al. in *Habits of the Heart*, famously describes how Ms. Larsen invented her own religion: "Sheila-ism."

22. von Balthasar, *The Scandal of the Incarnation*, 1.

23. Zizioulas, *Being as Communion*, 80. Here he describes how Irenaeus, "in his fight against Gnosticism, the most rationalistic movement of the period," emphasizes that Christ was the truth not only of the *mind*.

The Convertibility Of Being And Logos

To call being itself good, however, is to say that being and *logos* are convertible. This might sound absurd since one can observe quite easily the ways in which being is irrational. And yet a Christian understanding of being depends upon at least two key convictions. The first is creation *ex nihilo*; being as created "out of nothing" names a relation between Creator and creation. That is, all being is logically ordered to God; as Augustine famously states, "My heart is restless until it rests in Thee, O Lord." This relation is not at the level of will (we do not choose it) but is constitutive of being itself. It is thus not an optional "value" but the logic of creation irrespective of whether one acknowledges it or not. One of the key implications of this understanding for the academy is that the goodness of being-as-relation pertains to all that is: to all spheres and all disciplines. Such an understanding does not negate or suppress the distinctiveness of varieties of disciplinary knowledge but rather attunes them more fully to a larger whole: the logic of being and knowing as creation, as relation.

A second conviction, one emphasized by Irenaeus in his fight against the early Gnostics, is that "the flesh is the hinge."[24] Irenaeus thus emphasizes that "God's own creation, which depends for its existence on God's power and art and wisdom, has borne God."[25] To say creation has borne God is to point to a *logos* not in the purely spiritual realm, nor only in the world of the mind, nor merely in the world of facts. The *logos* rather includes the purpose of all creation. What is logical cannot be separated from creation as communion with God, revealed and realized most fully in Christ. As Samuel Kimbriel puts it, "Loving and knowing become identified precisely because the deepest contours of reality are those defined by divine love, whether that be within God himself or as displayed in creation."[26] Rightly understood, knowing cannot be separated from being as communion with God and others in and through creation. The excellent academy will thus embrace all knowing as a way of being in communion with others, creation, and ultimately God. Knowing, like being, is always first a gift of love. This leads to the challenging

---

24. *The Scandal of the Incarnation*, cited by Balthasar, 4. This saying is originally attributed to Tertullian but had decisive influence on Irenaeus.

25. Ibid., 54.

26. Kimbriel, *Friendship as Sacred Knowing*, 5. Schindler also emphasizes the convertibility of *logos* and love. See especially *Heart of the World*, 166–76.

conclusion that being and knowing at bottom "manifest as acknowledgment, as thanking."[27]

Some might worry that this understanding of being is not objective and this would be right. But objectivity understood as the flip side of subjectivity is determined by an understanding of being as itself closed, or what Stratford Caldecott describes as flat:

> A popular misconception has it that medieval man thought the world was flat, and modern science gave us a round world floating in an infinite space. But the truth is almost the opposite of this. Medieval man inhabited a three-dimensional cosmos which has now been largely replaced by a flat universe, with no ontological depth. It is not a question of size, or even of infinite spaces. An infinite field is still essentially flat. In pure modernity there can be no up or down, no getting closer to hell or heaven, and there are no sacred places and times which participate in the divine.[28]

In a flat universe, one imagines space in terms of what is "out there" (objective) or "in here" (subjective), body versus spirit. In an ontology of communion, however, "objectivity" is replaced by faithfulness. It is in this light that Michael Polanyi claims that in all our knowing we "strive under the guidance of antecedent belief . . ."[29] So understood, knowing entails a logic of affirmation that transcends "the disjunction between subjective and objective."[30] Whereas gnosticism is trapped in a flat ontology of the objective versus subjective, an ontology of communion sees all knowing as a way of living faithfully before others, and ultimately before God.

Some might be concerned that the particularity of this ontology is exclusive and thus shuts down the free exchange of ideas so central to academic being. And yet an ontology of communion (no more particular that the dominant gnostic ontology) actually allows for greater freedom and diversity. This is because freedom is not so much about choice as it is about becoming the kind of person and institution one is created and called to be. Created being, as I have argued, is being as communion. To live into this is to see the other as well as oneself as gift, as participants in God's own giving and receiving. Irenaeus describes this communion in terms of a great symphony: "Created things, in their great number and

27. Stines, in Cannon and Hall, eds., *Recovering the Personal*, 109.
28. Caldecott, *Beauty for Truth's Sake*, 139.
29. Polanyi, *Personal Knowledge*, 266.
30. Ibid., 300.

diversity, fit beautifully and harmoniously into the creation as a whole . . . [T]he same Artist was responsible for the wisdom, justice, goodness and munificence of the whole work."[31] Diversity, so understood, is not about individual choice or self-expression; it is rather a reception and participation in the love and wisdom of God. This does not erase the self but makes it more fully possible, as being is realized through communion.

As I have argued, however, gnostic convictions have blinded the modern academy to the goodness, truth, and beauty of its own being. To the extent this is true, we have failed to be faithful. Such failure could lead to pessimism or even hopelessness. To say the flesh is hinge, however, is also to say that all creation, including the academy, has been renewed in and through Christ. How do we reconcile the radical disconnect between creation's renewal and our failure to live into it? Thomas Merton has said that even the desire for prayer is itself a kind of prayer, both already responses to God's grace. Applied analogously to the academy, even the faintest awareness of our academic unfaithfulness is itself a response to grace, and thus a sign of hope. And hope is always possible because God, who does not abandon us, can use human failure to renew our lives for the sake of the world. Such a way of seeing, however, calls for patience and forebearance. But this is exactly the way we learn to receive our being and knowing as gift.[32] As such, it is already an alternative to our gnostic failure.

Bibliography

Bellah, Robert N., et al. *Habits of the Heart: Individualism and Commitment in American Life.* Berkeley, CA: University of California Press, 1985.
Burtchaell, James T. *The Dying of the Light, The Disengagement of Colleges and Universities from their Christian Churches.* Grand Rapids: Eerdmans, 1998.
Caldecott, Stratford. *Beauty for Truth's Sake, The Re-enchantment of Education.* Grand Rapids: Brazos, 2009.
Cannon, Dale W., and Ronald L. Hall, eds. *Recovering the Personal: The Philosophical Anthropology of William H. Poteat.* Lanham, MD: Lexington, 2016.
Farley, Edward. *Theologia: The Fragmentation and Unity of Theological Education.* Eugene, OR: Wipf and Stock, 2001.

31. Irenaeus in von Balthasar, ed., *The Scandal of the Incarnation,* 41.

32. Simone Weil captures this understanding in her well-known essay "Reflections on the Right Use of School Studies with a View to the Love of God," where she states, "We do not obtain the most precious gifts by going in search of them but by waiting for them." In Weil, *Waiting on God,* 56–57. I also develop this analysis in my book *Divine Abundance.*

Gleason, Philip. *Contending with Modernity: Catholic Higher Education in the Twentieth Century.* New York: Oxford University Press, 1995.
Grant, George. *Technology and Justice.* Notre Dame, IN: University of Notre Dame Press, 1986.
Hauerwas, Stanley. *The State of the University, Academic Knowledges and the Knowledge of God.* Oxford: Blackwell, 2007.
Hesburgh, Theodore, ed. *The Challenge and Promise of a Catholic University.* Notre Dame, IN: University of Notre Dame Press, 1994.
Kimbriel, Samuel. *Friendship as Sacred Knowing: Overcoming Isolation.* Oxford: Oxford University Press, 2014.
Marsden, George. *The Soul of the University, From Protestant Establishment to Established Nonbelief.* New York: Oxford University Press, 1994.
Newman, Elizabeth. *Divine Abundance: Leisure, the Basis of Academic Culture.* Eugene, OR: Cascade, 2018.
O'Brien, David J. "A Catholic Academic Revolution." In *Mission and Identity: A Handbook for Trustees of Catholic Colleges and Universities,* 23–35. Washington, DC: Association of Jesuit Colleges and Universities, 2003.
Pabst, Adrian, ed. *The Crisis of Global Capitalism: Pope Benedict XVI's Social Encyclical and the Future of Political Economy.* Cambridge: James Clark & Co., 2012.
Polanyi, Michael. *Personal Knowledge: Towards a Post-Critical Philosophy.* Chicago: University of Chicago Press, 1958.
Poteat, William H. *Recovering the Ground: Critical Exercises in Recollection.* New York: SUNY Press, 1994.
Schindler, David L. *Heart of the World, Center of the Church.* Grand Rapids: Eerdmans, 1996.
Sloan, Douglas. *Faith and Knowledge: Mainline Protestantism and American Higher Education.* Louisville, KY: Westminster John Knox, 1994.
von Balthasar, Hans Urs, ed. *The Scandal of the Incarnation, Irenaeus Against the Heresies.* Selected and introduced by Hans Urs von Balthasar. San Francisco: Ignatius, 1990.
Weil, Simone. *Waiting on God.* London: Routledge and Kegan Paul, 1951.
Zizioulas, John D. *Being as Communion.* Crestwood, NY: St. Vladimir's Seminary Press, 1985.

Part 4

Failure and Liberation

16.

Rival Powers

US Catholics Confront the Climate Crisis

ROSEMARY P. CARBINE

AFTER HIS INAUGURATION IN 2017, US President Donald Trump nominated and received US Senate confirmation for climate change deniers to join his cabinet, such as former CEO and chairman of ExxonMobil Rex Tillerson for Secretary of State, and Oklahoma Attorney General Scott Pruitt for the head of the Environmental Protection Agency. Tillerson is under investigation by state attorneys general for miseducation about the risks of climate change, and Pruitt openly supports environmentally dangerous methods of mining such as fracking (which caused earthquakes in his home state). He has also sued the EPA fourteen times to block or overturn clean air and water regulations that impact oil, gas, energy, agriculture, and other industries, in some cases based on campaign contributions to him from those same industries.[1] Both confirmed by the Republican-dominated US Senate for their respective cabinet posts, Pruitt implemented President Trump's cuts to the EPA's staff and budget, which will diminish its ability to enforce regulations that limit greenhouse gas emissions or to promote education about clean power; will roll back some of those same environmental safeguards; and, will involve vetting any EPA scientists' publications, especially the National Climate Assessment to be released by more than a dozen federal agencies in fall

---

1. Lipton and Davenport, "Scott Pruitt." Schaeffer, "Reject Scott Pruitt."

2017,[2] to avoid conflict with corporate, agricultural, mining, and other initiatives already proven to be hazardous to public and environmental health, especially among low-income communities and communities of color who suffer from environmental racism and other eco-injustices. Indeed, in his administrative role at the EPA, Pruitt delayed or rolled back, mainly in consultation with industry lobbyists and representatives, more than thirty environmental regulations of energy, oil, gas, chemical, and agricultural industries that protect both environmental and public health.[3] In addition, President Trump has withdrawn the US from international climate accords, such as the Paris Climate Agreement of 2015, favoring his American exceptionalism foreign policy but damaging the longtime role of the US in global leadership and governance.[4]

The current US administration thus demonstrates *both* the government's existential failure to confront the climate crisis because it dismisses domestic and international regulations as alleged threats to US economic supremacy and political sovereignty, *and* the apparent failure of political, corporate, activist, and religious leaders' moral and political authority and influence to open US leaders' eyes to this crisis. Utilizing popular strategies in the history of US social movements that especially involved scientists such as the anti-nuclear movement, scientists and their allies marched in Washington, DC, and in parallel marches nationwide during two weekends in April 2017 to coincide with Earth Day and with President Trump's one-hundreth day in office. Together, the March for Science and the People's Climate March validated the scientific consensus about climate change, emphasized the integral value of science to public and environmental health, and called for public support of science and technology in the face of proposed cuts to the EPA, the NIH, and other federal agencies and organizations, which will only reinforce race, gender, and economic inequalities amplified by climate change.[5] Taking a page from the US conservative playbook, about 300 cities, a dozen states, eighty university presidents, and dozens of corporations have asserted a states-rights approach and recommitted to implementing the Paris accord limits on greenhouse gas emissions at the local, state, college,

2. Friedman, 'Scientists Fear Trump Will Dismiss Blunt Climate Report"; Shear and Plumer, "Climate Report."

3. Davenport, "Counseled by Industry."

4. Shear, "Trump Will Withdraw US from Paris."

5. St. Fleur, "Scientists, Feeling Under Siege"; Fandos, "Climate March Draws Thousands of Protesters."

and corporate levels, igniting a Green Energy Revolution with positive ecological and economic results.⁶ Paralleling these social movements but from a faith-based perspective, eco-public theological strategies that emphasize ecological concerns and solutions as well as analyze and confront both types of failure are also urgently needed.

Drawing on the perspectives of feminist, ecological, and public theologies, this essay interprets the reactionary religious and political responses from the US political right to Pope Francis's encyclical on the climate crisis, *Laudato Si'*. The papal letter underscores anthropogenic causes of climate change, emphasizes personal and inter/national moral failure to recognize ecological responsibilities, and replaces prevalent notions of global technocratic power with intergenerational and ecological solidarity. Citing Catholic bishops' statements from the Global South (e.g., Africa, Latin America, the Caribbean, the Philippines) effectively situates the climate crisis in a global context of injustice and inequality. Yet, this prophetic letter tests the limits of papal influence on American bishops and US presidential candidates: as this essay will discuss, bishops tout religious liberty to oppose abortion, contraception, and same-sex marriage, and candidates rely on Catholicism to fuel these sexual culture wars but distance themselves from or outright denounce Catholic social teaching, thereby attempting to privatize religion from sociopolitical, economic, and ecological issues.

This essay offers an alternative path via feminist public theology, which joins the personal, the political, and the planetary. As I argue, Francis's failure to reach and persuade US Catholic conservative politicians and their party about global climate change illustrates a counterhegemonic theological strategy with an eschatological edge: an inbreaking, fleeting, and far from fully realized possibility for imagining alternative ways of being and living together at the intersections of and interdependence among social, political, and earthly life: "The new heaven and the new earth that Christians are expecting can certainly not be reduced to earth ecological healing, but such earthly ecological healing is equally a clear sign of the very visible consequences of this great vision."⁷ Papal encyclicals alongside global bishops' pastoral letters and nuns who have ecologically reinterpreted their vows, daily spiritual practices, and locally sustainable agriculture still express "lived practices of hope" because they

---

6. Tabuchi and Fountain, "Bucking Trump"; Thompson and Bajaj, "The Green Energy Revolution."

7. Bedford-Strohm, "Public Theology," 54.

"continue to reshape an ecologically conscious social imaginary [and] are, in this sense, effective practices of hope."[8]

Pope Francis as Eco-Public Theologian

Pope Francis's US visit in fall 2015 included invited addresses to a US Congressional joint session and the UN General Assembly, alongside visits to the White House, Independence Hall, the World Meeting of Families, as well as homilies and reflections at masses, memorial services, schools, and prisons in Washington, New York, and Philadelphia. In his address to Congress,[9] Francis defined politics as the defense of the transcendent dignity of citizens made in the image and likeness of God and as the basis of the pursuit of the common good. All people play a role in sustaining common life through work, voluntary associations, and social/public service in solidarity. To reinforce this religio-political grounding and goal of common life, Francis drew on the "historical memory" and "deepest cultural reserves" that in his view shaped fundamental US values, highlighting Abraham Lincoln, Martin Luther King, Dorothy Day, and Thomas Merton. "A nation can be considered great when it defends liberty as Lincoln did, when it fosters a culture which enables people to dream of full rights for all their brothers and sisters as Martin Luther King sought to do, when it strives for justice and the cause of the oppressed as Dorothy Day did by her tireless work, the fruit of a faith which becomes dialogue and sows peace in the contemplative style of Thomas Merton." These historical examples show that religion can foster both solidarity and the common good, which combine to shore up and support US society. For instance, religious pluralism and interreligious dialogue contribute to "new policies and new forms of social consensus" about the need for all citizens to "sacrifice particular interests in order to share, in justice and peace, its [the nation's] goods, its interests, its social life," especially civil rights for African Americans, First Nations, immigrants, and refugees. Moreover, religion helps develop solutions to the current climate crisis by reflecting on "the right use of natural resources, the proper application of technology, and the harnessing of the spirit of

---

8. Dalton and Simmons, *Ecotheology and the Practice of Hope*, 105. Also, Taylor, *Green Sisters*.

9. Francis, "Transcript: Pope Francis's Speech."

enterprise" to promote the common good, which expands and extends to include our common social, political, and earthly life.

In his address to UN General Assembly,[10] Francis characterized our present moment as "marked by our technical ability to overcome distances and frontiers and, apparently, to overcome all natural limits to the exercise of power." He then cited the UN's role in significantly shaping international humanitarian law that promotes human rights, justice, and peace, and thereby effectively limits as well as distributes power, whether political, economic, military, technological, and so on. Nonetheless, Francis pointed out that the natural environment and marginalized peoples stand as contemporary "victims of power badly exercised . . . The sectors are closely interconnected and made increasingly fragile by dominant political and economic relationships. That is why their rights must be forcefully affirmed, by working to protect the environment and by putting an end to exclusion." For Francis, theological claims about the intrinsic value, interdependence, and sacredness of all life endowed and sustained by the Creator foster ecojustice, namely the rights of the environment and of the excluded. While global governments have taken concrete political steps to ensure integral human development through access to basic goods (e.g., education, housing, work, food, and water), Francis mobilized this creation-centered theology to resist "a selfish and boundless thirst for power and material prosperity [that] leads both to the misuse of available natural resources and to the exclusion of the weak and disadvantaged . . . [who] are cast off by society, forced to live off what is discarded, and suffer unjustly from the abuse of the environment. They are part of today's widespread and quietly growing culture of waste."

Francis addressed the US Congress and the UN General Assembly in ways that resonated with his landmark 2015 environmental encyclical, *Laudato Si'*.[11] The letter outlined an integral ecology that emphasizes the intersections of religious, socioeconomic, political, and ecological justice grounded in a creation-centered theology. In Francis's view, an integral ecology takes "an integrated approach to combating poverty, restoring dignity to the excluded, and at the same time protecting nature" (139). Minoritized communities in the global economy are most gravely affected by degrading or disappearing ecosystems, which cause further disasters such as refugees from resource-based conflicts (25, 48, 57). When inter-

10. Holy See Press Office, "Address to the United Nations."

11. Francis, *Laudato Si'—On Care for Our Common Home*. All paragraph numbers are referenced in text from this point onwards.

preted by a creation-centered theology that unites religious, economic, and ecological commitments, sins against the sacramentality of creation (84–86) can now be construed as sins of current economic models against a creator God and poor marginalized peoples (48, 56, 75), especially indigenous peoples (146) and women. An integral ecology also highlights our comprehensive responsibility to the sustainability of present and future generations, and urges not only solidarity with the present-day poor or intragenerational solidarity, but also intergenerational solidarity (159, 162). Inspired by this integral ecology, Francis proposed new international relations and policies that recognize the "ecological debt" that the Global North owes the Global South for its disproportionate consumption and consequent harm (51, 95, 143–144). Global Northern economic interests have fueled the deregulation of multinational corporations and the weakening of international climate agreements (51, 54, 56). In coalition with the US bishops, Francis recommended "differentiated responsibilities" and practices to restore economic and ecological civil society: limited consumption by the Global North (52, 104–105), and sovereignty as well as sustainable development in the Global South (172).

Technocracy vs. Biocracy: Conservative US Catholic Backlash and Ecofeminist Responses

When the long awaited environmental encyclical was released, US Catholic Republicans denounced it either by apathetically not commenting on it at all, like Ted Cruz, Bobby Jindal, and Marco Rubio, or by aggressively challenging religion's prophetic role in US public life. Then US presidential candidate Rick Santorum rebuffed it in a radio interview and discredited Pope Francis's credentials to even write it. Even though Francis trained and worked as a chemist, Santorum delegitimized Francis's role as major religio-political public figure on these issues by citing the Catholic Church's uneven relations with modern science and by claiming that Francis should "leave science to the scientists" and instead restrict his public witness to theology and morality.[12] By contrast, Bishop of Des Moines Richard Pates urged presidential candidates prior to the Iowa caucuses to stop downplaying or outright denying the established science of global climate change.[13] Nonetheless, similar to the majority

12. Hale, "Rick Santorum."
13. Roewe, "Iowa Bishop to Presidential Candidates."

of US Catholic conservative politicians,[14] Santorum preferred Francis, bishops, and official Church spokespersons to blend religion and science in ways that addressed what US Catholic bishops called the five non-negotiables for US Catholic voters, namely, abortion, euthanasia, embryonic stem cell research, human cloning, and same-sex marriage,[15] while forgetting that Catholic social teaching broadly promotes and upholds the dignity and flourishing of all life, human and other-than-human, as created, loved, and declared intrinsically good by God. As historian Martin Marty poignantly observes, "some Catholic critics of the critics of *Laudato Si'* remind us that for a century Vatican social documents have been repudiated, neglected, misrepresented, or unrecognized, often by precisely the same set of politicians and interest groups who most ostentatiously wear the insignia and bear the banners of papal authority on some other topics."[16] Just as Catholic conservatives like Michael Novak and Richard John Neuhaus faulted the US Catholic bishops' pastoral letter on the economy in the 1980s, so too these contemporary Catholic conservative politicians accept capitalism and the creative production of wealth, rather than distributive justice alongside democracy (read for them as equal opportunity) and religious freedom (but without attention

---

14. Climate change creates religio-political and partisan divides among Catholics. A Pew Research Center poll shows that 62 percent of Catholic Democrats agree with anthropogenic climate change, whereas only 24 percent of Catholic Republicans do. See Goldenberg, "Pope Francis Faces Challenge"; Davenport, "Pope's Views on Climate Change."

15. "Climate change continues to be seen as a justice issue, and not a life issue, like abortion and marriage. Reframing climate change as a life issue would command more resources, according to some within the church. Until then, climate change takes second place to abortion and same-sex marriage for many in the US church leadership." Goldenberg, "Pope Francis Faces Challenge." By contrast, the US Bishops at their spring meeting in 2015 questioned these limited priorities, which are often narrowed further to religious liberty since the passage of the Affordable Care Act and which prompted the annual USCCB's Fortnight for Freedom since that same time. At this meeting, many bishops lobbied for a broader focus on economic justice, immigration, and climate change. The USCCB general assembly in fall 2015 and in fall 2016 ultimately approved its 2017–2020 strategic priorities that included "human life and dignity: uphold the sanctity of human life from conception to natural death with special concern for the poor and vulnerable" alongside other priorities regarding evangelization, family and marriage, vocations and clergy formation, and religious freedom understood as free exercise in the US and abroad. "Bishops Vote on Pastoral Statement on Pornography, Faithful Citizenship, Revise Strategic Priorities at General Assembly," and "Bishops Vote on 2017–2020 Strategic Plan."

16. Marty, "Encyclical."

to other virtues of justice or of just persons), as the best means to address and alleviate social injustices and poverty.[17]

Similar to the reception history of US Catholic social teaching on the economy, then US presidential candidate Jeb Bush at a town hall gathering in New Hampshire contested the ways in which Francis's encyclical situated ecological problems within economic structures of unchecked free market capitalism that controls and exploits people and resources for profit, individualist consumerism that hones and drives our knowledge and desires to objectify, commodify, possess, and ultimately master others including nature, and global inequalities.[18] Invoking President John F. Kennedy's strategy to assure the American public that papal teachings would not influence US policy, Bush claimed in his campaign's initial days that "I don't get economic policy from my bishops or my Cardinals or my Pope," and stressed that religion should humanize rather than politicize issues.[19] Ironically, Archbishop Thomas Wenski of Miami enacted a diocesan strategic plan to implement the encyclical throughout summer sermons and public press events, especially since the 2014 National Climate Assessment listed Miami among the most ecologically endangered US cities as a result of global warming.[20] Moreover, sharpened in the Vatican II Pastoral Constitution on the Church in the Modern World and in subsequent papal as well as episcopal statements, Catholic social teaching pivots precisely around the principle of humanization, of integral human development. This principle provides both theological and political inspiration and impetus for the Church's public engagement that engenders and enhances solidarity with marginalized peoples not only affected by worker's rights, war and peace, the death penalty, racism, immigration, sex trafficking, and so on, but also disproportionately impacted by the global climate crisis.

In advance of Pope Francis's US visit, Catholic and Republican Congressman Paul Gosar pledged to boycott the Pope's Congressional address as part of his longtime trenchant criticism of the Environmental Protection Agency's policies and regulations founded on what he called the "questionable science" of climate change. Taking a tactic from the civil rights-era activist's toolkit to protest the environmental encyclical,

17. Curran, "The Reception of Catholic Social and Economic Teaching," 481–83.

18. Shiffman, "Between the Knower and the Known."

19. Hale, "Jeb Bush's Response"; Goldenberg and Siddiqui, "Jeb Bush Joins Republican Backlash."

20. Davenport, "Pope's Views on Climate Change."

Gosar commented in his op-ed that "if the Pope stuck to standard Christian theology, I would be the first in line . . . If the Pope spoke out with moral authority against violent Islam, I would be there cheering him on. If the Pope urged the Western nations to rescue persecuted Christians in the Middle East, I would back him wholeheartedly. But when the Pope chooses to act and talk like a leftist politician, then he can expect to be treated like one."[21] Here, political party interests trumped Catholic social teaching's integral, not accessory or additive, links between sociopolitical and environmental concerns.

Current environmental crises—such as rising and more acidic oceans, intensifying storms and droughts, deforestation, desertification, decreasing biodiversity, glacier melt, species extinction, unsustainable rates of production and consumption, increasing greenhouse gases, and increasing pollution of land, air, and water with attendant diseases—together reveal polarizing contrasts between technocratic and feminist eco-public theological views of biocratic power at work in these Catholic debates: de-creation and co/re-creation.[22] Conservative Catholic backlash to Francis's environmental encyclical and US visit shows how Christian eco-public theology endures, navigates, resists, and eventually seeks liberation and transcendence from hegemonic power, which Francis defines as the techno-economic or technocratic paradigm. Technocracy is characterized by the collusion of modern individualism and consumerism, the un/underregulated capitalist and corporate exploitation of environmental resources aided and abetted by rapid technological progress, and the Western imperialist, neocolonialist, and exceptionalist consumption of those resources to the detriment—that is, the de-creation—of global peoples and ecosystems. In *Laudato Si'*, Francis described the "techno-economic paradigm" as the globalized logic of control and consumption of the world's water, forests, terrestrial, marine and ocean life (14, 28, 30, 38, 41) for mainly the Global North's interests and profits at the expense of the poor (53, 95, 106, 109, 145, 170, 210). For Francis, the objectification of other-than-human life for its instrumental value to human life and needs (11) trades on a flawed Christian anthropology of mastery (116), thrives on a "throwaway culture" (22), and treats marginalized peoples as dominated and disposable (82, 106). Treating all nonhuman and some human life as resources only engenders global patterns of inequality

---

21. DeBonis, "Catholic Congressman Boycott Pope Francis."
22. Carpenter, "Rushing Winds," 326–27, 330–34.

(33, 81–82), leading to environmental racism, modern-day slavery, and sexual exploitation, for example (45–46, 123).

As Kwok Pui-lan puts it in ecofeminist terms, "technological control, a Western-oriented model of development, and patriarchy form an 'unholy trinity' dominating the lives of marginalized women."[23] Tackling a technocratic anthropology that aligns with anthropocentric Christian anthropologies, ecofeminist theologian Rosemary Radford Ruether synthesized feminist, liberationist, and environmental movements in order to challenge how globalization is premised on a hierarchical dualistic worldview and sociopolitical order of race, class, and patriarchal power and privilege that instrumentalizes (ab/uses and discards) rather than intrinsically values women, subjugated peoples, and nature.[24] In a similar ecojustice vein, ecofeminist theologian Sallie McFague critiqued corporate globalization and its attendant economic systems that legitimize and reinforce gender and social injustices along with ecological degradation. McFague traced the roots of corporate globalization to medieval and modern European mechanistic and consumerist views of the earth and of progress, which prioritize the human self-interested production of goods through the exploitative control of the earth's limitless resources for profits.[25]

By contrast, Francis in *Laudato Si'* recognizes the created subjectivity of all life and assigns intrinsic rather than instrumental worth to all life as profoundly interrelated, whether inhabiting social ecologies or natural ecosystems (140). Similarly, self-identified geologian Thomas Berry, together with physicist Brian Swimme, encouraged Earth's evolutionary history toward an Ecozoic era that values all planetary and cosmic life as an organic communion of subjects-in-relation with subjectivity and agency, in contrast to the Technozoic era which pathologically prizes individualist, economic, and nationalist growth at the expense of ecocide.[26]

As Ruether, McFague, Berry, and others like Elizabeth Johnson have argued, countering technocracy and its multiple facets requires retelling, or better re-placing, the Earth story in an evolutionary, ecological,

---

23. Pui-lan, "Ecology and the Recycling of Christianity," 108.

24. Ruether, *Gaia and God*; Dalton and Simmons, *Ecotheology*, 48–49, 63–66.

25. McFague, *Super, Natural Christians* and *Life Abundant*. See also Zimmerman, "God, Creation, and the Environment," 256–61; Dalton and Simmons, *Ecotheology*, 61–63.

26. Deane-Drummond, *Eco-Theology*, 40–42; Ellard, "Thomas Berry," in *Confronting the Climate Crisis*, 302–3, 310; Scheid, *The Cosmic Common Good*, 64–81.

embodied, and ultimately holistic cosmic context that, collectively, stresses the co-original, co-evolutionary, interrelated, interdependent, intersubjective, and integrated nature of all embodied life involved in co/re-creation in order to overcome human-nature oppression and all its multiple attendant aggressive forms (racism, sexism, classism, ableism, religious xenophobia).[27] In contrast to technocracy, eco-liberation theologian Leonardo Boff elaborated a biocratic sociopolitical order in which social and ecological intrinsic interconnectedness and interdependence spurs on attendant rights—personal rights (social and economic rights, including rights to cultural respect, diversity, and positive reciprocity), national rights (civil and political rights to equality and citizenship), planetary rights (the option for the poor is situated within a primary option for the planet), and cosmic rights (the kinship of all life in its origins and its destiny).[28]

Similarly, eco-ethicist Jame Schaefer extended selected core principles of Catholic social teaching—solidarity, subsidiarity, and option for the poor—to further situate these rights in a co/re-creative context. Solidarity mandates "informed decisions for the common good of all people in the present and the future through dialogue, collaboration, aid to the poor, and service to one another individually and collectively."[29] Subsidiarity urges personal and associational rights to social, cultural, economic, and political participation so that all people "at increasing levels of governance" contribute freely, creatively, and responsibly to the common good. "Thus, from the individual to the highest level of association formed, each has its own purpose, purview, task, and authority to address issues that the individual or lower association is incapable of addressing to achieve the good of all."[30] Finally, the option for the poor ties together poverty and ecological degradation, and focuses on empowering resistance to environmental racism and other eco-injustices in order to mitigate negative effects on present and future generations. Schaefer also engaged with the anthropocentrism of these principles, and "expand[s]

---

27. Johnson, *Quest for the Living God*, 181–201. Dalton and Simmons, *Ecotheology*, 44–47, 74–75, 79–80. For more on ecofeminist theories of place, see Dalton and Simmons, *Ecotheology*, 99–100.

28. Deane-Drummond, *Eco-Theology*, 46–49. Scheid summarizes these ultimately theocentric and cosmocentric rights and associated responsibilities as the cosmic common good; see Scheid, *The Cosmic Common Good*, 23–44.

29. Schaefer, "Solidarity," 395.

30. Ibid., 401.

solidarity to include other species and ecological systems, reconfigure[s] the principle of subsidiarity so decision-making and acting is based on biological regions and the biosphere, and consider[s] endangered species and degraded ecological systems among the poor and impoverished."[31] In all these ways, a biocratic sociopolitical order interlinks, in ecofeminist fashion, the personal, the political, and the planetary—even unto the cosmic in co/re-creative ways.

Doing Effective Eco-Public Theology

Elaborated by Celia Deane-Drummond and Heinrich Bedford-Strohm, eco-public theology recovers and reconstructs religious traditions into a civil-society–based language that is publicly accessible across pluralistic worldviews and that persuasively demonstrates the role of religious peoples and traditions in addressing pressing public questions—in this case, the ways in which religions edge public discourse and policy from technocracy toward biocracy, toward a new social, economic, political, and environmental order founded on ecological justice.[32] To do so, eco-public theologians need to develop a polyglot ability and agility to engage in global public discourse and in doing so envision public policies about ecological issues in ways that illustrate religion's credibility and relevance across multiple communities that address similar issues with their own specialized systems of communication.[33] For example, as Peter Beyer contends,

> religious speaking for the environment . . . invariably translates environmental questions into specifically religious idioms and symbolic clusters. Environment becomes "creation," "Gaia" or "Mother Earth"; ecological problems become religio-moral justice issues. These translations allow one to express ecological matters in religious terms and thereby permit the connectivity with religious remedies . . . Secular systems do something analogous: they also "translate the environment" into their own idioms to render them communicable in terms of their own rationales.[34]

31. Ibid., 410.

32. Deane-Drummond and Bedford-Strohm, "Introduction," 4–5; Beyer, "Who Shall Speak?," 25.

33. Beyer, "Who Shall Speak?," 22–24; Bedford-Strohm, "Public Theology," 46–48.

34. Beyer, "Who Shall Speak?," 29.

As demonstrated by Trump's environmental policies and US Catholic conservative backlash to *Laudato Si'*, dominant economic systems discuss environmental concerns in relation to a free-market–based economy that aims at generating capital and prosperity amid uneven, unequal development and unsustainable patterns of consumption and growth given the planet's carrying capacity. Similarly, prevalent political systems interpret environmental issues in terms of fostering national interests and preserving the Global North's dominance while negotiating transnational relations. By contrast, scientific systems measure, interpret, and publish data, which contribute to a growing global consensus in the scientific community about the impacts of climate change even amid persistent climate change denial. Therefore, eco-public theology needs to bring religio-linguistic flexibility and theo-political savvy to talk across these particular and seemingly incommensurable ways of communicating about environmental concerns, as well as grapple with religion's differential or outright marginal power to address these same concerns alongside global economics, politics, and science.[35]

Francis's eco-public theology engaged in polyglot public discourse, and communicated effectively about religious responses to eco-crises using both economic and scientific discourse. *Laudato Si'* is addressed to all people (3) and encouraged international political, economic, religious, and scientific dialogue (chapter 5). Moreover, the encyclical outlined a cogent and compelling interpretation of various environmental crises (chapters 1 and 3), and emphasized the contribution of Christian claims and practices to address those crises (chapter 2). However, he failed to transform status quo US conservative economic and political discourse and policy in the pursuit of ecojustice due to those discourses' long-standing policies and ties to transnational technocratic power relations.

Nonetheless, effective "public theology is liberation theology for global civil society"[36] that opposes oppressive sociopolitical, economic, or religious powers and that prophetically challenges those same powers to reorient sociopolitical, economic, and religious institutions and structures toward social *and* ecological solidarity,[37] toward biocracy. Liberation theologies in the United States have more recently incorporated an intersectional analysis of poverty affected by race/ethnicity, gender, class,

---

35. Ibid., 35.
36. Bedford-Strohm, "Public Theology," 46.
37. Ibid., 52.

sexual and reproductive justice issues, and ecology. For public theology to lead as a new paradigm for global eco-liberation theology, liberation theologians need to sustain communities of accountability through relevant lived relationships with social movements, such as women's movements, environmental movements, antiracist movements, and LGBTQIA movements. "Lack of dialogue and cooperation between liberation theology and new social movements may thus result in liberation theologians lack of credibility in major contemporary social issues, such as sexual ethics, racism, religious syncretism, environmental issues and popular religion; all relevant for women, indigenous, and African-American people."[38] Just as the US Catholic bishops' pastoral letter on the economy in the 1980s failed to deal with grassroots community-based power mobilized from below—that is from social movements, to bring about prophetic social structural and economic change[39]—so too Pope Francis fails to articulate a public eco-liberation theology, because his faith-rooted eco-advocacy at least in *Laudato Si'* is fundamentally grounded in global bishops' statements but less so in global religious environmental movements.

Naming the anthropocentric sins of environmental injustice and simultaneous anthropogenic causes of climate change may have highlighted human failures to meet our social economic, political, and ecological responsibilities. But, it also may have too soon disregarded the patriarchal theological anthropologies underlying our eco-crises. As Elina Vuola claims, "The *anthropos* in what has been named anthropocentrism may in fact have been the classical subject of Christian theology: white, male, and European. To move away too fast from reworking this *anthropos* from the perspective of colonized, racialized, and gendered subjects also makes it difficult to reconceive human beings' relation to nature in radically new terms."[40] Feminist political mottoes hold that the personal is political, that personal experiences both shape and are shaped by larger social, economic, and political structures. Thus, revisioning eco-politics and effective eco-public theology requires further rethinking of theological anthropology.

Similar to ecofeminist theological anthropologies, Francis rejected all sorts of anthropocentric dualisms between heaven/earth, spirit/matter, soul/body, and leisure/labor (98), which fuel the interconnections

---

38. Vuola, "Latin American Liberation Theologians," 96.
39. Curran, "The Reception of Catholic Social and Economic Teaching," 483.
40. Vuola, "Latin American Liberation Theologians," 108.

between ecological degradation and the subjugation of oppressed peoples, including women. Also, his creation theology linked the universal indwelling of the Spirit with the cultivation of ecological ethics (88). Francis expanded this creation-based pneumatology into a practice of ecological citizenship and its associated civic and political virtues of loving care, responsibility, and solidarity (210–11, 219–20, 229, 231), out of which a new "shared identity" and "social fabric emerges" (232). Nevertheless, in *Laudato Si'*, an integral ecology still trades on and reinforces all sorts of patriarchal hierarchical dualisms that further widen, rather than bridge, long held dominative, dualistic, and divisive gaps in God-human-earthly relations. As I have elaborated elsewhere,[41] Francis foregrounds paternal language for an all-powerful, absolute creator father God (73, 77, 96, 220, 226) as a theological symbol to reject anthropocentric dualisms between human and other-than-human life (89). However, this dominating father God "who alone owns the world" (75) functions as the theological bedrock for the interrelatedness and interdependence of all life in God, but retains patriarchal theo-logics of social, political, economic, and even ecological power and mastery that in turn perpetuate hierarchical human-earthly relations, all of which the letter's theology aims to undo.

By contrast, more effective eco-public theology will deconstruct anthropocentric patriarchal hierarchical dualisms that falsely separate and alienate us from one another and from all life, and will simultaneously reconstruct our mutual and healing interlocking interconnections with as well as responsibilities to all creation, so needed now as a result of various human-induced and human-magnified environmental crises.[42] For example, many ecofeminist theologies turn to incarnational or body theology, specifically the panentheistic metaphor of the world as the body of God;[43] to Sophia, particularly to the personification of God as a woman in the biblical Wisdom tradition who co-creates, binds together, and sustains the diversity and future destiny of all life;[44] or to the Spirit whose creative power inspires and renews all life, who confounds dualisms with mutuality, and who permeates or indwells in all life, the world,

---

41. Carbine, "Imagining and Incarnating an Integral Ecology," 47–66.

42. Franck, "Sophia Wisdom and Climate Change,", 47–52.

43. McFague, *Super, Natural Christians*, 1–9, 12–16, 20–22, 24–25, 32–39, 164–75, and Gebara, *Longing for Running Water*, 75, 82, 84–92, 94, 97, 103, 105, 140–41, 151, 155.

44. Deane-Drummond, "Sophia," 11–31.

and the universe as a radical sign of sacrality.⁴⁵ These ecofeminist theologies reevaluate God-talk to propose a theocentric and biocentric, rather than egocentric, theological anthropology that affirms *both* the inherent equality and sacramentality of all life to reveal the divine presence *and* the relational subjectivity of all life within the *imago Dei*. Foregrounding biocratic rather than technocratic power will require a theological anthropology, as Celia Deane-Drummond contends based on a paraphrase of early Christian anthropology, that "the glory of God is the cosmos fully alive."⁴⁶

Bibliography

Bedford-Strohm, Heinrich. "Public Theology of Ecology and Civil Society." In *Religion and Ecology in the Public Sphere*, edited by Celia Deane-Drummond and Heinrich Bedford-Strohm, 39–56. London: T & T Clark International, 2011.

Beyer, Peter. "Who Shall Speak for the Environment? Translating Religious, Scientific, Economic, and Political Regimes of Power and Knowledge in a Globalized Society." In *Religion and Ecology in the Public Sphere*, edited by Celia Deane-Drummond and Heinrich Bedford-Strohm, 21–37. London: T & T Clark International, 2011.

"Bishops Vote on Pastoral Statement on Pornography, Faithful Citizenship, Revise Strategic Priorities at General Assembly." USCCB News Release November 17, 2015. http://www.usccb.org/news/2015/15-160.cfm.

"Bishops Vote on 2017–2020 Strategic Plan, Encountering the Mercy of Christ and Accompanying His People with Joy, at General Assembly." USCCB News Release November 15, 2016. http://www.usccb.org/news/2016/16-151.cfm.

Carbine, Rosemary P. "Imagining and Incarnating an Integral Ecology: A Critical Ecofeminist Public Theology." In *Planetary Solidarity: Global Women's Voices on Christian Doctrine and Climate Justice*, edited by Grace Ji-Sun Kim and Hilda P. Koster, 47–66. Minneapolis: Fortress, 2017.

Carpenter, Colleen. "Rushing Winds and Rising Waters: Seeking the Presence of God in a Radically Changing World." In *Confronting the Climate Crisis: Catholic Theological Perspectives*, edited by Jame Schaefer, 323–38. Milwaukee: Marquette University Press, 2011.

Curran, Charles E. "The Reception of Catholic Social and Economic Teaching in the United States." In *Modern Catholic Social Teaching: Commentaries and Interpretations*, edited by Kenneth R. Himes, 469–92. Washington, DC: Georgetown University Press, 2005.

Dalton, Anne Marie, and Henry C. Simmons. *Ecotheology and the Practice of Hope*. Albany, NY: State University of New York Press, 2010.

Davenport, Coral. "Counseled by Industry, Not Staff, EPA Chief Is Off to a Blazing Start." *The New York Times* July 1, 2017. https://www.nytimes.com/2017/07/01/us/politics/trump-epa-chief-pruitt-regulations-climate-change.html.

---

45. Johnson, *Women, Earth, Creator Spirit*; Carpenter, "Rushing Winds," 330–34.
46. Deane-Drummond, *Eco-Theology*, 185.

———. "Pope's Views on Climate Change Add Pressure to Catholic Candidates." *The New York Times*, June 16, 2015. https://www.nytimes.com/2015/06/17/us/politics/popes-views-press-gop-on-climate-change.html.

Deane-Drummond, Celia. *Eco-Theology*. Winona, MN: Anselm Academic, 2008.

———. "Sophia: The Feminine Face of God as a Metaphor for an Ecotheology." *Feminist Theology* 16 (1997) 11–31.

Deane-Drummond, Celia, and Heinrich Bedford-Strohm. "Introduction." In *Religion and Ecology in the Public Sphere*, edited by Celia Deane-Drummond and Heinrich Bedford-Strohm, 1–14. London: T & T Clark International, 2011.

DeBonis, Mike. "Catholic Congressman Says He Will Boycott Pope Francis Over Climate Change Stance." *The Washington Post*, September 18, 2015. https://www.washingtonpost.com/news/post-politics/wp/2015/09/18/catholic-congressman-says-he-will-boycott-pope-francis-over-climate-change-stance/.

Ellard, Peter. "Thomas Berry as the Groundwork for a Dark Green Catholic Theology." In *Confronting the Climate Crisis: Catholic Theological Perspectives*, edited by Jame Schaefer, 301–20. Milwaukee: Marquette University Press, 2011.

Fandos, Nicholas. "Climate March Draws Thousands of Protesters Alarmed by Trump's Environmental Agenda." *The New York Times*, April 29, 2017. https://www.nytimes.com/2017/04/29/us/politics/peoples-climate-march-trump.html.

Francis, Pope. *Laudato Si'—On Care for Our Common Home*. Huntington, IN: Our Sunday Visitor, 2015.

———. "Transcript: Pope Francis's Speech to Congress." *The Washington Post*, September 24, 2015. https://www.commonwealmagazine.org/pope-franciss-us-visit.

Franck, Suzanne. "Sophia Wisdom and Climate Change." In *Confronting the Climate Crisis: Catholic Theological Perspectives*, edited by Jame Schaefer, 39–54. Milwaukee: Marquette University Press, 2011.

Friedman, Lisa. "Scientists Fear Trump Will Dismiss Blunt Climate Report." *The New York Times*, August 7, 2017. https://www.nytimes.com/2017/08/07/climate/climate-change-drastic-warming-trump.html.

Gebara, Ivone. *Longing for Running Water: Ecofeminism and Liberation*. Minneapolis: Fortress, 1999.

Goldenberg, Suzanne. "Pope Francis Faces Challenge Persuading US's Catholic Leaders on Climate Change." *The Guardian*, September 16, 2015. https://www.theguardian.com/environment/2015/sep/16/us-catholic-leadership-pope-francis-climate-change.

Goldenberg, Suzanne, and Sabrina Siddiqui. "Jeb Bush Joins Republican Backlash Against Pope on Climate Change." *The Guardian*, June 17, 2015. https://www.theguardian.com/us-news/2015/jun/17/jeb-bush-joins-republican-backlash-pope-climate-change.

Hale, Christopher. "Jeb Bush's Response to Pope Francis's Climate Change Encyclical is Hogwash." *Time*, June 17, 2015. http://time.com/3924287/pope-francis-climate-change.

——— "Rick Santorum Wants Pope Francis to Leave Science to Scientists Only When It's Convenient for Him." *The Washington Post*, June 4, 2015. https://www.washingtonpost.com/news/acts-of-faith/wp/2015/06/04/rick-santorum-wants-pope-francis-to-leave-science-to-scientists-only-when-its-convenient-for-him/.

Holy See Press Office. "Address to the United Nations General Assembly." September 25, 2015. https://www.commonwealmagazine.org/pope-franciss-us-visit.

Johnson, Elizabeth. *Quest for the Living God: Mapping Frontiers in the Theology of God*. New York: Continuum, 2007.

———. *Women, Earth, Creator Spirit*. New York: Paulist, 1993.

Lipton, Eric, and Coral Davenport. "Scott Pruitt, Trump's EPA Pick, Backed Industry Donors Over Regulators." *The New York Times*, January 14, 2017. https://www.nytimes.com/2017/01/14/us/scott-pruitt-trump-epa-pick.html.

Marty, Martin E. "Encyclical." *Sightings*, July 13, 2015. https://divinity.uchicago.edu/sightings/encyclical.

McFague, Sallie. *Super, Natural Christians: How We Should Love Nature*. Minneapolis: Fortress, 1997.

———. *Life Abundant: Rethinking Theology and Economy for a Planet in Peril*. Minneapolis: Fortress, 2001.

Pui-lan, Kwok. "Ecology and the Recycling of Christianity." In *Ecotheology: Voices from South and North*, edited by David G. Hallman, 107–11. Eugene, OR: Wipf & Stock, 1994.

Roewe, Brian. "Iowa Bishop to Presidential Candidates: It's Time to Talk Climate Change." *National Catholic Reporter*, July 2, 2015. https://www.ncronline.org/blogs/eco-catholic/iowa-bishop-presidential-candidates-it-s-time-talk-climate-change.

Ruether, Rosemary Radford. *Gaia and God: An Ecofeminist Theology of Earth Healing*. San Francisco: HarperCollins, 1992.

Schaeffer, Eric. "Reject Scott Pruitt for the EPA." *The New York Times*, January 18, 2017. https://www.nytimes.com/2017/01/18/opinion/reject-scott-pruitt-for-the-epa.html.

Schaefer, Jame. "Solidarity, Subsidiarity, and Preference for the Poor: Extending Catholic Social teaching in Response to the Climate Crisis." In *Confronting the Climate Crisis: Catholic Theological Perspectives*, edited by Jame Schaefer, 389–425. Milwaukee: Marquette University Press, 2011.

Scheid, Daniel. *The Cosmic Common Good: Religious Grounds for Ecological Ethics*. New York: Oxford University Press, 2016.

Shear, Michael D. "Trump Will Withdraw US from Paris Climate Agreement." *The New York Times*, June 1, 2017. https://www.nytimes.com/2017/06/01/climate/trump-paris-climate-agreement.html.

Shear, Michael D., and Brad Plumer. "Climate Report Could Force Trump to Choose Between Science and His Base." *The New York Times*, August 8, 2017. https://www.nytimes.com/2017/08/08/us/politics/climate-trump-scientists-supporters.html.

Shiffman, Mark. "Between the Knower and the Known: *Laudato Si* and the Limits of the Scientific Spirit." *Commonweal*, March 8, 2016. https://www.commonwealmagazine.org/between-knower-known.

St. Fleur, Nicholas. "Scientists, Feeling Under Siege, March Against Trump Policies." *The New York Times*, April 22, 2017. https://www.nytimes.com/2017/04/22/science/march-for-science.html.

Tabuchi, Hiroko, and Henry Fountain. "Bucking Trump, These Cities, States, and Companies Commit to Paris Accord." *The New York Times*, June 1, 2017. https://www.nytimes.com/2017/06/01/climate/american-cities-climate-standards.html.

Taylor, Sarah McFarland. *Green Sisters: A Spiritual Ecology*. Cambridge, MA: Harvard University Press, 2007.

Thompson, A., and Vikas Bajaj. "The Green Energy Revolution Will Happen Without Trump." *The New York Times,* June 20, 2017. https://www.nytimes.com/interactive/2017/06/20/opinion/green-energy-revolution-trump.html?mcubz=1.

Vuola, Elina. "Latin American Liberation Theologians' Turn to Eco(theo)logy—Critical Remarks." In *Religion and Ecology in the Public Sphere*, edited by Celia Deane-Drummond and Heinrich Bedford-Strohm, 91–110. London: T & T Clark International, 2011.

Zimmerman, Kari-Shane Davis. "God, Creation, and the Environment: Feminist Theological Perspectives." In *Green Discipleship: Catholic Theological Ethics and the Environment*, edited by Tobias Winright, 242–65. Winona, MN: Anselm Academic, 2011.

17.

The Body of Christ Given Up for the Ashamed

Rethinking Shame after the Sinking of the Ferry Sewol

Min-Ah Cho

[T]he shame which the just man experiences when confronted by a crime committed by another, and he feels remorse because of its existence, because of its having been irrevocably introduced into the world of existing things, and because his will has proven nonexistent or feeble and was incapable of putting up a good defense.
—Primo Levi.[1]

I could not celebrate the Easter Vigil in 2014. Easter Sunday was only three days after the sinking of the Sewol ferry that eventually took the lives of 304 people, mostly high school students who were en route to a field trip to Jeju Island off South Korea's southern coast.[2] CNN's breaking

---

1. Levi, *The Drowned and the Saved*, 73.
2. The sinking of MV Sewol occurred on April 16, 2014. The ferry capsized while carrying 476 people, killing 304 passengers and crew members, mostly high school students from Danwon High School in Ansan, South Korea. The disaster resulted in broad social and political reaction within and beyond South Korea. Criticism focused

news relentlessly showed the images of my homeland with the families of the missing people crying and screaming out in pain at a harbor near the disaster area. It seemed like Holy Saturday was never ending the night the ferry sank. I could not muster the courage to see the Easter lights and listen to the Easter Proclamation, while the capsized ship carried the lives of hundreds of people into the cold water and their families desperately waited for them to be saved.

A few years have passed since that bleak Easter. As the investigation efforts proceeded with tedious slowness, the disaster has exposed the ugly underside of Korean society, including government corruption, lack of safety regulations, and the indiscretion of political leaders. The disaster was not a mere accident. It announced the failure of the system and of Korean leadership. To this day, the families of the victims are still fighting for a thorough inquiry, a proper governmental response, and the establishment of safety systems—all while learning to live without their beloved.

As a theologian and a person of faith, I have been struggling with the discontinuity that I experienced on that night and beyond—the fracture between the excruciating pain of the Sewol families and the joy and grace of Easter. What has kept me in anguish is a kind of shame for being unable to do anything but watch the numerous lives drowning and their families writhing with pain in the harrowing hours of the night and in their ongoing struggle. Akin to Holocaust survivor and writer Primo Levi's quote above, my capacity was disgracefully "feeble," if not "nonexistent," in the face of this event. I felt shame, as if I was somehow involved, and I sensed that it was "irrevocable."[3]

In fact, such shame was a collective emotion of many Koreans in their response to the systemic failure revealed by the ferry disaster. The shame experienced after the disaster shook the calm of many people's daily lives and triggered additional post-traumatic events including

---

on: 1) the actions of the captain and most of the crew who escaped from the ferry while hundreds of passengers remained trapped inside; 2) the ferry operator and the regulators who oversaw its operations; 3) the South Korean government's failure to rescue the victims and to take responsibility for the failed safety systems; and 4) South Korean media for its disaster response and attempts to downplay government culpability. The families of the victims continue to protest, demanding the government investigate the disaster to the fullest extent and establish laws and systems to prevent reoccurrence of such a disaster. Korean citizens have supported the families by holding nationwide and international protests.

3. Levi, *The Drowned and The Saved*, 86.

depression and suicides. Nonetheless, it has also intensely motivated people to move beyond their comfort zones in order to protest against the wrongful system and to faithfully support the victims' families.

Focusing on the experience of Koreans after the Sewol tragedy, this chapter explores various facets of shame after failure. In particular, it uncovers how to channel the destructive power of shame into conscientious self-reflection and compassionate authority to stand with those who suffer. Theologian Edward Schillebeeckx's view on the Eucharist is particularly instrumental for this discussion. Based on his insights, I suggest the Eucharist as a powerful symbol that invites us into a process of transforming shame into constructive remembrance of our suffering and the anticipation of solidarity with the suffering of others.

Shame as a Moral Emotion: "We Ought to Be Ashamed…"

Shame is defined as an "acute arousal or fear of being exposed, scrutinized, and judged negatively by others" after one becomes aware of her failure.[4] The experience of shame includes feelings of regret, anxiety, anger, embarrassment, disgust, indignity, and withdrawal. While shame is initially a reaction to public disapproval, the self in shame is affected not only by the disapproval of others, but also by an "internalized observing 'other'" because she judges and feels about herself according to how others judge and feel about her.[5]

Such role of self in shame as "both agent and object of observation and disapproval" distinguishes shame from guilt, which often arises together with shame.[6] Guilt concerns a rule that one has broken while shame hinges upon a profound sense of diminishment of self encroached by both external and internalized "others."[7] Shame can be even more damaging than guilt, because it looks primarily to the entire self and

---

4. Fischer and Tangney, eds., *Self-Conscious Emotions*, 3–22.

5. Lewis, "The Role of the Self in Shame," 1181; "Self-Conscious Emotion," 83, 68–78.

6. Lewis, "The Role of the Self in Shame," 1181.

7. To briefly note the distinction between guilt and shame, I take the point described by Williams, Lamb, and Manion. They pursue the distinction between guilt and shame in parallel with the distinction between rules and ideals. For more discussion on this subject, see Williams, *Shame and Necessity*; Manion, "Moral Relevance of Shame"; Lamb, "Guilt, Shame, and Morality"; Lewis, *Guilt and Shame in Neurosis*; and Baumeister, Stillwell, and Heatherton, "Guilt."

could entail a collapse of self, whereas guilt looks to an individual act and rarely infringes on self-boundaries.

The aspect of shame that affects the sense of one's agency makes shame a precarious subject to deal with, especially for a feminist theologian. The doctrine of original sin has assigned women misdirected guilt and false shame, consequently trapping them in the confinement of Christian patriarchy.[8] Misplaced shame is painful and bitter not only for women, but also for people of color, the disabled, sexual minorities, victims of sexual violence, and whoever lives outside the "norms" imposed by society. By focusing on aspects over which one has no control, the Christian discourse of shame leads her to a sense of isolation, self-revulsion, and even to a destructive relationship with herself and with God.

However, shame also refers to the "ability" to look back at ourselves after a failure, which gives us authority to admit the failure and respond to it. As Mark Twain says, the human being is "the only animal that blushes."[9] Shame makes a human being more human. Shame attunes our sensitivity toward others. Several scholars of psychology and philosophy have identified this constructive aspect of shame and re-evaluated it as a moral emotion. Scholars who promote the positivity of shame point out that most accounts of shame hardly differentiate its moral aspects from false or dysfunctional ones. Shame—in its constructive aspect—according to Carl D. Schneider for example, is a "mark of the human," which leads toward an authentic dimension of self-awareness and value integration in relation to others.[10] Helen M. Lynd further argues that shame has "revelatory potential," because it exposes one to her unknown aspect of self and invites her to self-assessment.[11] These scholars propose that shame can "motivate a person positively to make changes in her moral character" and "to forge positive bonds with others."[12] It generates a powerful self-reflective force that can challenge our highly ego-centered culture.

---

8. For a classical example of feminist criticism against the doctrine of original sin, see Plaskow, *Sex, Sin, and Grace*.

9. Twain, *Following the Equator*, 256.

10. Schneider, *Shame, Exposure and Privacy*, 4–5.

11. Lynd, *On Shame and the Search for Identity*, 20; McNish and Dayringer, *Transforming Shame*, 52.

12. Manion, "Moral Relevance of Shame," 79–80.

The shame experienced by a number of Koreans after the Sewol tragedy points to the need for a positive reconsideration of shame. Beyond question, the Sewol ferry disaster has drawn a flood of emotional responses from the entire Korean society, varying from shock and fear to sorrow and sympathy. As a part of those reactions, shame was apparent in the groups and individuals who have firmly stood in solidarity with the families of victims.

Before discussing the shame experience of Koreans after the disaster, it is worth mentioning how shame instigates the shared sense of responsibility in a collectivistic culture like Korea.[13] Although the difference between the collectivistic culture and the individualistic culture is only in degree and not in kind, the two cultures show variations in perspectives about the relationship between shame and moral responsibility. In the individualistic culture moral responsibility is concerned mostly with guilt and has a "robust control condition." To put it another way, "in order to be blameworthy for a state of affairs, [one] must have played an active role in bringing it about."[14] In the collectivistic culture, however, moral responsibility is concerned not only with guilt, but also with shame, and is extended to the entire people who belong to the culture. The members of the collectivistic culture tend to feel responsible for another member's failure, misfortune, indignity, and wrongness even if they have not intended to bring it about. The emphasis on shame leads the people of collectivistic culture to feel responsible or even atone for public acts over which they have little or no control.[15]

The reactions of many Koreans to the ferry disaster showcase how such a collective shame can develop into a shared sense of moral

13. While Ruth Benedict differentiates the shame culture from the guilt culture and offers a description of the distinctive character traits in each culture in her controversial book *The Chrysanthemum and the Sword*, I disagree with her dichotomous distinction between the two cultures, particularly in regard with her discussion on the difference of moral sentiment in the two cultures. Benedict's view ignores shame's influence upon the sense of the shared responsibility, while emphasizing external force to do good things and attempt to save face in the shame culture.

14. Sommers, *Relative Justice*, 2.

15. The reaction of many first generation Korean Americans to the shootings at Virginia Tech University in April 2007 stands as an example. As the anthropologist Kyeyoung Park points out, Korean Americans wanted to do something about the incident because they felt ashamed of the fact that the shooter was a South Korean citizen with US permanent resident status. "Some of them feel truly responsible, even though they had nothing to do with it." Park, "Where Do We Go From Here?," 89–120. For more discussion on this subject, see Sommers, *Relative Justice*.

responsibility. Shortly after the disaster, contrite and remorseful statements of shame have burst forth, such as: "I would die of shame if I do nothing to support the families," "I feel ashamed of enjoying a comfortable life when my neighbors are suffering that hard," "I am ashamed for having been complacent to the unjust powers of society, even if I knew I could have countered," and "we ought to be ashamed of having ignored the corruption of the system up until this point." Shame even manifested in the families of the victims who called for acts of solidarity. They cried with pain, "I can't give up the protest because I don't want to be a shameful parent again when I reunite with my child in heaven," and "until now that I lost my child, I had never fought for others. I feel so embarrassed and guilty for having sought the safety and prosperity of only myself and my immediate family."[16]

As the investigation effort was delayed due to government neglect, the collective shame of South Koreans has grown particularly distinct and strong. While sympathetic reactions withered and turned into exhaustion, apathy, and even reprimand against the victims' families, shame developed into a more specific moral influence.[17] Noteworthy above all is how, after the disaster, shame pushed South Koreans to recognize that all of us were responsible for the failure of the leadership of the society and also tied to the families' suffering which is a consequence of the failure. Shame urged us to reflect on the collective failure and pain of our nation. In the wake of the tragedy, shame thus prompted the demand for shared responsibility and reinforced the rise of different movements and shared action including protests, religious rituals, prayers, artistic works, and performances.

The Sewol tragedy illustrates that shame can bring about deep accountability, reflection, and act of solidarity, which mere sympathy and pity cannot. Susan Sontag's critical view on sympathy is accurate in this regard: "So far as we feel sympathy, we feel we are not accomplices to what caused the suffering [. . .]. To set aside the sympathy, we extend to others beset by war and murderous politics for a reflection on how our privileges are located on the same map as their suffering, and may—in

---

16. Statements were taken from Korean newspapers and social media. See articles published in English on the collective shame after the disaster: "Ferry disaster fills South Korea with shame," *Los Angeles Times*, April 22, 2014; "South Koreans blame themselves for ferry tragedy," *Public Radio International*, April 17, 2014.

17. "Families of South Korea ferry victims still fighting for investigation one year later," *Los Angeles Times*, April 11, 2015.

ways we might prefer not to imagine—be linked to their suffering."[18] True and enduring compassion requires a sense of responsibility, and it is inseparable from reflective thinking provoked by shame. Beyond sympathy and pity, shame compels us as a community to admit our failure and transform it into something constructive and imperative, instead of simply releasing it or feeling less pain.

The philosopher Michael L. Morgan, whose research uncovers the collective shame of bystanders after inhumane events such as the Holocaust and the Rwandan genocide, would affirm the shame emotion of Koreans after the disaster.[19] Morgan explains that shared shame after such tragic events can involve the revision of our moral agency and can motivate us to attend to our responsibility to and for others. The thorough challenge that shame gives us can awaken our sense of who we are and what we hope to be. It can turn our conscience to an "invigorating force for moral action against the violence and enormity of the world in which we live."[20] It can enable us to be truly compassionate toward others by suffering with them and conducting ourselves with accountability.

Yet, despite such powerful potential, shame does not always move us into a constructive direction. Rather, it often undermines our confidence and courage and keeps us from facing the ordeals of life. Martha Nussbaum is acutely aware of this ambivalent nature of shame. In her book *Hiding from Humanity*, Nussbaum criticizes "primitive" or "narcissistic" shame and notes that this kind of shame manifests in the inclination to deny one's own weakness by projecting it onto others.[21] Such callous shame is a "threat to all possibility of morality and community, and indeed to a creative inner life."[22] It could lead to self-abnegation, obsession, defensive anger, and aversion for others, as demonstrated in numerous cases of "honor" killings. However, Nussbaum also clearly affirms the constructive aspect of shame in inciting moral responsibility. When shame is connected with norms that are "basic to the shared political conception" of public life, it is actually "anti-narcissistic, reinforcing a sense of common human vulnerability, a sense of inclusion of all human

---

18. Sontag, *Regarding the Pain of Others*, 102.

19. Morgan, *On Shame*. The phrase "collective shame" is coined by Theodor Heuss to describe the emotion of Germans who never ceased feeling ashamed for crimes the Nazis committed. Kansteiner, *In Pursuit of German Memory*, 207.

20. Morgan, *On Shame*, 54.

21. Nussbaum, *Hiding from Humanity*, 192.

22. Ibid., 208.

beings in the community, and related ideas of interdependence and mutual responsibility."[23]

As such, shame is complicated and uncertain. We cannot simply relieve or overcome shame. Our response to shame constantly wavers between a "productively transformative" potential and a range of "destructively inhibiting effects."[24] Thus we need to process shame and think through it within ourselves and with others. In this fashion, shame begs the question: How can we channel the negative and dysfunctional effects of shame into a positive and constructive direction? Instead of serving as a toxic and self-destructive force, in what way can shame be a productive search for integrity, a challenge to the grandiose ego, and a compassionate authority toward others?

In what follows, I suggest a process for positively transforming shame through Christian witness. Based on Edward Schillebeeckx's insights on the Eucharist, I delve into the ways in which the Eucharist invites the ashamed into the process of reclaiming their authentic self and expanding the boundary of their relationship to others through shame itself.

Shame and the Eucharist: The Body of God for the Ashamed

> After the disaster, I came to see the Eucharist in a different way. The bread dipped in red wine gave me the chills all of sudden. It looked exactly like a piece of Jesus' flesh covered in blood. Then I thought, "Ah, the disciples. How courageous and mercilessly firm they were! They ate the bloody body of Jesus at which they had *shamefully* peeped before. And engraved it on their own bodies." — Excerpted from a testimony of Eunhee Park, the mother of Ye-Eun Yoo, one of the victims of the Sewol ferry tragedy.[25]

Eunhee Park is a ferry victim's mother. Since the loss of her daughter in the disaster, she too has experienced shame, besides visceral pain and anger, for feeling so powerless to protect her daughter against the

---

23. Ibid., 213.

24. Burrus, *Saving Shame*, 4.

25. The original text of Park's testimony at *Kukminilbo*, July 12, 2016. Emphasis mine.

collective failure of the society. Yet, Park has earnestly promoted protests for demanding the truth of the disaster and installing safety systems to secure the lives of others. Park notes that since the disaster, the biblical stories of suffering became so impactful that they enabled her to reframe her story and gain the authority to interrupt and challenge competing narratives of her circumstances. By paralleling the conversion story of Jesus' disciples after the crucifixion with her own story after the disaster, Park's testimony above invites us to ponder her experience through the biblical narrative.

The story of the disciples on the night of Jesus' death is a story of failure and conversion, not of disloyalty and punishment. The disciples were not "the persecutors of Jesus." Instead, they failed to follow Jesus due to their weakness and limitation.[26] Just as in any other story of failure, the disciples experienced deep shame. Peter's denial of Jesus is a convincing example of how shame serves a significant role in the conversion of the disciples, as depicted in each of the four Gospels, which vividly describe Peter's failure and shame.

At the Last Supper, Jesus predicted that Peter would deny him three times. Peter rebutted. However, the night of torment came and Peter denied that he was with Jesus because he was afraid of being mocked and ashamed. After a rooster crowed, Peter became conscious of what he was doing and remembered the words of Jesus. He felt deeply remorseful for his weakness and cowardice. He "went out and wept bitterly" (Matt 26:69–75; Mark 14:66–72; Luke 22:54–62; John 18:15–27).

Peter's story reveals the ambivalence of shame that we have previously discussed.[27] Peter's first shame in front of the onlookers was a "primitive" and "narcissistic" shame that emerged out of his fear and weakness (Matt 26:69–74a; Mark 14:66–71; Luke 22:54–60a; John 18:15–17 and 25–26). This shame influenced Peter to not only deny Jesus, but also his own social identity and relationships. Nonetheless, his second shame, which arose after the crowing of a rooster, awakened him from self-denial and isolation (Matt 26:74b–75; Mark 14:72; Luke 22:60b–62; John 18:27). Unlike the first shame, the second shame was a moral emotion that developed from his failure to uphold his inner values and integrity in relation to Jesus and to his fellow disciples. Peter "wept bitterly"

---

26. Edward Schillebeeckx also reads the disciples' story as a story of failure. *Jesus*, 382.

27. Jacoby briefly mentions the ambivalence of Peter's shame in *Shame and the Origins of Self-Esteem*, 20.

because he was ashamed of himself for offending the truth, disowning Jesus, and violating his conviction. At last, however, he turned himself from the primitive shame and returned to the fellowship with Jesus.

As Park attests in her testimony, Peter's experience of failure and shame corresponds with her and her fellow protesters' experience, and thus provides us with hope for a positive outcome of their struggle. Still, however, questions remain: Peter and Park's shame needed a new direction if transformed into something constructive and life-giving. What happened while they were navigating between the two poles of shame? What motivated them to turn their primitive shame into a moral emotion? How were they able to break through the quandary of shame rather than falling into self-imprisonment? The immediate answer to these questions cannot be "the resurrection" because, as Edward Schillebeeckx points out, anyone who has at first disowned Jesus and subsequently confess him to be the "risen One" and the "bringer of salvation" has "of necessity undergone 'conversion process.'"[28]

I find Schillebeeckx's theology of the Eucharist helpful for this discussion. His profound sense of balance between the reality of suffering and eschatological hope holds an answer for pondering the ambivalence of shame. Schillebeeckx, who developed his theology during the midst of the failure of the World Wars, remained keenly sensitive toward the emotional pains of the afflicted. In his reading of the disciples' story after the crucifixion, Schillebeeckx perceptively attends to the failure and shame of the disciples. He underlines that Peter and the disciples were in need of conversion that would "resume the task of 'being a disciple' and 'imitating Jesus.'"[29] While emphasizing that their conversion was initiated by the unconditional mercy and forgiveness of God, he also illuminates what happened inside of these men in their process of conversion.[30]

Here, based on Schillebeeckx's account of the disciples, I suggest the twofold significance of the fellowship of Jesus that led them into conversion. This process is eventually brought into sharp focus through Schillebeeckx's theology of the Eucharist: the remembrance and anticipation of the communion with God.[31]

---

28. Schillebeeckx, *Jesus*, 381.
29. Ibid.
30. Ibid., 381–82; 390.
31. Jennifer Cooper names these two elements as the focus of Schillebeeckx's theology of the Eucharist. Cooper, "The Eucharist," 29.

First, the role of remembrance was critical in the disciples' conversion, because it awakened them from the deserted cell of shame. According to Schillebeeckx, the disciples—despite their failure—remembered their life shared in the fellowship with Jesus who also had been broken and humiliated and yet "[willed] only the well-being and not the destruction of [people]."[32] They retained in their mind Jesus' fellowship with the failed and ashamed like them, his eating and drinking with them, and his offer of salvation to them. The disciples recalled, most of all, the peculiar words of Jesus through the Words of Institution when he shared bread and wine at the Last Supper: "This is my body and blood given up for you." Jesus' offering of his body and blood in the face of death was by no means predicting a vindictive punishment and vengeful victory. It was a radical, unceasing invitation to a shared table and shared life. For the disciples, this remembrance was an experience of accompaniment that brought their heart to the heart of Jesus. It reopened their eyes from the solitary sphere of shame and compelled them to reassess their emotions and thoughts.

Remembering these aspects of Jesus' fellowship, in turn, drove the disciples to anticipate their communion, or salvation, with God. For Schillebeeckx, salvation is a "healed and reconciled life" that overcomes "all personal and social forms of alienation." It is the "being in wholeness" of one's life and her history.[33] The disciples already had a glimpse of it as they were offered a new relationship with Jesus whom they confessed as the Crucified and Risen One. The disciples carried their anticipation into action by assembling together, and their experience of God's forgiveness gathered them back into community. Thus their anticipation of communion with God evolved into seeking communities of Christians where Jesus' message of salvation remained alive. The reconciled life found in communion with God and with other human beings allowed the disciples to move beyond primitive shame and firmly continue the mission of proclaiming the Risen One.

For Schillebeeckx, the twofold significance of remembering and anticipating the communion of God merges into the enactment of the Eucharist. The relation between remembrance and anticipation runs as a theme throughout his theology of the Eucharist, while generating tension between each other. Schillebeeckx notes in his book *The Eucharist*:

---

32. Schillebeeckx, *Jesus*, 382.
33. Ibid., 624.

"Our personal relationship with the Lord is also essentially an *anamnesis*, a calling to mind of the historical event of salvation on the cross, not insofar as it is past, but insofar as it endures eternally in its completion. The eternity is, however, not situated behind history, but accomplished in history."[34]

The act of remembrance upholds the forgiving mercy of God, and yet it also reminds believers of their failure, weakness, and shame. Unless it is brought into action to meet the anticipation of communion with God, the act of remembrance exacerbates their wounds. It is, however, this paradoxical tension between remembrance and anticipation held in the Eucharist that draws the ashamed like the disciples and Park into processing their shame and reassessing it productively.

Borrowing from the words of theologian Susan Ross, Schillebeeckx's approach to sacramentality is marked by "a strong sense of ambiguity and tension, made more acute by his increasing focus on human suffering."[35] Schillebeeckx lays emphasis on the Eucharist not so much as the triumphalist or mechanical view in which the divine grace is automatically guaranteed precisely because he knew that it would not be helpful for people who must struggle with their suffering and shame even after they experience conversion.

The kind of shame that disciples and Park bear will persist for years to come. They have to endure it for their entire life because they cannot and do not want to forget. For Schillebeeckx, who himself was concerned with suffering, the Eucharist is an invitation for the failed and ashamed to endure their ongoing struggles yet remain in communion with God. The Eucharist, in its ordinariness and radical inclusivity, holds the ashamed firmly in their search for the truth of themselves and the world. The Eucharist constantly reminds them that their failure may not be final and that the reconciled life, the communion with God and with other human beings, is possible and necessary—despite, or more precisely, because of their shame. "The living Christ identifies himself with the community at the table," says Schillebeeckx. Thus, "we can live in this community from his redeeming death and his being raised by the Father. This is sufficient for Christian life."[36]

---

34. Schillebeeckx, *The Eucharist*, 126.
35. Hilkert and Schreiter, *The Praxis*, 138.
36. Schillebeeckx, *The Eucharist*, 139.

Shame and the Eucharist: Holding and Moving Forward

In discussing the ambivalent nature of shame, we have taken a risk by looking into the painful emotion of shame after the Sewol ferry disaster in hopes of finding ways in which we can channel it from a dysfunctional force into a constructive and relational power. Building upon the Christian experience of a ferry victim's mother, I have argued that shame and vulnerability can expand into self-awareness, a redefinition of our capacities, and the authority to confront habitual injustice. Yet, shame also contains pitfalls. It is an unsettling and disquieting emotion that constantly vacillates between two extreme poles of toxicity and transformation. We cannot simply mitigate it lest we lose accountability for our failure.

Perhaps Park and her fellow protesters, including myself, must continue struggling with our shame. We may walk through the darkness of Holy Saturday haunted by the graphic memory and shame of the night the ferry sank. Perhaps the glorious Easter lights will continue flickering at us. Regardless of what happens, the Eucharist penetrates into the darkness of our days by inviting us to the reconciled life and by empowering us to build communities of compassion. In our yearning for the body of Christ broken and given up for us, we dream of a society where shame like ours can be productive, where we can reflect on our apathy to see the face of the suffering other, where we can challenge the misery and injustice of our failed systems. There we hope our shame may be embraced shamelessly.

Bibliography

Baumeister, R. F., A. M. Stillwell, and T. F. Heatherton. "Guilt: An Interpersonal Approach." *Psychological Bulletin* 115 (1994) 243–67.

Benedict, Ruth. *The Chrysanthemum and the Sword: Patterns of Japanese Culture.* Boston: Houghton Mifflin, 1989.

Borgman, Erik, and Paul D. Murray. *Sacramentalizing Human History.* London: SCM, 2012.

Burrus, Virginia. *Saving Shame: Martyrs, Saints, and Other Abject Subjects.* Philadelphia: University of Pennsylvania Press, 2007.

Cooper, Jennifer. "The Eucharist: Remembrance, Anticipation, Real Presence." In *Sacramentalizing Human History*, edited by Erik Borgman and Paul D. Murray, 25–31. London: SCM, 2012.

Fischer, K. W., and J. P. Tangney, eds. *Self-Conscious Emotions: The Psychology of Shame, Guilt, Embarrassment and Pride.* New York: Guilford Press, 1955. Cited in Paul Gilbert and Bernice Andrews, eds., *Shame: Interpersonal Behavior, Psychopathology, and Culture.* New York: Oxford University Press, 1998.

Hilkert, Mary, and Robert Schreiter. *The Praxis of the Reign of God: An Introduction to the Theology of Edward Schillebeeckx.* New York: Fordham University Press, 2002.
Jacoby, Mario. *Shame and the Origins of Self-Esteem: A Jungian Approach.* London: Routledge, 1996.
Kansteiner, Wulf. *In Pursuit of German Memory: History, Television, and Politics after Auschwitz.* Athens, OH: Ohio University Press, 2006.
Lamb, R. E. "Guilt, Shame, and Morality. *Philosophy and Phenomenological Research,* vol. 43, no. 3 (March 1983) 1–24.
Levi, Primo. *The Drowned and The Saved.* New York: Vintage, 1989.
Lewis, Helen Block. *Guilt and Shame in Neurosis.* New York: International University, 1971.
Lewis, Michael. "The Role of the Self in Shame." *Social Research* (Winter 2003)1181–2014.
———. "Self-Conscious Emotion," *American Scientist,* vol. 83, no. 168 (January–February 1995) 68–78.
Lynd, Helen Merrell. *On Shame and the Search for Identity.* London: Routledge, 1958.
Manion, Jennifer C. "Moral Relevance of Shame." *American Philosophical Quarterly,* vol. 39, no. 1 (January 2002) 73–90.
McNish, Jill, and Richard L. Dayringer. *Transforming Shame: A Pastoral Response.* Binghamton, NY: Routledge, 2004.
Morgan, Michael L. *On Shame.* New York: Routledge, 2008.
Nussbaum, Martha C. *Hiding from Humanity: Disgust, Shame, and the Law.* Princeton, NJ: Princeton University Press, 2004.
Park, Kyeyoung. "Where Do We Go From Here? The Virginia Tech Shootings and the Korean American Community." *Journal of Korean Language Education* 20, 89–120.
Plaskow, Judith. *Sex, Sin, and Grace: Women's Experience and the Theologies of Reinhold Niebuhr and Paul Tillich.* Washington, DC: UPA, 1979.
Schillebeeckx, Edward. *The Eucharist.* London: Burns & Oates, 2005.
———. *Jesus: An Experiment in Christology.* New York: Crossroad, 1981.
Schneider, Carl D. *Shame, Exposure and Privacy.* Boston: Beacon, 1977.
Sommers, Tamler. *Relative Justice: Cultural Diversity, Free Will, and Moral Responsibility.* Princeton, NJ: Princeton University Press, 2012.
Sontag, Susan. *Regarding the Pain of Others.* New York: Macmillan, 2003.
Twain, Mark. *Following the Equator: A Journey Around the World.* Hartford, CT: American Publishing Company, 1898.
Williams, Bernard. *Shame and Necessity.* Berkeley, CA: University of California Press, 1993.

18.

"Love Never Fails"

Rereading 1 Corinthians 13 with a Womanist Hermeneutic of Love's Struggle

Mitzi J. Smith

Love is patient; love is kind; love is not envious or boastful or arrogant or rude; It does not insist on its own way; it is not irritable or resentful; it does not rejoice in wrongdoing, but rejoices in the truth. It bears all things, believes all things, hopes all things, endures all things. Love never ends.... When I was a child, I spoke like a child, I thought like a child, I reasoned like a child; when I became an adult, I put an end to childish ways.... And now faith, hope, and love abide, these three; and the greatest of these is love.
—1 Corinthians 13:4–8a, 11, 13, NRSV.

This essay offers a reading of Paul's theology of failure (love never fails; Greek: *piptei*) to construct a hermeneutic of love that encourages violated, dispossessed, and subordinated persons, particularly non-white women and poor women, to participate in their own freedom. I read 1 Corinthians 13 through a womanist lens that prioritizes black women's experiences, traditions, and artifacts. I attempt to construct a liberating contextual literary analysis that acknowledges the complexity of embodied love and the organic relationship between love and active resistance to oppression. Love as expressed between and among human beings is embodied, imperfect love refracted by/through human fallibility. For non-white women, the impact of intersectional oppressions like racism, classism, and (hetero)sexism contributes to the complexity of embodied love. As Cheryl Townsend Gilkes states,

> All human experience is embodied experience and the consequences of cultural humiliation are most dramatically shown with reference to the body. Not only is experience embodied, but stereotypes, pernicious cultural representations of people, are also embodied images. All racial stereotypes are usually named images attached to an image of a body, and all of those named images are gendered.[1]

I also read 1 Corinthians 13 inter(con)textually, constructing a dialogue between the biblical text and cultural (con)texts. Proto-womanist and former enslaved African Howard Thurman's grandmother Nancy Ambrose rejected most of the Pauline corpus because of Pauline admonitions that slaves submit to their masters. The slave masters' preachers declared that according to Paul, God willed that Africans should be enslaved to whites. Thus, God expected enslaved Africans to be docile and obedient—never resisting their enslavement. Yet Ambrose saw fit to salvage chapter 13 of 1 Corinthians, removing it from its literary context and decontextualizing and recontextualizing the passage.[2] According to Alice Walker's definition, a womanist "loves struggle."[3] But love in 1 Corinthians 13 is contextually hierarchical, patriarchal, and anti-resistance of oppression. Walker's statement should not be understood in the sense of black women loving struggle for the sake of struggle and unaffected by the trauma inflicted on one's mind, body, and soul from engaging in the perennial struggle for freedom, voice, visibility, dignity, equal rights, equity, and justice. Black women love struggle because hatred and oppression yield nothing without a fight; it is through struggle—resistance, protest, and boycott—that black people have gained liberty and rights. Black women would prefer that they did not have to struggle against race, class, and gender bias. Struggle has yielded many casualties. Too often, women of color, especially poor black women, are asked to love and give sacrificially. And very often they sacrifice their own well-being, dignity,

---

1. Gilkes, "The 'Loves' and 'Troubles,'" 92–93.
2. Thurman, *Jesus and the Disinherited*, 30–31.
3. Walker, *In Search of Our Mothers' Gardens*, xi.

happiness, and vocation, for the sake of men, manhood, children, family, church, and other institutions while being treated oppressively.

The dominant society with the help of social scientific research has attempted to persuade black people to view their relationships through the lens of white patriarchal heteronormativity, which is often undergirded by a theology of failed love and/or a failed theology of love. Black women and women of color are accused of failing to love their men and communities if they do not imitate white patriarchal love inclusive of submission to male headship ideology. What does 1 Corinthians 13 have to say to black women and other women who live daily with the trauma of misogyny, racism, classism, dis-abilism, heterosexism, and the intersectionality of oppressions and violence? How do we love ourselves and others while rejecting our subordination and oppressions? A female child victimized by sexual abuse and neglect might find it confusing at the very least to be asked to embrace a love that is unconditionally long-suffering; that requires her to endure all things, to esteem others better than herself, including her abusers. Such a love would require a denial of her own experiences, abuse, and oppression. Women and children who have experienced abuse generally need time and space to recover a sense of self-worth and identity before they are able to risk loving others in wholesome ways. Most victims of sexual abuse are women, and most often they are victimized by men, men whom they know. Unbridled patriarchy takes and is never satiated, especially when men themselves struggle for wholeness due to the trauma of classism, racism, heterosexism, and other forms of oppression that diminish a man's sense of self and self-love. When that self is constructed as "manhood" predicated on the panacea of female submissiveness, women's sense of self-embodied wholeness must be sacrificed to the patriarchal gods.

First Corinthians and Gender Subordination

Theologies of love—love never fails—based on 1 Corinthians 13 generally neglect important aspects of the chapter's literary context. Reading 1 Corinthians 13 in its literary context demonstrates a theology of love that failed to transcend patriarchalism but was meant to reinforce it. I do not attempt a comprehensive literary analysis here; instead, I analyze three significant passages that contribute to an understanding of 1 Corinthians 13 within the framework of Paul's overall project in 1 Corinthians of subordinating women to men. The texts I discuss are: 1 Corinthians

1:10–17, the dis/appearance of Chloe's people, and 1 Corinthians 11:1–2, the ideological epistemology of headship or patriarchal hierarchy. These texts and the immediate context (addressed below) demonstrate that 1 Corinthians 13 is part of Paul's rhetorical agenda promoting a gender hierarchy that privileges maleness while encouraging the submission of women to men for the sake of unity and order among the Corinthian believers.

1 Corinthians 1:10–17. Paul apparently wrote his first letter to the Corinthians to address the report he received from Chloe's people informing him of theo-political divisions among the believers (1:1). Readers might assume that the omission of Chloe from the list at 1:10–17 demonstrates that she was not one of those leaders to whom believers in Corinth attached themselves because of her charisma (gifts) and teachings; that her people were marginal tattle-tellers and not agentive participants, forming their own community of believers. That is an impression Paul's letter gives. But reading with a hermeneutics of suspicion that interrogates the rhetorical silencing of women and the bait (report of Chloe's people—she has people) and switch (she is excluded from the Androcentric list of party leaders who also have people: "I belong to Paul, ... to Apollos, ... to Cephas, ... or to Christ," 1:12), we are able to uncover another story. The omission of Chloe from the list is the first hint of and step toward the subordination of women among the Corinthian believers so as to achieve and/or recover order and patriarchal authority; Chloe is a leader, unacknowledged by Paul, among the Corinthian prophets.[4] Both Jesus Christ and Paul have been subordinated to a status parallel to Apollos and Cephas (and Chloe too) as party leaders among the Corinthian believers. At stake is the headship of Jesus and more significantly Paul as the flesh-and-blood or earthy "father" of the Corinthian believers (4:15; 8:6), despite having baptized only Crispus and Gaius (1:14).

Without having received some kind of communication from Chloe's people—those who belong to Chloe, Paul would not have written his first letter to the believers at Corinth about the existence of party divisions and/or strife among them. Chloe's people are perhaps a group of slaves and/or disciples who have adhered to Chloe's understanding of the Gospel of Jesus Christ, perhaps because she owns them, and/or they belong to or reside in her household, and/or they are drawn to her charisma

---

4. I first suggested this possibility in a 2015 Society of Biblical Literature panel response to Wire, *The Corinthian Women Prophets*.

(gifts).⁵ Perhaps Paul wants his readers to see Chloe, a gifted woman with a following, as part of the problem, along with women mentioned in chapters 11 and 14 of the letter. To neglect or fail to acknowledge the existence of Chloe and her people beyond revealing them as the source of the rumored divisions among the believers in Corinth renders them invisible and divests them of authority and agency.

Complicating and contributing to women's autonomy and giftedness in Corinth may be the presence of materially wealthy and educated women and men, as well as female and male slaves and former slaves hoping for and experiencing some measure of liberty and autonomy. If all are equal, why shouldn't they expect the same freedoms? Slaves and freed-persons were gifted people too and perhaps some could have been wealthy despite their social status as slaves and/or freed-persons.⁶

1 Cor 11: 2–16. At 11:2–16 Paul delineates an epistemology of hierarchical headship—a way to understand (*eidon*) order and subordination particularly in regard to praying and prophesying. The hierarchy goes like this: Christ heads biological man (*aner*); biological man being the image (*eikon*) and glory (*doxa*) of God is the head of woman (*gyne*); biological woman is, in her very being, the glory (*doxa*) of man (*aner*), as she is from man and was created for man (there is no mutuality here). Thus, to remind everyone, including herself, that she is subordinate to man, a woman ought to wear a symbol of her subordination on her head—a veil. This ideology would apply to silent, private, and public prayers and prophesying. The veil as the symbol of this ideological epistemology of headship/hierarchy serves as a visible reminder of women's innate and divine subordination to men and of women's submission to her subordination. Men must not cover their heads or grow their hair long as a visible reminder that they are the head of women. A mutual interdependence exists between women and men, but within the ideological epistemology of hierarchical headship.

Paul's acknowledgement of the interdependence of men and women and of the fact that only women give birth is summed up with the statement that "all things come from God" (11:11). Paul rhetorically places the seal of God on the gendered hierarchical order. After arguing for what Paul understands to be a natural theo-anthropological hierarchy of

---

5. In my 2015 Society of Biblical Literature panel response to Wire, *The Corinthian Women Prophets*, I suggested that Chloe has people in the same way that Apollos, Cephas, and Paul have people who say that they "belong" to them.

6. Smith, "Slavery in the Early Church," 14.

gender, he invites the Corinthians to "judge for yourselves" whether or not nature (*physis*) supports his argument, asserting human constructed biases about women and men with long hair, and using the same or similar evaluative language he has already employed: It is disgraceful for a man to pray or prophesy with covered head (11:4) and long hair on a man is degrading (11:14). Equally so, a woman's long hair is her glory, and it is disgraceful for her to shave off her hair or to pray or prophesy with her head/hair uncovered (11:5, 15). Christine Amjad-Ali argues that Paul is trying to adhere to traditional, cultural symbols that validate the subordination of women to men "while transforming the substance."[7] Paul acknowledges the equality of men and women but preserves traditional symbolism that reflects women's subordination. But the theological justification Paul uses for retaining the symbolism later becomes justification for silencing women and prohibiting them from leadership roles.[8] On the one hand, Paul states that factions are to be expected in order to distinguish imposters from the genuine believers in Corinth (11:19). Yet, other kinds of divisions must be done away with by establishing hierarchy and order.

1 Corinthians 13 and its Immediate Literary Context

Chapter 13 is sandwiched between Paul's chapter 12 on spiritual gifts and chapter 14 regulating the gift of prophecy and the use of gifts in worship, including the subordination and silencing of women. First Corinthians 13, the so-called love chapter, is predicated upon the rhetorical and ideological subordination of women to men.[9] Paul attempts to construct a

7. Amjad-Ali, "The Equality of Women," 192.
8. Ibid.
9. As he has done elsewhere in 1 Corinthians, Paul employs the first-person singular in 1 Corinthians 13. By using the first-person singular Paul demonstrates that he is theologically and ideologically invested in the situation in Corinth and in the outcome he wants to achieve there, which appears generally to be a kind of unity among the believers. Paul personally stands behind the theology and ideology he offers as a solution to the situation in Corinth. Paul's letters are situational and were not meant to be universally applicable but applicable to given situations/issues. When Paul says, "If I speak . . . and have not . . ." he is, I assume, hypothesizing that *if* he were in his audience's shoes, he would behave as he suggests that they should behave (but of course he is not). This rhetorical strategy does not negate or mitigate the gender hierarchy that Paul promotes throughout the letter and that constitutes the context and pretext for his love chapter. Also, I think that Paul is particularly concerned with prophesying and any disorder connected with it in Corinth, particularly with respect to women

prescriptive definition of love that will temper the arrogant and boastful display of spiritual gifts, perhaps by wise prophesying women.[10] The Spirit can distribute gifts to Corinthian believers and yet they can use those gifts without love. Paul is not seeking to create a panacea or a universally applicable definition of love; nor is it prescriptive for everyone, but it targets that which ails the divided Corinthian believers. The exercise of spiritual gifts seems to be one source of strife and disorder. Apparently, according to Paul's argument, the charisma (gifts) that the Spirit provides cannot ensure that people will be loving toward one another in the way described by Paul—at least not in Corinth!

The only way that one can acknowledge Jesus as "Lord" (*kurios*, also translated *master*) or refrain from cursing Jesus' name (12:3) is by God's Spirit. From the Spirit originates, discriminately, a variety of gifts, services, activities that are provided for the common good of all (12:7, 11). The gifts Paul lists to make his point are wisdom, knowledge, faith, healing, working of miracles, prophecy, discernment of spirits, tongues/languages, and interpretation of languages (12:8–12:10). Everyone belongs to one body; in Christ all members are baptized into the body of Christ. This specifically includes "Jews or Greeks, slaves or free," 12:13.[11] However, the phrase "women and men" does not here constitute a social category that is transcended or overcome by inclusion in the body. Paul seems to intentionally omit the phrase "men and women" despite its inclusion in the pre-Pauline baptismal formula that we find in his Letter to the Galatians (3:28): "there is neither male nor female, slave nor free, Jew nor Gentile." Thus, at 12:13, Paul argues for a unity that erases ethnic (Jew and Gentile) and social (slave and free) hierarchies, at least concerning spiritual gifts, but not those based on gender. Jouette Bassler argues that Paul most likely omitted the gender binary "because including it would

---

prophets. I doubt that the words "And if I have prophetic powers . . ." at 1 Corinthians 13:2 is a self-description of Paul! I am not suggesting that Paul demonstrates this gender bias in all of his correspondence, but it is certainly present in 1 Corinthians. Neither am I suggesting that Paul does not "think that love is a universal issue" but I do not believe that universal love is Paul's goal in 1 Corinthians. It may be the goal of many readers, but that does not make it Paul's.

10. Wire, *The Corinthian Women Prophets*.

11. These same two social categories are addressed in Paul's admonition that believers remain in the social condition that they were when God call them: uncircumcised/circumcised and slave/free (7:17–24). Since only men were physically circumcised or uncircumcised, it stands to reason that Paul has in mind only men when he speaks of slave and free in the same context. He does not include the male/female gendered binary that is included in his earlier letter to the Galatians (3:25–26).

undermine his already torturous argument in Chapter 11 concerning the wearing of status-marking veils."[12] If Paul had included the erasure of gender hierarchy in his baptismal formula in 1 Corinthians, he would have undermined rhetorical arguments constructed throughout the letter, both explicit and implied subordinating women to men.

Paul says each and every body part belongs to the whole body and is necessary for the functioning of the body; an interdependency exists among the parts, just as it does among men and women as noted in chapter 11. Paul implicitly argues that some are weaker, *less* honorable, and *less* respectable than others, and some are even inferior to others (12:22–25). The weaker are indispensable, the less honorable are clothed with more honor, and the less respectable are treated with more respect. To combat dissension or division, God has given more honor to the inferior members. Perhaps Paul has in mind that the women are the weaker, less honorable, less respectable members of the body. As noted above, in chapter 11 the honor that women exhibit is in the covering of their hair while praying and prophesying, which is also a symbol of their subordinate (inferior, weaker) status in relation to men as the head. The body respects women's gifts; it rejoices in their honor, despite them being inferior, less respectable, and weaker (12:26).

The image of body parts, despite their interdependence, does not encourage a vision of wholeness for the individual reader who may be suffering from a fragmented life caused by oppression and violence. To see one's self a (weak, less honorable, inferior) part of a body or community and not as fully embodied is to see one's self in a fragmented way connected to others in terms of one's own weakness and the other's strength; one's own lack of honor and another's honor; one's own lack of respect and the respectability of others. This is the way in which black women and men, people of color and poor people, have been encouraged to see themselves in relation to their enslavers, their oppressors, and the larger white dominant patriarchal society. Black people, people of color, and black women more specifically have been taught implicitly and explicitly to be conscious of or to hate their body parts within the ontological or being-ness of their blackness. Emilie Townes asserts that "To love the mouth, the eyes, the hands, the neck, the heart—to love the body is radical ontology within structured domination and control. The concerns for concrete material well-being *and* spiritual wholeness are

---

12. Bassler, "1 Corinthians," 557–65 esp. 564.

imperatives in the post-modern context for African Americans."[13] Gilkes avers that "where our bodies and our appearance are concerned, because of the many mixed messages from within and outside of African-American culture, we are loved and troubled almost constantly."[14]

Paul does not emphasize love among members of the body, but his focus is love in relation to the function of spiritual gifts. He equates the body with the *ekklēsia* (usually translated as *the church*; it could simply refer to any public or private and religious or civic assembly) and the greater gifts presumably are those mentioned in the order of priority: apostles, prophets and teachers, are to be coveted. If we accept that Chloe was one of the charismatic leaders to whom also some believers "belonged," then she would have been elevated among her people to the status of Paul, Apollos, and Cephas, as an apostle. But Paul's rhetoric would take her down a few notches along with the other female prophets, teachers, and apostles.

Since Paul is ostensibly trying to combat strife and division in the *ekklēsia*, to "strive for the greater gifts" may mean to honor them according to the gift recipient's gender. Prophesying women would be most impacted by Paul's rhetoric. It is the gifts of tongues, prophecy, mysteries, knowledge, faith that Paul sets in opposition to love. Love is not presented as a gift of the Spirit (14:1). The kind of love that Paul is pushing in 1 Corinthians 13 is one framed by the gifting, exercise, and honoring of gifts; beyond that love is not contextualized for oppressive social circumstances. Nothing about the love Paul prescribes makes room for active resistance. Civil and voting rights activist Fannie Lou Hamer said that her Christian mother taught her to practice active resistance but never without love. Love functioned as a powerful, freeing, truth-telling, and resistance-to-the-death weapon with divine force promoting the full humanity of oppressed and oppressor.

1 Corinthians 14:26–40—Orderly worship—the instructions about spiritual gifts, love, and the hierarchy of prophesy over tongues leads to what the Corinthian believers should do when they gather for worship. At 14:1, Paul advises them to "pursue love *and* strive for the spiritual gifts, and especially that you may prophesy." In other words, they are to

---

13. Townes, "To be Called Beloved," 190. In this essay Townes explores lynching in the eighteenth and nineteenth centuries and racism in both north and south; the dumping of toxic waste in poor black communities, poverty, and the impact of black neoconservatism.

14. Gilkes, "The 'Loves' and 'Troubles,'" 84.

temper their exercise of gifts with love as Paul has prescribed. It is acceptable for women to strive for prophesy as long as they do so within the framework of their subordination to men. Love is not described as a gift of God's Spirit or as a fruit of God's Spirit as in Galatians (5:22–26). In Galatians where the abolishing of social divisions includes gender (male and female), love, gentleness, kindness, longsuffering are all equally fruit of the Spirit. But in 1 Corinthians 13, kindness and long-suffering are manifestations of love. Paul prescribes a kind of love that is deferential, submissive, and long-suffering and when considered in its literary context is directed more at women's behavior in relationship to men than a mutuality among women and men. Paul's prescribed love is directed at independent, gifted, wise women (freeborn, enslaved, and freed) in deference to male headship. Copeland writes that in "their resistance, black women's suffering redefined caricatured Christian virtues. Because of the lives and suffering of black women held in chattel slavery, the meanings of forbearance, long-suffering, patience, love, hope, and faith can never again be ideologized."[15]

At 14:12 Paul advises the believers to strive to excel in spiritual gifts to build up the *ekklēsia*. Paul argues that "all things" should be done for that purpose (14:26). Only two or three prophets are to speak and they are to speak one by one, 14:29–31; God does not sanction disorder, 14:33. Verses 14:33–35 constitute a parentheses that commands women to be silent in the churches; women who desire more knowledge about something said or prophesied at worship should inquire of their husbands at home. This mandate implies that women will not be allowed to prophesy in public worship. Some scholars take this instruction to be a later addition that is not authentically Pauline. But whether Paul himself wrote it or a scribe inserted it later, the mandate reflects the overall epistemological strategy and ideological framework of the letter, which silences women, attempts to convince women to silence themselves and to accept or acquiesce to the subordination of their bodies and prophetic and praying activity to that of men, especially to their husbands or fathers in the case of single virginal women. This may be most easily accomplished by requiring women to be silent during the worship services, which may effectively exclude them from *ekklēsia* leadership. The *ekklēsia* publicly mirrors the hierarchy of the private household. Chapter 14 continues the pattern of silencing persons who fail to submit to what Paul teaches in chapter 12: If someone speaks in a language for which no one is present

15. Copeland, "Wading through Many Sorrows," 153–54.

to interpret, they are to be silent, 14:28; if revelation is directed to one person, let others be silent, 14:30; women are to be silent altogether in order to support a gendered social hierarchy; otherwise, women contribute to disorder, 14:33–36, 40.

When my ex-husband and I divorced, it was stated that my marriage did not work because there were "two bosses in the house." In other words, my very presence as an educated, intelligent woman must have introduced disorder into the home. A relative who never set foot in our home offered this reason for the demise of my marriage to visitors in her home. In her mind, I did not bear and endure all things expected of me as wife; I must not have relinquished enough of my voice and agency to save my marriage. Women, in my experience, are more often encouraged and expected to silently bear and endure all things in their personal and social relationships in both private and public spaces (i.e., in the home, at work, in the church). M. Shawn Copeland argues that virtues like patience, long-suffering, forbearance, love, faith and hope must be reevaluated in the context of black women's experiences.[16] A theology that asserts that love never fails without regard for context is often used to promote silence and forbearance as the ultimate godly response to intimate partner violence, racism, sexism, classism, and other oppressions resident in church, home, and society.

Anyone among the Corinthian believers who fails to comply to the order of gifts and worship is to be marginalized, rendered invisible, and ineffective. To fail to comply is to fail to allow "all things" to be done orderly and to oppose God, 14:33, 37–40. Paul is promoting a one-way flow of knowledge reception, void of dialogue. Love cannot exist without dialogue. Real dialogue cannot exist in a context of gender subordination and silencing. Paulo Freire argues,

> Love is at the same time the foundation of dialogue and dialogue itself. It is thus necessarily the task of responsible Subjects and cannot exist in a relation of domination. Domination reveals the pathology of love: sadism in the dominator [oppressor] and masochism in the dominated [oppressed]. Because love is an act of courage, not of fear, love is commitment to others. No matter where the oppressed are found, the act of love is commitment to their cause—the cause of liberation. And this commitment, because it is loving, is dialogical. As an act of bravery, love cannot be sentimental; as an act of freedom, it must not serve as a

---

16. Copeland, "Wading through Many Sorrows," 151.

pretext for manipulation. It must generate other acts of freedom; otherwise, it is not love.[17]

Black women in America have always had to struggle for love, through love, and in love. As enslaved Africans and as African Americans they have been coerced and forced into loveless, illicit sexual relationships with white slave masters; coerced and forced to breed with enslaved males to increase the property holdings of their enslavers. Black women have been prohibited from marrying the black men (or white men) they have loved, encouraged to stay in relationships where love went south or sour, told that they as a racial gender group are unlikely to marry or find love, and diagnosed as being emasculators of black men and the cause of decline in the black nuclear family. Black women have been encouraged by religious folks to stay in loveless, violent marriages for the sake of children and black men's souls. Upon earning graduate degrees or answering the call to ordained ministry, black women continue to be told that they can kiss goodbye to any hope of finding love or getting married. Too many battered, abused women have been admonished to develop the type of love advocated in the Apostle Paul's First Letter to the Corinthians. In that chapter (13), Paul rhetorically separates the possession and demonstration of spiritual gifts from possessing love. One can be gifted and loveless. Love is presented in black and white terms without regard for the reader's context. Regardless of context, readers are encouraged to bear, believe, hope, and endure "all things" in demonstration of and in order to possess a love that will not fail (13:7–8).

Human love is embodied love. Embodiment cannot escape the particularity of the individual or collective body, its situatedness. A beloved community should not be grounded in hierarchy. What does it mean for me to be in relationship with God through Christ—to love myself first, to seek wholeness for myself and through that wholeness be in relationship with others? Any fragmentation, brokenness that I embody will be reflected and refracted in my relations with others. The somatic community Paul seeks for the Corinthians is being built on the backs of women, freeborn, enslaved, and freed, gifted women who are encouraged to be silent and to treat their gifts as secondary to those of men and to wear visible symbols of their secondary status. Yung Suk Kim argues that "embodying Christ means living and dying like Christ" as expressed in

---

17. Freire, *Pedagogy of the Oppressed*, 70–71.

the crucified Christ.¹⁸ But Christ did not teach in the canonical Gospels that man is the head of the woman because man was created first or that he was the head of a new church. Kim further argues that "the language of embodiment is relational: from God's love to Christ's faithfulness to Paul and the believers. It is a chain of life or embodiment, not the chain of command based in status or authority." Kim admits to the presence of hierarchy in 1 Corinthian in terms of

> recognizing the higher place of others and God, and if heteronomy is understood as a mode of voluntary sacrifice, we can hardly say that this hierarchy is negative. Moreover, hierarchy and heteronomy are understood through the lens of Christic embodiment[;] they are a hardly coercive means of control, but are invitational challenges that both Paul and the Corinthians reconfigure their relationships based on this image of Christ crucified.¹⁹

But Paul does maintain in implicit and explicit ways his authority over the believers. He is father. Man is the head of woman. To extend an invitation by use of coercive words and theologies that reinscribe social oppression is quite negative; some persons are dispossessed and silenced based particularly on gender, race, and class, while others are elevated. And to imitate Paul while he imitates Christ is to ask the believers to accept Paul's interpretation of Christ, despite that Paul was not one of the disciples who followed the historical Jesus during his life and ministry on earth.

Womanist Love Ethic Promoting Wholeness and Liberation in a Hostile World

Jesus summed up the relationship between embodied self-love and love of the other: "You shall love your neighbor as yourself" (Mark 12:33; Luke 10:27; Matt 19:19, 22:39). The Hebrew Bible and the Gospels prioritize loving self and loving neighbor conjunctively, meaning both are necessary in order to demonstrate a God-like love; one must love one's self to know how to and to be able to love others divinely. In Paul's First Letter to the Corinthians what seems to matter most is order and to achieve this order Paul promotes patriarchal hierarchy. What seems to matter

---

18. Kim, *Christ's Body in Corinth*, 125.
19. Ibid., 130.

most is the equilibrium of patriarchy or, as bell hooks puts it, "patriarchal approval . . . [I]f we step outside of the approval circle, we will not be loved."[20] Hooks continues that

> [p]atriarchy has always seen love as women's work degraded and devalued labor. And it has not cared when women failed to learn how to love, for patriarchal men have been the most willing to substitute care for love, submission for respect. We did not need a feminist movement to let us know that females are more likely to be concerned with relationships, connections, and community than are males. Patriarchy trains us for this role. We do need a feminist [or womanist] movement to remind us again and again that love cannot exist in a context of domination, that the love we seek cannot be found as long as we are bound and not free.[21]

But "love and domination do not go together."[22] Howard Thurman states that "love is possible only between two freed spirits."[23] Perhaps this is why enslaved Africans privileged hope (for freedom) over love.

For womanists, respect and equity are non-negotiables. Clenora Hudson-Weems argues that an Africana woman is both spiritual and ambitious.[24] Hudson-Weems further states, "If all Africana men respected the original reality of the equality of both sexes in African cosmology, then they would refuse to continue to allow external forces, such as non-traditional African religions and alien political family structures wherein female subjugation is inherent, to influence their lives and ways. The end result would be that Africana people (men and women) the world over would then collectively struggle toward recovering their natural birthright as determiners of their fate as a liberated people, dedicated to their families and their future generations."[25]

In this era of Trump, black women and other peoples of color must find a way to keep hope alive in a way that embodies self-love, a self-love that extends itself toward others. African American pastor ordained in AME Zion Church Frances Spearing Randolph (1866–1951) preached a sermon from 1 Corinthians 13:13 entitled "Hope." She proclaimed that "when all else has gone out of life, hope is still left." Randolph argued

20. hooks, *Communion*, xv.
21. Ibid., xvi–xvii.
22. Ibid., 6.
23. Thurman, *Jesus and the Disinherited*, 101.
24. Hudson-Weems, *Africana Womanism*, 143.
25. Ibid., 144.

that human beings "would die but not [for] hope sustain[ing]" them, for when all else fails, hope remains. What the "Negro race" needed, according to Randolph, in the twentieth century, facing the problem of the color line, was hope, which engenders perseverance; success, she argued "is gained only by perseverance." [26]

Gilkes states, "If, through loving ourselves 'regardless' and repairing our inner visions, we save our own lives, we have taken the first step toward our 'response-ability' to save our brothers and sisters. Self-love then is probably the most critical task we complete in establishing our commitment to survival and wholeness of entire people, male and female."[27] When one tries to practice other-centered love without self-love, that other-centered love will be fractured and distorted to the degree that we fail to love self and sooner or later the other will be a source and object of contempt and hate.

Emilie Townes asserts that a "womanist ontology is a radical concern for is-ness in the context of African American life . . . [Rejecting dualism, it] argues for wholeness. . . . Being is physical and spiritual in a womanist ontology . . . [A] womanist ontology advocates the self-other *relationship*, for it is in the relational matrix that wholeness can be found for African Americans."[28] Sometimes wholeness requires that one separate oneself for a while—be a separatist to engender certain aspects of wellness, to safeguard or to regain one's sanity. Townes wishes to draw attention to the complexity of African American culture, the diversity of voices and their challenges and hopes. "At the heart of a womanist ontology is the self-other relation grounded in concrete existence and succored in the flawed transcendent powers of our spirituality."[29] We must guard against individualism and a disavowal of the significant self. Townes further writes that "To remember our fleshiness is to recognize that dualistic oppositions such as self-other, egoism-altruism, theory-practice, individual-community, and mind-body are interactive and interdependent in an ontology of wholeness."[30] Each informs the other

---

26. Randolph, "Hope," 119–20.

27. Gilkes, "The 'Loves' and 'Troubles,'" 97.

28. Townes, "To be Called Beloved," 184–85. In this essay Townes explores lynching in the eighteenth and nineteenth centuries and racism in both north and south; the dumping of toxic waste in poor black communities, poverty, and the impact of black neoconservatism.

29. Ibid., 200.

30. Ibid., 201.

and impacts the other, in positive and negative ways. It is important to remember our stories of resistance and rebellion, Townes asserts, for "defining Black people's otherness or subjectivity as victimization is a hollow and incomplete description of is-ness. We have narratives of resistance and rebellion as part of our story as well . . . [A] womanist ontology of wholeness is, finally, radically relational . . . We are, in the most basic sense, each other's keeper."[31] It is equally important that we continue to make *her-stories* of resistance and rebellion as expressions of embodied self-love. Too often the only stories told are those of the oppressor, from the perspective of the oppressor, *his*-stories, but women of color and their communities have untold stories of both resistance and creativity in the midst of oppression. Her-stories of resistance and rebellion are often stories of survival and evidence of healing and wholeness, and as such encourage hope in the present and for the future. Her-stories can encourage others in their struggle to survive and thrive. Townes states that a "womanist ontology of wholeness is founded on the belief that values like hope, virtue, sacrifice, risk accountability have had a different cast in the Black community. The reinterpretation of these values has helped to hold Black folk in their sanity and determination."[32]

Black women, and their communities, experience racism, sexism, and classism as mutually impacting forms of oppression that daily threaten to diminish our civil and human rights and to undermine our ability to be and remain whole, to be confident in our giftedness, and to exercise our gifts in the context of an embodied love of self. It is an act of resistance and love, divine Goddess love, for black women to wholly love ourselves and to celebrate that love. It is, as Michelle Obama stated, an act of going high, when the world around us takes the low path in its approach to our existence and thriving. Gilkes posits that

> A womanist approach to life and living underscores the importance of self-love for celebrating and resisting in a hostile society. . . . The ethical challenge to live out the mandates of love in a hateful and hate-filled world is a constant struggle and demands an attitude of resistance that must be embraced through what bell hooks calls "a process of critical remembering."[33]

---

31. Ibid.
32. Ibid.
33. Gilkes, "The 'Loves' and 'Troubles,'" 82.

A womanist approach to life emphasizes and affirms the necessity of re-membering or embodying that which a hostile world has attempted to dismember through racism, classism, neo-colonialism, and (hetero) sexism. A womanist approach resists attempts to render black women ontologically and existentially loveless or loved or lovable only in relation and/or in subordination to men. We re-member that we are gifted; we are beautiful; we are smart; we are capable; we are loved; and we are loving.

Bibliography

Amjad-Ali, Christine. "The Equality of Women: Form or Substance (1 Corinthians 11.2–16)." In *Voices from the Margin: Interpreting the Bible in the Third World*, edited by R. S. Sugirtharajah, 185–93. Maryknoll, NY: Orbis, 1995.

Bassler, Jouette. "1 Corinthians." In *Women's Commentary of the Bible*, edited by Carol A. Newsom, Sharon H. Ringe, and Jacqueline E. Lapsley, 557–65. Louisville: Westminster John Knox, 2012.

Copeland, M. Shawn. "'Wading through Many Sorrows': Toward a Theology of Suffering in a Womanist Perspective." In *Womanist Theological Ethics: A Reader*, edited by Katie G. Cannon, Emilie M. Townes, and Angela D. Sims, 135–54. Louisville: Westminster John Knox, 2011.

Freire, Paulo. *Pedagogy of the Oppressed*. New York: Continuum, 1997.

Gilkes, Cheryl Townsend. "The 'Loves' and 'Troubles' of African-American Women's Bodies: The Womanist Challenge to Cultural Humiliation and Community Ambivalence." In *Womanist Theological Ethics: A Reader*, edited by Katie G. Cannon, Emilie M. Townes, and Angela D. Sims, 81–97. Louisville: Westminster John Knox, 2011.

hooks, bell. *Communion: The Female Search for Love*. New York: Perennial, 2002.

Hudson-Weems, Clenora. *Africana Womanism: Reclaiming Ourselves*. Troy, MI: Bedford, 1995.

Kim, Yung Suk. *Christ's Body in Corinth: The Politics of a Metaphor*. Minneapolis: Fortress, 2009.

Randolph, Frances Sperry. "Hope." In *Daughters of Thunder: Black Women Preachers and Their Sermons, 1850–1979*, edited by Bettye Collier-Thomas, 101–47. San Francisco: Jossey-Bass, 1998.

Smith, Mitzi J. "Slavery in the Early Church." In *True to Our Native Land*, 11–23. Minneapolis: Fortress, 2007.

Thurman, Howard. *Jesus and the Disinherited*. Boston: Beacon, 1976.

Walker, Alice. *In Search of Our Mothers' Gardens: Womanist Prose*. San Diego: Harcourt Brace, 1983.

Townes, Emilie M. "To Be Called Beloved: Womanist Ontology and Postmodern Refraction." In *Womanist Theological Ethics. A Reader*, edited by Katie G. Cannon, Emilie M. Townes, and Angela D. Sims, 183–202. Louisville: Westminster John Knox, 2011.

Wire, Antoinette Clark. *The Corinthian Women Prophets: A Reconstruction through Paul's Rhetoric*. Minneapolis: Augsburg Fortress, 1990.